Recipient of the 1992 ALAN Award for outstanding contributions to the field of adolescent literature, Donald R. Gallo is the editor of a number of award-winning books for young people as well as for their teachers. He has compiled and edited seven other collections of short stories for Bantam Doubleday Dell, including *Short Circuits, Join In,* and *No Easy Answers.* His first collection, *Sixteen: Short Stories by Outstanding Writers for Young Adults,* was named by the American Library Association as one of the 100 Best of the Best Books for Young Adults published between 1967 and 1992. His most recent book for teachers, coauthored with Sarah K. Herz, is *From Hinton to Hamlet: Building Bridges Between Young Adult Literature and the Classics.*

ULTIMATE
SPORTS

**Short Stories
by Outstanding Writers for Young Adults**

Edited by Donald R. Gallo

LAUREL-LEAF BOOKS

Published by
Bantam Doubleday Dell Books for Young Readers
a division of
Bantam Doubleday Dell Publishing Group, Inc.
1540 Broadway
New York, New York 10036

ISBN: 0-440-22707-0

RL: 6.5

Reprinted by arrangement with Delacorte Press

Printed in the United States of America

November 1997

10   9   8   7

OPM

For Cheryl Karp Ward,
who provided the motivation
for this collection

and

in memory of my former coaches
at Eastside High School,
Henry Rumana
and
Joseph Frank

Acknowledgments

Thanks to all of the following for their roles in the formation and production of this book:

teacher Sarah K. Herz and her students in Westport, Connecticut; teacher Bill Mollineaux and his students in West Hartford, Connecticut; library/media specialist Cheryl Karp Ward and her students in Windsor Locks, Connecticut; and my students at Central Connecticut State University for their help in choosing the title for this book . . .

sports fan Dan Ward for his assessments of several of the stories submitted for this collection . . .

and Michelle Poploff for her publishing direction, judgments, and support.

Contents

CONTENTS

Introduction

Millions of teenagers, as well as adults, participate daily in some kind of athletic activity, whether through being a student in a phys ed class, playing on an interscholastic sports team, taking an aerobics class, weight-lifting at a neighborhood gym, or zipping around the local park on Rollerblades. And if we're not actively participating in some organized sporting activity, we're watching one in a stadium or on television. We also read about sports: in the daily newspaper, in magazines, and in books—fiction as well as nonfiction.

Although mysteries and horror stories, along with stories about the supernatural, top the lists of teenagers' reading preferences, ask any group of boys in grades six through twelve what else they prefer to read—when they do read—and they'll say "Sports!" Girls, of course, will read sports books and articles too.

During the first half of the 1990s a significant number of first-rate sports novels were published, each featuring teenagers in a variety of athletic pursuits: baseball, basketball, running, ice hockey, boxing. . . . But there hasn't been a good collection of interesting and insightful short stories about teenagers in sports in a long time. I decided it was time for a new collection of sports stories for young people—not just a slapped-together handful of stories taken from previously published books and magazines, but new, exciting, never-before-published stories written especially for this book.

So I contacted a variety of well-known authors who have written award-winning novels about sports—such as Robert Lipsyte and Chris Crutcher—along with a few other writers who are not known for their sports books but whose novels have gained special attention and who have inside information about sports, as well as an understanding of teenagers.

I told these writers that I wasn't looking for stories about how to play specific sports, or stories that contain blow-by-blow accounts of sporting events that bore everyone except the most avid practitioners. Instead I asked them to write stories that were more about the teenagers involved in sports activities than about the conduct of the sports themselves. I wanted stories about believable teenagers involved in challenging activities that reveal their motivations and show their emotional as well as their physical conflicts as they prepare for and participate in a variety of athletic activities.

Here, then, are the results of my requests: an unprecedented collection of sixteen stories about teenage athletes written by the best authors in the field.

It is important to note that almost every one of these writers participated in one or more sports as a teenager—usually the traditional team sports of baseball, basketball, football, and track. And almost every one of them today participates in some kind of athletic activity—from basketball and racquetball to swimming and triathlon to walking for exercise. Because the writers, for the most part, have themselves been participants in the sports they are writing about, the feelings and actions in these tales are realistic.

The stories in this book deal with a variety of team and individual sports, though not every major sport is covered. It is, perhaps, fitting that there is no baseball story in this collection, since these stories were written during the summer of 1994, when professional baseball disappeared from television screens and ballparks across the country and there was no World Series. But you will find in these pages stories about basketball, football, tennis, boxing, wrestling, sailing, racquetball, running, fishing, and a few other sports, some of which you've probably never even considered, along with one that author Robert Lipsyte envisions as an interscholastic sport of the future.

But the inclusion or omission of any particular sport is not what matters in a collection of stories like this. It's not the details and statistics about a specific sport that give a story life and relevance, that make it important or memorable. It's the way the characters—the young men and women—deal with the challenges those athletic events pose for them: how they prepare for the activities; how they react to the physical pain; how they deal with winning and losing; how they interact with teammates, adversaries, friends, and family. In short, it's not the sport that makes the story, but the people, and their actions and reactions. And it's the quality of the writing that brings us as readers into the heart of the action and the emotions.

So, sports fans, get comfortable in your seats—you've got an unobstructed view, as close to the action as you can be. Enjoy this ultimate sporting activity.

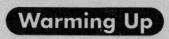

Warming Up

In piano competitions, Peter is always a runner-up. Perhaps he can learn to be more successful by studying the techniques of the cross-country runner who glides effortlessly past his house every day.

Joyriding

Jim Naughton

Peter glanced at the clock on the bookshelf. It was quarter after four. "Fifteen minutes to freedom," he said to himself. Fifteen minutes until he could turn off the metronome—*two, three, four*—and stop moving his fingers across the keys.

For Peter the best part of the day began at the moment he stopped practicing the piano. Beginning at four-thirty each day he had an entire hour to himself. He could read science fiction. He could play video games in the den. He just couldn't leave the house.

This had never really bothered him until the afternoon three weeks earlier when he'd seen the runner gliding up Putnam Street hill. Something about the way the older boy looked, something about the way he moved, drew Peter away from his music and out onto the porch to watch the runner race by in his maroon and gold Darden High School sweat suit.

That night at dinner his mother had said, "Mrs. Kennedy says she saw you on the porch this afternoon. I hope you weren't neglecting your music."

"I was just saying hello to a friend," Peter lied. He didn't even know the other boy's name.

Intimidated by his mother's intelligence network, Peter had not ventured back onto the porch for three weeks, content to watch from his bench as the older boy churned up the hill and off to the oval behind Peter's junior high school. But the previous afternoon, as he'd watched the second hand on the parlor clock ticking away the final seconds of his captivity, *two, three, four,* Peter had decided to go back out on the porch. He thought he might wave as the runner strode by, but instead he studied the older boy in silence.

The runner was tall, lean, and broad-shouldered. *I am none of that stuff,* Peter thought.

The runner had sharp features. Peter's nose looked like he had flattened it against a window and it had stayed that way. The runner had a clear, steady gaze. Peter was near-sighted and tended to squint. The runner had a shock of copper-colored hair. Peter had a frizz so fine it was hard to say what color it was.

In spite of these differences, Peter could have imagined himself in the other boy's place were it not for the runner's grace. The way the boy moved reminded him of music. His legs had the spring of a sprightly melody. His arms pumped a relentless rhythm. He ascended the hill almost effortlessly, as though gravity were no greater hindrance on this steep incline than it had been on the prairie-flat main street below.

He must never lose, Peter thought.

That was another way in which they were different. Peter had just come in third in the piano competition sponsored by the university, after coming in second in the contest sponsored by the orchestra and third in the contest sponsored by the bank.

"Peter," his mother said, "you are a perpetual runner-up." Then she decided that rather than practice for one hour every day, he should practice for two. Two hours!

But two hours were now up. And as Peter stopped the metronome, he spotted a familiar figure in a maroon sweat suit at the bottom of the hill.

• • •

Who is this kid? Kevin asked himself.

Kevin McGrail had not yet reached the crest of Putnam Street when he noticed the pudgy boy in the orange T-shirt on the porch of the white stucco house.

At least he's on the porch today, Kevin thought. For three weeks the kid had watched him from his piano bench. Every day as he pounded up the hill Kevin would hear this weird tinkly music coming from the stucco house across the street. Then there would be a pause as he passed by, and he would see the little frizzy-headed kid looking at him through the window. Then the weird tinkly music would begin again.

At first Kevin felt kind of spooked when the music stopped, like maybe Freddy Krueger was going to jump out of the bushes or something. But after a while he just wondered why the kid was so interested in him.

It wasn't like he was a big star or anything. Kevin was the number three man on the Darden cross-country team, a nice steady runner who could be counted on to come in ahead of the number three man on the opposing team. Coach Haggerty always told him he could be the number two man if he worked at it, but Kevin thought working at something was the surest way to turn it from a pleasure into a chore.

Just look at what happened with Mark Fairbanks. He and Kevin used to hang out together, but that was before Haggerty had convinced Mark that if he devoted his entire life to cross-country he could be a star. Well, Markie was a star all right. He was the fastest guy on the team and one of the top runners in the district. But he was also the biggest drone in the school. Every day at the beginning of practice he would shout, "Okay, men, it's time to go to *work!*"

Kevin felt the strain on his legs lighten as he reached the top of the hill. He saw the road flatten before him and felt the crisp autumn air tingling pleasantly in his lungs. *As soon as this becomes work,* he said to himself, *I quit.*

• • •

"Mom," Peter said at dinner, "I want to go out for the football team."

His mother looked up from her Caesar salad with an expression of exaggerated horror. "Think of your hands!" she said.

Peter had known she would say that. "Well, maybe basketball then," he replied.

"That is every bit as dangerous."

Peter had kind of figured she would say that too. "Well, I want to do something," he said. "Something where there's people. Where there's guys."

His mother put down her fork, pressed her palms together in front of her face, hooked her thumbs under her chin, and regarded him from over her fingertips. *Now we are getting serious,* Peter thought.

"What about choir?" his mother proposed. "I haven't

wanted you exposed to a lot of influences. Musically, I mean. But I am not insensitive to your need for companionship."

Peter shook his head. "How about cross-country?" he asked. "It's only running. How about that?"

"Sports are nothing but trouble," his mother said. "Trouble and disappointment. I think you will agree it is much more satisfying to devote yourself to something at which you can really excel."

"There is a boy on the high-school team who runs up at the oval every day," Peter said. "He told me I could practice with him."

His mother pursed her lips. If Peter could only have explained his plan to her, he was certain she would have said yes. But he wasn't ready to try that. He could barely make sense of it himself.

One thing he was sure of: That boy who ran past the house every day was a champion. He would know what separates winners from perpetual runners-up. And if Peter could learn that, well then, his mother would be happy, and if his mother was happy, well then, everything would be okay again. All she had to do was say yes.

"You still owe me two hours at that piano every day," she said.

• • •

Kevin was surprised to see the little piano player up at the oval the next day. The kid was dressed in one of those shapeless sweat suits they wore in junior-high-school gym class.

Looks like he's already winded, Kevin thought as he watched the kid struggle through about a dozen jumping jacks. *I hope he doesn't hurt himself.*

8

Kevin was beginning his second lap when the kid fell in beside him.

"Hi," the boy said.

"Hey," said Kevin without slowing down.

"I'm getting in shape for next season," said the boy, who was already breathing heavily and losing ground.

"It's good to give yourself a lot of time," Kevin said, not meaning to sound quite so smart-ass.

"See you around," the boy called as Kevin opened up the space between them.

Every day for the next three weeks the routine was the same: The kid was always waiting when Kevin arrived. He would puff along beside Kevin for a few strides, try to start a gasping conversation, and then fall hopelessly behind. The kid was obviously never going to be a runner, Kevin thought, and he sure didn't look like he was enjoying himself. Yet there he was, grinding away, just like Fairbanks only without the talent.

You're a better man than I am, Kevin thought. *Or a sicker one.*

That Friday when Kevin got to the oval the chubby kid took one look at him and started to run. It was as though he were giving himself a head start in some kind of private race. The thought of some competition between the two of them made Kevin laugh, because he generally lapped the kid at least five or six times each session.

He put the little piano player out of his mind and tried to focus on the rhythm of his own footfalls. The following weekend he and the rest of the Darden team would be competing in the district championships, and Kevin had begun to think it might be a good time to answer a question that had been nagging at him for the last month. He wanted to know how good he was—not how good he could be if he devoted his entire life to cross-country, but how good he was at that moment. What would happen, he wondered, if he ran one race as hard as he could?

Part of him did not want to know. Suppose he beat out Billy Kovacs, the number two man on the Darden team? That would mean Coach Haggerty would be all over him. He'd expect Kevin to have a big season in his senior year, maybe even make it to the state championships. Just thinking about the way Haggerty put his gaunt face up next to yours and shouted "Go for the goal!" was enough to stop Kevin in his tracks.

On the other hand he might not beat Billy Kovacs, and that would be depressing too. Kevin liked to think of himself as somebody who *could* run faster if he *wanted* to run faster. But if he went all out and still finished in the middle of the pack, it would mean he was just another mediocre high-school runner.

Maybe I should just run a nice easy race and forget about this, Kevin thought. *It would be less complicated.*

As he began the seventh of his eight laps, Kevin noticed that the chubby kid was still running—puffing and panting and lurching from one foot to another. "This is my bell lap," he gasped as Kevin trotted by.

Kevin chuckled at the idea of the little piano player in a race, but when he finished his workout he stopped to watch the other boy circle the track one last time. This was the kid's fourth lap. Kevin had never seen him run a mile before, and he felt a sneaky sense of pride in his training partner's accomplishment.

The kid came chugging down the track, gulping huge bites of air and clutching his right side. But when he reached his imaginary finish line, he threw both hands into the air and held that pose for a moment before collapsing onto the grass. Kevin was about to jog over when he heard a voice in the stands announce: "And the winner in the Pudge Ball Olympics: Peter Whitney."

Kevin turned quickly and recognized three kids from the freshman class at school. "Hey, why don't you bozos take off," he said sharply, and looked at them long enough for the kids to understand that he meant it.

The piano player was still lying flat on his back when Kevin reached him and extended a hand to help him to his feet.

"Thanks," the boy said, in a barely audible voice.

• • •

Hours after he had gotten home, Peter kept replaying the details in his head to see if there was something he had missed. First the fudge-brains from the ninth grade had made fun of him and the runner had taken his side. Next the older boy had waited around while Peter caught his breath. Then they'd walked down the hill together all the way to Peter's house. It was almost like they were friends.

But things had begun to go wrong as soon as Peter tried to ask him his secret. The trouble was he couldn't figure out how to put the question in his own words, and so he began talking like the books his mother read to help her get ahead at her office.

"Do you visualize your goals?" he blurted.

The boy looked at him quizzically.

"Some people do that," Peter continued, eager to fill the silence. "But other people, they say that you should concentrate on developing the habits of a highly effective person."

The runner didn't respond, so Peter felt compelled to keep talking. "Do you think your habits are effective? I mean, are they consistent with your aspirations? You know?"

The other boy shrugged. "You still play the piano?" he asked.

"Two hours a day," Peter said.

"You like it?"

"No," Peter said. "I mean, yes. I used to."

"But now you don't?"

Peter did not want to waste time talking about himself, but the older boy seemed genuinely interested. "Before we came here I had a different teacher," he said, and as he did every time he sat down at the piano, he began to think of Mickey Ray.

Mickey was his teacher back in Rochester. He taught part-time at the university and at night he played in clubs. Peter's mother didn't like him because he wore a ponytail. But everybody told her that he was the best teacher in town. She let Peter take lessons from him on one condition: that they play only "performance pieces"—compositions Peter might later play in a competition.

But Mickey did not always abide by this condition. Every once in a while he would pull a new piece of music from his satchel, wink conspiratorially at Peter, and ask him to give it a try. This was how Peter got to know jazz and ragtime and gospel music.

After Peter played through the piece once, Mickey would sit down on the bench beside him. "Next time," he would say, "a little more like this." And off he would go, playing the same notes in the same order, but making the piece sound more fluid, more powerful, more alive.

"It is not about hitting the right key at the right time," Mickey used to say. "It is about taking this baby for a ride." Peter began to tell the other boy about Mickey Ray.

"He sounds cool," the runner said.

"My teacher now is better," Peter said. Actually he wasn't sure if that was true. "Mr. Brettone is a superior musical pedagogue," his mother had said. But lately Peter had found himself imagining that Mr. Brettone had tiny pickaxes attached to his fingertips and that each time he struck a key it would crack and crumble.

They were standing in front of the house by the time Peter finished the story, and he was no closer to learning the other boy's secret than he had been before all those grueling afternoons on the oval. Finally, just as the other boy was about to leave, he blurted: "How do you do it?"

"Do what?"

"Win."

"I don't know anything about winning," the runner said. "I just know about running."

Then came what Peter found the most puzzling exchange of all. "I hope you win at the districts," he said as the boy jogged away.

"Now what would I want to do that for?" the runner called back.

• • •

Kevin stood among the throng of two hundred runners packed into a clearing just off the first fairway at the Glen Oaks Golf Club. At the crack of the starter's pistol they would all surge forward onto the manicured expanse of the fairway. The sight of all those bodies churning and all those bright uniforms bobbing up and down was so captivating that during his first two seasons Kevin had hung back at the beginning just to take in the spectacle.

Not this year, though. He had decided to run the race of his life, and moments after the gun was fired, he found himself in the first fourth of the great mob of runners struggling for position as they tore toward the first green, where the course cut sharply downhill and into the woods. As he hit what he thought of as a good cruising speed for the first stage of the race, Kevin couldn't help wondering if he would wear himself out too quickly or collapse on the grass at the finish line like that crazy little piano player.

It was strange to be thinking of him at a time like this. Or maybe it wasn't. Because what Kevin had been trying to figure out all along was whether excelling at his sport would somehow ruin it for him, the way excelling at the piano had ruined it for Peter. He half suspected that it would, but something the kid had told him that day Kevin had walked him home had given him a half-assed kind of hope.

In the pack just ahead of him Kevin picked out Mark Fairbanks, Kovacs, and a couple of the top runners from other schools he had raced against during the year. No question—he was a lot closer to them than he usually was at the half-mile mark.

• • •

As the runner streaked by, Peter cheered and pointed his friend out to his mother. It had taken heroic persuasion to get Mom to come out to a cross-country meet on a Saturday morning, but now he was sure that everything would go just the way he planned. His friend would win the race and then Peter would introduce him to Mom.

He wasn't really certain what would happen after that. He couldn't really explain why he wanted them to meet. It wasn't so that Mom could see that he was making friends at school, because she thought friends only distracted him from his piano. And it wasn't because he thought she would be impressed by a cross-country champion, since Mom didn't really appreciate sports.

Peter wanted them to meet so that Mom could see that he had a little of the runner in him, a little bit of the champion, a little bit of something that would lift him beyond the status of a "perpetual runner-up." If he could only convince her of that, maybe it wouldn't be so hard to keep sitting down alone at the piano. Or to keep sitting down to dinner with her.

"He's not winning," Peter's mother said as they watched the runners cut off the fairway and into the woods.

"It's strategy, Mom," Peter told her, though he too was wondering why his friend was not at the head of the pack.

• • •

They were tearing along an old railroad bed at the top of a ridge near the fourth tee. Kevin's legs still felt strong. His breath came easily. Fairbanks, who was fighting for the lead, was just a speck up along the train tracks, but Billy Kovacs was only twenty yards or so ahead of Kevin.

I can take him, Kevin thought, *but then I'll have to hold him off the rest of the way.* He hesitated for a second, and then decided to pick up his pace.

• • •

A single runner in the maroon Darden uniform came streaking out of the woods and onto the tenth fairway. There was only a half mile remaining in the race.

"That isn't your friend," Peter's mother said.

Another runner in red and white charged out of the woods a few yards behind. In a few moments there were six, seven, and then eight other runners pounding the last half mile toward the finish line. Peter didn't recognize any of them.

"I'm sorry, dear," his mother said, rummaging in her purse for her car keys.

Peter felt as though he had bet a lifetime of allowances on the wrong horse.

• • •

As he tore out of the woods and onto the tenth fairway, Kevin began counting the people ahead of him, a feat made more difficult by the sweat dripping into his eyes. There were fifteen of them, as nearly as he could tell. The top ten finishers went on to the state finals. Somewhere up along the railroad tracks the desire to be in that group had seized him and he had picked up his pace. Now the wind burned in his lungs and the acid burned in his calves. His Achilles tendons felt like guitar strings being tightened with each footfall. He had less than half a mile to make up six places.

He glanced quickly across the fairway and saw Fairbanks dueling for the lead with Pat Connors of Tech. In the crowd behind them he saw the little piano player. He was gazing in Kevin's direction, disappointment etched on his face.

I'm running the race of my life and it isn't good enough for him, Kevin thought. He could feel the anger rising inside him. The race was ruined for him now, and he began to doubt his motives. Was he really running all out just to see what it felt like, or had the attention of this peculiar little kid made him hungry for more?

Kevin wanted his sense of purity back. He wanted to stop caring whether he finished in the top ten. Something inside him whispered, "Slow down," but instead he emptied his mind and kept running.

Into that emptiness floated the memory of the conversation he and the little piano player had had just a few days before. The kid had been talking about his old teacher, the one who liked to take the piano "for a ride." *I can't play*, Kevin thought, *but I can run. This can be my ride*.

Imagining that he was Mickey Ray, Kevin focused his eyes on the ground in front of him and sprinted the last two hundred yards, unaware of the screaming fans or the other runners on the course.

• • •

Peter couldn't understand what the big fuss was about. The kid had come in eleventh. That wasn't even good enough to qualify for the state finals, yet people were acting like that was a bigger deal than Mark Fairbanks, who had come in second. It was pretty cool to take a minute off your best time, he supposed, but still, eleventh place wasn't worth all the cheering the Darden fans did when the kid crossed the finish line.

Besides that, Kevin McGrail looked like hell. When he had glided up Putnam Street six weeks ago he had been so smooth, so poised. Now he was bent over, walking like he had a sunburn on the bottoms of his feet.

Peter saw the boy's coach, a gaunt man wearing a baseball cap, put an arm around Kevin's shoulder. "You dug down deep and you came up big," the coach barked.

Kevin drew a few rapid breaths. "I was joyriding," he said.

"Joyriding," Peter repeated to himself as he sat at his piano later that afternoon. "Joyriding lands you in eleventh place." He stood up, opened the piano bench, and withdrew the exercises Mr. Brettone had assigned for that week. Beneath it he found *The Fats Waller Songbook*. Mickey had given it to him as a going-away present. Peter thumbed through the pages until he found "Your Feet's Too Big." Just the title made him laugh. And the way Mickey used to play it—

He looked up to see his mother standing in the doorway. "What are we featuring this afternoon?" she asked.

"Exercises for the left hand," Peter said, and he sat down to work.

Jim Naughton

As a sports reporter, Jim Naughton covered the Mets for the New York *Daily News* in 1986, the year the Mets won the World Series. The holder of a B.A. in journalism and an M.A. in American history from Syracuse University, he has also covered sports for *The New York Times* and worked as a feature writer for *The Post-Standard* in Syracuse and *The Washington Post*. He is the author of three sports books for young adults: two novels and a biography of Michael Jordan.

My Brother Stealing Second, an American Library Association Best Book for Young Adults, is about a sixteen-year-old baseball player who has trouble dealing with the death of his older brother, who had been a star shortstop. As he slowly starts to heal with the help of a girlfriend and an older male friend, he learns the truth about the mysterious accident in which his brother was killed.

Taking to the Air: The Rise of Michael Jordan examines the basketball star's life, as well as the social, cultural, and commercial forces that helped shape his legend. This was selected as a New York Public Library best book for teenagers in 1993.

Mr. Naughton's most recent novel, *Where the Frost Has Its Home,* features a seventh-grade hockey player.

In high school, Jim Naughton helped found his school's cross-country team. But, he says, when he was growing up "my heart belonged to baseball. Unfortunately I wasn't much good at it." As an adult living in Washington, D.C., he now walks and swims for exercise.

Harlow sees the potential in Randy, who is insensitive, impulsive, and in trouble. If only Randy can learn to control his temper . . .

Fury

T. Ernesto Bethancourt

➤ **It** was after midnight when Harlow Fuller heard his dog barking in the front yard. He was in his bedroom, in the neat, five-room brick house he'd owned for years. He put down the magazine he'd been reading and went cautiously to the front door. A baseball bat stood in the corner behind the door. South Jamaica was a bit safer than ghetto Brooklyn, but here, where people owned their homes, the burglary rate was higher.

Harlow peeked through the drawn curtains on his barred windows. He saw a large young man standing at his front gate. From behind the gate, Emile, Harlow's huge Doberman, was barking wildly. Harlow went to the front door and opened it a crack.

"Who's out there? What do you want at this hour?" he called.

"Uncle Harlow? It's me—Randy Fuller."

"What are you doing out here in Jamaica?"

"I can explain, if you let me in."

Harlow stepped outside. "Emile!" he said softly.

21

"Place!" The dog stopped barking immediately and trotted over to Harlow's side, where he sat down and looked up at his master. "Good boy," Harlow said, rubbing the dog's ears.

"It's okay, Randy," Harlow called to the boy at the gate. "You can come in. Emile won't bother you now." He turned and went inside. Randy entered the yard and followed his uncle into the house.

Once inside, Harlow said, "Well, let's have a look at you, boy. Last time I saw you, you were . . . ten years old, I think. At your daddy's funeral. You've sure grown."

There was no denying Randy's size. He stood two inches over six feet. When Randy took off his light windbreaker, under which he wore a T-shirt, Harlow noticed the young man's barrel chest and thickly muscled arms. He whistled softly.

"Seems we got us a heavyweight in the family," Harlow observed. "I can't believe how much you look like your daddy. He could have been a fine boxer, you know. I offered to train him, but your mamma was dead against it.

"So your daddy stayed on, driving a truck. And what happened? He gets hit by a drunk with no insurance. Some safe job.

"I said that to your mamma at the funeral. Bert would have been safer in the ring. She hasn't talked to me since. I'm not welcome at your mamma's house. That's why I'm so surprised that you showed up here. And at this hour. What's going on, Randy?"

Randy shifted in the chair, facing Harlow. "I'm in bad trouble, Uncle Harlow. Police are looking for me."

"What did you do, boy?"

"Nothing, really. I was just there when something happened."

Harlow threw back his head and laughed loudly. "Half the cons in the joint say the same thing, Randy. Suppose you back up a bit and tell me just what went down."

"I was helping out a pal," Randy said. "His name is . . . *was* Eddie Sanger. Some dude owed Eddie some money. Eddie asked me to come with him to collect it."

"Hold on," Harlow said. "What did this 'dude' owe Eddie the money for?"

Randy avoided his uncle's eyes. "That's what Eddie does for a living—he loans out money."

"And this was the first time you ever went with Eddie to collect?"

"Uh . . . no. I done it before."

"And Eddie paid you, right?"

"Uh-huh."

"Then let's get things straight, boy. You were strong-arming for a loan shark when this 'something' happened."

"I wouldn't put it that way," Randy said.

Harlow smiled. "I can think of a half dozen judges and DAs who *would*. But go on with your story."

"When me and Eddie found the guy, I had to run him down. He was taking off on us. I knocked him down on the sidewalk, right off Ralph Avenue and Jefferson Street.

"All of a sudden, the dude pulls out a piece and starts shooting. I didn't know Eddie had a gun, too. Before I know it, there's bullets flying all over. I got out of there, fast. I took in a movie over on Broadway." He reached over to his jacket and took out a ticket stub.

"Figuring that if anyone came looking for you, you'd say you were at the movie all along?" Harlow asked.

Randy nodded. "When I got back to my street, there was talk already. Eddie was dead. The other guy was in the hospital in bad shape. But word on the street was that he's saying Eddie shot at him first. And the cops are looking for me."

"I'm not a bit surprised. But what brought you out here to me, Randy?"

"Well, Mamma always talks about how you were in trouble once. That you did time, upstate. I thought maybe you, knowing about these things, could tell me what to do."

Harlow shook his head. "Francie always had a mouth on her. Did she ever tell you what I was in for?"

"No."

"I was in for being stupid, that's what for. I did six years out of eighteen for manslaughter. I killed a man with these." Harlow held up two knotted fists. "Some fool got wise with my woman one night at a restaurant. He swung at me when I told him to buzz off. I punched him out. But he hit his head on a table when he fell. He died."

"Then it wasn't your fault," Randy said.

"Oh, but it was. I was a pro—a boxer. To the law, my hands were deadly weapons. And it was my fault, too. I could have talked my way out of it. But a hot temper runs in the Fuller family. Your daddy had it too. It could have made him great in the ring. But it's no good if you can't control it outside the ring. That's what happened to me."

"And you did all that time for it."

"Nowhere near what it could have been. After a few years, I got another lawyer and a new trial. When I came out, I was an ex-con. I lost my license to fight. It was hard to stay straight. Then I started in training young fighters that I thought looked good—kids who could be champs. I've done okay. I get respect as a businessman these days. But I still haven't found my champ—that kid who can make it all the way to the top."

"So you never were a real criminal, were you?"

"Sorry to let you down, Randy. I was stupid and made a bad mistake. I paid for it, too. Even one day in a cage would be too much. I did over two thousand days. Most hotheaded kids never know what it's like inside—until it's too late."

Harlow got up from his chair. "Now, what am I going to do with you, kid?" He saw the look on Randy's face. "Don't worry—I ain't going to turn you in. But it's a matter of time before the police start checking out the whole family. They *will* come here, sooner or later."

"If I can stay a few days . . . ," Randy began.

"Are you hungry, kid?" Harlow asked. "Did you eat at all today?"

"Not since breakfast."

"You go on into the kitchen. Help yourself to what's in the freezer. You know how to run a microwave?"

"Yeah."

"Get yourself something, then. I have to go down to the basement and set up a place for you to sleep."

"In the basement?"

"Can't have you up here. I got a finished basement down there, though. I got a door that locks from the outside. If anyone checked, they could see no one's using my other bedroom. I'm gone in the daytime, at my gym on Jamaica Avenue. Emile keeps people away from the place while I'm out."

"He's some kind of dog."

"Ain't he ever? I named him for Emile Griffith. That's what Emile looked like when he was welterweight champ. All muscle, steel wires, and teeth. Now, you get something to eat while I go downstairs."

A half hour later, Randy followed his uncle down the

basement stairs. Harlow swung open a door to a large, wood-paneled room. There was a mattress in one corner. A heavy bag hung from a chain in the center of the room, and a light speed bag was in the far corner. On the walls were bright, shiny weights for bodybuilding. Between two paneled doors was a rowing machine. The only light came from a bare bulb that hung from the low ceiling.

"Okay, kid," Harlow said. "It ain't much, but it's going to be your home for a time. You can't keep the light on at night—people could see it through the basement windows." He waved at the barred windows set high in the walls. "Once the sun comes up, you'll have light enough down here."

"But what will I do down here?" Randy protested. "There's no radio, no TV—"

"What do you think you'd have in jail, boy?" snapped Harlow. "You want to do something, hit the speed bag or the heavy bag. There's a pair of workout gloves in that closet and some sweats that should fit you. They're mine. There's a little john behind that other door. I'll bring you a toothbrush and some shaving stuff when I get back from work tomorrow. Now I have to get some sleep."

Harlow closed the door and shut off the light switch alongside it. "But this is like jail!" Randy protested from behind the door.

"You don't know what jail is," Harlow said. "You got your own health club in there, kid. Use it."

He went upstairs, brushed his teeth, and went to bed. As he turned out the light, he heard a slow, regular thumping sound from the basement. He smiled. "Fool kid's hitting that heavy bag in the dark," he thought as he drifted off. "Yeah, no doubt of it. He's got that Fuller hot blood."

• • •

Early the next morning, Randy was awakened by a rough hand on his shoulder. Without thinking, he swung hard at its owner. His large fist hit nothing but air. He opened his eyes, for a moment not remembering where he was. He saw his uncle standing over him, smiling.

"You do wake up a bit sudden, don't you, Randy?" Harlow said.

"What time is it?"

"Six o'clock. Time to be up and doing, boy!"

"Leave me alone," Randy grunted, rolling over. "I don't get up at home until noon."

"This ain't home, kid," Harlow said. He grabbed at one corner of the mattress on the floor and tugged mightily. Randy rolled out onto the hard tile. The young man got to his feet with fists at the ready. Harlow laughed.

"Come on, kid. Anytime you're ready."

Randy rushed at the older man, swinging a wild, overhand right. Harlow barely moved. As the force of the blow carried Randy past him, Harlow gave the younger man a hard shove that sent him sprawling onto the floor.

Harlow then threw the mattress over Randy. As the young man got to his hands and knees under the mattress, Harlow placed a well-aimed kick on his padded rear. Even through the mattress, he could hear Randy's grunt of surprise and pain.

"This is no way to treat somebody who's brought you breakfast, Randy," Harlow said to the form on the floor. "Aren't you hungry?"

"Mmmmph" came from under the mattress.

"I guess that means yes," the older man said. He walked to the open door and picked up a tray from the bottom step of the stairs. When he returned, Randy was sitting up in the center of the floor. Harlow set the tray before him.

"What's this?" Randy asked, eyeing the tray.

"High-protein drink, high-fiber cereal, and skim milk. Some complex carbohydrates and a handful of vitamins."

"This is garbage," Randy said. "Ain't you got any Froot Loops?"

"You're something else, boy," Harlow answered. "Here you show up at my house, on the run. I take you in, give you a nice place to stay, and you try to punch me out. Then you complain about the eats. You sure got a short grip on being grateful, boy." He pointed to the tray. "If you're hungry, eat it. If not, I'll be taking it with me, along with the mattress."

"What are you taking that for?" Randy asked. He had secretly intended to go back to sleep once his uncle had left.

"I got it off the bed in my spare room. If anyone came by to look for you, they'd wonder where the mattress was.

"I'm going to be gone for most of the day. When I get back, we'll have dinner."

"But what will I do for lunch?"

"That's why I gave you such a big and healthy breakfast. Eat it, or don't." Harlow grinned widely as Randy began to try the cereal. He was still smiling as he locked the heavy door behind him and tugged the mattress upstairs. As he reached the top step, he heard Randy call out through the door.

"What am I supposed to do in here all day?"

"You could do a couple of things," Harlow called back. "You could think on how you got yourself into this mess. And you could also do your body some good. You may look okay, but you're slow on the punch. The only thing you could hit for sure is the floor."

As Harlow left the house, he could hear thumping coming from the basement. He paused outside to feed Emile before getting into his car. He patted the dog and whispered, "You take care of things around here, Emile. I think we got us a heavyweight, all right."

• • •

It was growing dark when Harlow returned to his home. He was greeted by Emile. He reached into his car, took out a large paper sack, and walked into the house. He checked his answering machine, then went downstairs. As he did, he heard the *rat-a-tat* of the speed bag. It didn't last long. But then it began again, after some muffled curses from Randy.

Harlow unlocked the door to find Randy flailing away at the speed bag. "I told you that you had slow hands," Harlow said, setting the paper sack on the floor. "Didn't anyone show you how to use that bag right?"

Randy turned and looked at his uncle sullenly. "Nobody ever showed me nothing. But I had to do something. I'm going crazy down here."

"After only one day? What do you think you'd do in a jail cell?"

"Maybe I'd have somebody to talk to there."

"Maybe you would. But I'll tell you this: In the six years I listened to jail talk and yard talk, I never heard anything worth two cents. And best you get used to being here. It may be a while before you see the outside."

"What are you talking about?"

"That 'dude' you told me about. His name was Arnold Jensen—the homeboys called him Zipper, right?"

"Yeah. How did you know?"

"He's in the papers, Randy. He died last night from the gunshots. Now the cops really want to talk to you."

Randy sat down on the floor and put his head in his hands. "What am I gonna do?" he moaned. "I told you I didn't have nothing to do with the shooting part."

"I believe you. But the police might not. That's why I bought this today." He reached into the paper sack and took out a long yellow legal pad.

"You're going to write down exactly what happened. Then you're going to sign it. After that, I'll send it to the police."

Randy got to his feet. "Are you crazy? Soon as they get that, they'll be here!"

"Oh, I don't think so," Harlow said. "I'll mail it to one of the kids I used to train. He lives in Detroit. He'll send it from there. With no return address, all the cops will have is a Detroit postmark."

"That's great of you, Uncle Harlow! Now, when can I get out of this room?"

"Hold on! First, the cops won't stop looking until after they get this paper from Detroit, and probably not even then," Harlow looked up at the ceiling. "In fact, they could show up here anytime. The best place for you right now is here in the basement. Now, let's get started on getting your story on paper."

A half hour later, Randy crumpled up another yellow page and threw it across the room. "It's no good!" he complained. "I can't write this out myself."

"Didn't they teach you anything in school? Or didn't you pay attention?"

"Didn't see no need for school," Randy grumbled.

"Okay. I'll write it down and you copy it, word for

word. It's got to be in your handwriting. It will give you something to do tomorrow." Harlow pointed to the paper sack. "I got you a razor and shaving cream and a toothbrush. There's some new underwear in there, too. I got extra-large. Is that right?"

"I don't know. Mamma buys all that."

Harlow roared with laughter. "Some tough guy you are. What are you? Eighteen . . . nineteen years old and your mamma still buys your clothes!"

Randy jumped to his feet. "You got no call bagging on me."

Harlow backed off in mock fear. "Oh, please don't hit me, Mr. Tough Guy," he moaned. "Otherwise, I'll have to tell your mamma!"

With a roar of rage, Randy rushed at Harlow. The older man ducked under a roundhouse right hand and stepped lightly to one side. Then he hit Randy in the gut with a blow that caused the younger man to let out his breath in a giant *whoosh!* Randy fell to his hands and knees, gasping for air.

Harlow stood over him. "Not only do you have slow hands, you got a soft belly, boy. Must be all those Froot Loops you eat. I hope I didn't spoil your dinner with that punch. I got you something real healthy tonight."

"Like that breakfast?" asked Randy from the floor.

"Much better. You be nice to me, I'll let you have some extra wheat germ on it. And if you eat it all up, I'll show you how to work that speed bag."

• • •

The next morning when Harlow awoke, he heard the speed bag going like a machine gun. "The boy learns fast," he thought. "If he keeps it up, it ain't going to be so easy keeping him down there—Oops! almost forgot!"

Harlow took a book from the shelf alongside his bed. Then he went downstairs and opened the door. Randy was at the speed bag, his hands moving just as Harlow had shown him the night before. He looked up as Harlow entered. The older man tossed the book to him.

"What's this?" Randy asked.

"When you get all punched out, you could look it over," Harlow said. "It helped me when I was in the joint."

Randy looked at the thin book. Painfully, he formed his lips around the words on the cover. *"Yes . . . I . . . Can . . . R-Read."*

• • •

It was four days later when Harlow came running down the stairs. Randy was working out in silent fury. He barely looked up when Harlow burst into the room.

"Quick, Randy—into the shower stall!" Harlow commanded.

"What for? I ain't finished working out."

"There's a police car just pulled up in front. Do what I say. I'm going to open up this room. Show them the closet, too. With the john door open, I don't think they'll check the shower stall. Pull the curtain closed, though." From the floor above, the doorbell began to ring. "No more time," Harlow whispered. "Be cool, kid."

Harlow quickly locked the door and ran up the stairs. Randy heard voices and the heavy tread of feet above him. He remained inside the shower stall. A few moments later, he heard footsteps coming down the stairs.

"What's in there, Mr. Fuller?" Randy heard a strange voice saying.

"My private workout room. I'll show it to you."

"You don't have to, sir. We have no warrant—"

"No, I insist." The lightbulb went on in the basement room. "No one can say I didn't cooperate with the Police Department."

Randy pressed himself tightly against the wall of the shower stall, hoping it would make him appear smaller. Was Uncle Harlow going crazy? Why was he bringing the cops downstairs?

"What's behind that door?" Randy heard the policeman say.

"A closet," Harlow answered. "I'll show you."

"No need," the cop said. "I've seen enough. Thank you for your help, Mr. Fuller. And if you do see Randy . . ."

"I'll be sure to call you."

The light went out again, and Randy heard the door being locked. He stood inside the stall for the longest time, shaking all over. After what seemed like years, the footsteps overhead stopped and he heard the front door close heavily. Shortly after that, he heard Harlow coming downstairs.

"Okay, Randy," Harlow said softly. "You can come out." Still unsteady, Randy came out into the main room. "That was awful close, Uncle Harlow," he said. "Why'd you bring him down here? I heard him say he didn't have no warrant."

"Use your head. If I told him he couldn't look, he'd have gone to a judge and got the papers. This way, I showed him I have nothing to hide."

"I guess they didn't get that letter from Detroit yet," Randy said.

"Even if they did, they probably wouldn't give up. This is a murder case. That stays on the books forever."

"Then what am I going to do? I can't stay down here for the rest of my life."

"You won't have to. Once things blow over a bit, we'll get you a good lawyer. In the meantime, you got no choice but this." Harlow looked around at the small room.

"But I can see why you feel boxed in down here. Now that the cops won't be back, maybe we can start you on some roadwork. You can run off some of that anger of yours."

"But where? Won't someone see us?"

"Baisley Park is four blocks from here. We'll run early in the morning while it's still dark."

"I heard about Baisley Park. That's a dangerous place after dark."

Harlow laughed loudly. "You mean you're scared? The reason people stay away from the park is they don't want to run into someone like *you*! You're the one who's on the run from the police.

"Besides, we'll take Emile with us. He needs to run, too. I figure two guys our size and a dog like Emile, no one's going to mess with us."

And so began a regular routine of roadwork and body-building for Randy. Each morning, Harlow would drive to the park and the two men and the dog would run until nearly sunrise.

Harlow noted that it helped Randy's spirits. The young man no longer complained about being cooped up. His body shed fat and gained hard ropes of muscle. Randy continued to work endlessly on the two punching bags and the rowing machine. Often, Harlow would hear Randy continuing to work out in the dark.

What made Harlow feel best was that Randy had finished *Yes, I Can Read*. But at the end of each day, Randy would have the same questions: "When do I get out of here? When are we going to get that lawyer?"

Each time Harlow said, "When I think it's cool, and no sooner." Randy would grow more restless. Finally, one night in early September, he exploded.

"I don't care what you say!" he shouted at Harlow. "I'm leaving. It's been almost four months. I'll take my chances outside. Anything is better than this!"

"You watch yourself, boy," Harlow said, "or I'll take away your roadwork. How would you like that?"

"How would you like me to walk right over you?" Randy growled.

"You think you're man enough?"

In a dark rage, Randy sprang at him. A looping left hand banged into Harlow's ribs, and like lightning, a stiff right hand to his head followed.

As Randy was about to throw another punch, Harlow dodged, hooked a foot behind the younger man's left ankle, and tripped him. Randy tried to regain his balance, but Harlow stepped in and with three short punches knocked him to the floor.

His head buzzing from the blows, Randy looked up at his uncle. "You cheated!" he cried.

"You bet I did," Harlow answered. "No way I'm going to bust my hands on your hard head. And there's not enough room down here to fight. But if that's what you want, that's what you'll get. Tonight I'll sneak you over to my gym. We'll put on the gloves and settle this right!"

• • •

The gym was on the second floor of a run-down building, in the shadow of the el. Harlow opened the double-locked steel door and hit a light switch inside the doorway. "Go through that door behind the ring," he said. "The lockers are in there."

In a few minutes, Harlow had pieced together shoes, shorts, and sixteen-ounce gloves for Randy and himself. "One more thing," he said to the younger man. "Put this on, too." He handed Randy some headgear.

"What do I need that for?" Randy asked.

"We already know you can hit hard," Harlow said. "But we don't know how hard a punch you can take. I don't want to scramble the inside of your head."

The two men climbed into the ring. "We don't have a bell or timekeeper," Harlow said, "so there won't be any rounds. When I say 'go,' you start fighting. When you're ready to quit, just say 'when.' Ready?"

"Yeah, I am."

"Then go!"

As Harlow expected, Randy came on in a rush, swinging wildly. For the first few minutes, all Harlow did was avoid the rushes and tag Randy with a left or right hand as he went past. But after a time, Randy stopped being wild. A cold, hard look came over his face and he began to stalk Harlow.

Seconds later, Randy connected with a straight left hand that rocked his uncle. He held on, then wrestled Randy into the nearest corner.

Once his head cleared, Harlow put together a savage left, then a right to Randy's body. He finished with a stinging left hook that caught Randy square on the headgear. Randy went down.

"Had enough?" Harlow asked, standing over his nephew.

"I'll say when," Randy growled, getting up.

It began again. Was it his imagination, Harlow wondered, or was the kid getting stronger? Over the next ten minutes it took all of Harlow's skills to hit and not get hit. And still the boy came on. He shook off punches that would have taken him out only months before.

For all of Harlow's coaching in the basement, Randy seemed to learn better by doing, in the ring. He connected with a solid right to the middle of Harlow's chest. It felt like a small car had hit him; he was actually pushed back a few steps by the force of the blow. And still Randy came on!

Harlow felt his strength fading—an experience he hadn't known in years. He had always kept himself in superb shape. But this nephew of his didn't seem human. Harlow showered a group of punches on Randy, finishing with a right cross that knocked the younger man to his knees.

Breathing hard, Harlow said, "Had enough yet?"

To his amazement, Randy was getting up again! "I'll say when," he said.

This time, Harlow didn't back off and allow Randy to regain his senses. With all he had left, Harlow hammered his nephew to the canvas. Again, he stood over the young man.

"Enough?" he asked. Randy shook his head and tried to get to his feet! Harlow put a hand on his nephew's headgear and pushed him to the canvas. "Well, *I've* had enough," he said. "You got heart, boy. Seems to beat you, I'd have to kill you. And I'm not ready to do that."

Randy stayed down. Harlow pulled off his gloves and

reached a hand out to help him up. To his surprise, a thundering right hand caught him flush on the chin, knocking him onto the seat of his shorts. Randy was on his feet like a cat. He looked down at Harlow.

"I been trying to catch you standing still all night," he said. "Now I did."

"You cheated!" Harlow accused.

"You bet I did," Randy replied. "Same as you did, back at your house. But I got to say you did beat me, fair and square."

Harlow sat up and roared with laughter. He took the hand that Randy extended and got to his feet. As they left the ring, Harlow began talking. "See, you couldn't get at me because of the way I was moving. And you got to stop dropping that left jab after you throw it. I came over that left with my right all three times I dropped you.

"That left jab has got to snap out straight and come back just as fast. You practice and you can double up the jab. That's a real setup for a right hand." He rubbed his rib cage. "And you got some right hand on you, kid. I'm going to get you a mirror for the basement, so you can see what you're doing better."

"The basement again!" Randy moaned. "When do I get out of there? When do we get that lawyer?"

"I'll make you a deal, Randy. When you beat me, you're out of that room."

"You got a deal, Uncle. When's our next fight?"

Harlow groaned in mock pain. "Soon as I get over this one." Both men laughed, then walked together to the locker room.

The next three weeks marked an even greater change in Randy. Harlow had given him a copy of *The Ring Encyclopedia*. Though Randy had shown some interest in easy-to-read stories, this new book was something different.

Randy began asking Harlow to help him sound out words in the book. And it seemed that Randy could remember almost everything he read—so long as it was about boxing.

As always, he went at his workouts in a rage, but it was different now. It was a cold anger. Randy stopped wasting his moves. He paid attention to every detail.

When he and Harlow ran in the park, Randy would reel off the names, dates, and winners of title fights, going back for years. Sometimes he seemed to know more than Harlow about the subject.

Every time Randy would ask a question about boxing history that Harlow couldn't answer, it pleased the younger man. It was as though he had won something personally over Harlow.

But on the subject of leaving the basement room, Randy was unchanged. It was in early October that he greeted his uncle with: "I'm ready for that rematch. We still have the same deal?"

"Same deal," Harlow answered. "You beat me—we get the lawyer, and you get out of the downstairs."

• • •

When they came up the stairs and Harlow simply pushed the door to the gym open, Randy looked at his uncle in surprise. "Did you forget to lock up?" he asked.

"I'd sooner forget my head," Harlow replied. "I called someone to be here. To keep time and count for knockdowns. We're going to go six rounds, boy."

As the two men entered, an attractive woman of about

thirty came out of Harlow's office. She was over five feet seven inches, Randy judged, and her well-muscled form was properly shown off by the jeans and light sweater she wore.

"Hey, Danielle," called Harlow. "I got someone I want you to meet." Harlow saw the look of near panic on Randy's face and whispered as Danielle approached. "It's okay. She's cool."

"But she's a woman!" Randy whispered.

"Sure is, isn't she?" Harlow said, grinning. "And she knows her boxing, too. Try some of your questions on her."

"What questions are those?" asked the young woman.

"This is my nephew Randy. I told you about him on the phone. He's some kind of expert on the fight game, Danielle."

Danielle looked Randy over with a cool gaze. "Good-sized kid," she said to Harlow. "How much do you weigh, Randy?"

"Two-ten. But don't you say 'hello' or 'pleased to meet you,' lady?" asked Randy.

"I don't get social with fighters," Danielle answered. "Bad enough I go out with Harlow. But what did you want to ask me?"

Randy was silent for a moment, his mind racing. "Who beat Tommy Burns for the heavyweight title in 1908?"

Danielle laughed. "You joking? Jack Johnson. He held the title from 1908 to 1915.

"Let me ask *you* one. Name the only heavyweight champs who retired undefeated."

"That's easy. Rocky Marciano and Joe Louis."

"Wrong!" crowed the woman. "You forgot about Jim Jeffries. He quit the fight game in 1905."

"I ain't that far back in the book," grumbled Randy. "Besides, I ain't into any of the fights before black men had a chance at the titles."

"I don't know what book you're reading, but you better read it better. There were other black men in boxing before Jack Johnson. Check out the other weight divisions, Randy."

"I told you she knew her stuff," Harlow said. "Now, let's get set for our little rumble, okay? You hit the locker room. I'll be there in a minute. And don't forget your headgear."

When Randy had left, Danielle fixed Harlow with a hard look. "Are you sure you know what you're doing, Harlow? You told me that kid's been in heavy training for almost six months. And you've been teaching him all you know.

"You got a few pounds on him, that's true. But face it, man, you're forty. If he's got any real stuff, that kid can do you world-class harm."

"Now, that's real caring of you, Danni," Harlow responded, "looking out for an old man. But I didn't say I showed the boy *everything* I know. I still got some stuff he's never seen."

"I'm looking out for the fancy dinner you promised me. And I want both of us in shape to eat it. Now how about you get ready, too?"

In a few minutes, Harlow and Randy were standing in the middle of the ring, with Danni between them. "All right, you two," she said. "I can't be in the ring and work the bell, too. And all I can time rounds with is my watch." She raised her wrist to show a sports watch with a built-in stopwatch.

"When I say 'fight!' you go at it. If you clinch and I say

'break!' you break, and break clean. When I holler 'stop!' you quit, or I'll take points away. I keep score, and whoever I say wins is the winner. You got that?"

Both men nodded. "You're going to be your own seconds. And you won't get to sit down between rounds. I can't be shuffling buckets and stools around. If there's a knockdown, you get to the nearest neutral corner. I won't start counting till you do. Now, go to your corners and don't come out till I say so."

The two men went to opposite corners. Danni raised her hands over her head, then brought them down, smacking her palms together. "Fight!" she cried out.

Randy moved in fast. Harlow began a circling motion, blocking or slipping past Randy's punches. Each time Randy would be about to get set, Harlow would hit him with a quick left, then circle again, always keeping the younger man off-balance.

As he continued the pattern, Randy's punches kept getting closer. Still, the only solid blows struck were by the older man. Ten seconds before Danni cried "Stop!" Randy missed a punch aimed at Harlow's head, and instead caught him on the left shoulder.

Harlow felt like he'd been hit with a hammer. For a second, he lost feeling in his left arm. "I got to slow this kid down," Harlow thought as he stood in his corner, his mouthpiece in his hand.

Almost before he knew it, Danni had called out "Fight!" again, and Randy was closing in. This time Harlow appeared to stand his ground. As the younger man closed, Harlow moved his left shoulder but threw a hard, right-hand lead that caught Randy flush on the button. The younger man was knocked onto the seat of his pants in the center of the ring.

Danni waved Harlow to the far corner and began a count. But by the time she got to four, Randy was on his feet. "Hold on!" Danni cried to Harlow. "Standing eight count here!"

She finished the count and cried "Fight!" Randy moved in again, this time keeping his hands higher. As Harlow began to circle again, Randy kept after him, cutting off the ring and working his uncle toward a corner. It was there that Harlow experienced the roughest few seconds of his entire career.

Randy let loose a series of lightning-fast short blows to Harlow's body. Every time Randy hit him, Harlow felt the pain. But when Randy shifted his attack "upstairs," Harlow slipped two blows. Bouncing off the ropes, he punched his way out of trouble. As he moved away, he connected with a straight left hand that he felt hit the mark.

For years Harlow had practiced this "going away" punch, made famous by the great Sugar Ray Robinson. He had knocked men cold with it. Now Harlow felt the force of the blow throughout his whole body. But Randy just took the shot, blinked, and moved in—just as Danni called "Stop!"

As Harlow stood in his corner, breathing heavily, Danni approached him, with one eye on her stopwatch. "You okay?" she asked.

"Yeah," Harlow said. "But you didn't do me no favor with that standing eight."

"Don't complain," Danni said. "The way it's going, you might need one yourself. That kid is real good. A little green, but he's good. You take care of yourself, Harlow."

"I'm trying! I'm trying!"

Danni called "Fight!" and it began again. After the harm done in the corner, Harlow wasn't moving well. His ribs hurt, and his punches were slower. Still Randy came on. Harlow landed a three-punch combination that should have knocked the younger man down. It didn't even slow Randy.

Harlow got set to try the right-hand lead that had floored Randy earlier, and suddenly his world exploded in a shower of bright light. When he opened his eyes, he was looking into Danni's. "What? . . ." he said.

"What do you think?" Danni replied. "He tagged you. Before you could throw that right, he put a straight left in your dumb face. You scared me, man. You were really out."

"Where's Randy?"

"I told him to hit the showers. You going to be all right?"

"Yeah . . . I think so. Man, that boy can hit!"

Harlow got to his feet and walked with Danielle to his office, where he sat down heavily at his desk. Danielle took off his gloves, then talked with Harlow for the next few minutes. Finally, cleaned up and wearing street clothes, Randy came into Harlow's office.

"Are you okay, Uncle Harlow?" he asked.

"Fine, boy . . . just fine. I got to admit you beat me."

"Hard not to admit," said Danni, "when they scrape you off the canvas."

"This might not be the time," Randy said, "but how about that lawyer?"

Harlow waved a hand at Danielle. "Go ahead and talk. You're looking at her."

"You're a lawyer?" Randy gasped at Danni.

"One of the best," Harlow said. "She gave me a lot of help in getting your case together."

"Case?"

"Yes, Randy," Danni said. "I've been involved since last June. That's when Harlow told me what had happened with you in Brooklyn."

Randy turned to Harlow. "But you told me . . ."

"It's complicated, Randy," Harlow said. "Why don't you just listen to what Danni has to say?"

"You're in trouble, all right, Randy. But not as big as you think," Danni said. "Yes, you were at the scene of a crime. And your connection to it isn't the cleanest. But you didn't do the crime.

"As to that, both people involved in the double murder—Eddie and Zipper—are dead. I talked to the police and to a judge. Nobody is going to miss either one of them too much. But you saw it all happen, Randy. Did you ever hear of a material witness?"

"No . . ."

"Well, that's what you were. In fact, some of Zipper's friends were looking for you. The police only wanted your statement as to what happened. Zipper's friends were after your head. There were two things the police could have done. One was lock you up to keep you safe."

"In jail?"

"No place safer, except if you were being hidden by a responsible person. In your case, you had a family member—Harlow—who is also an assistant probation officer."

Randy turned to Harlow. "You're a cop!" he accused. "And all that time you had me in that little room, you were lying to me! And you lied about you getting into trouble, I bet!"

"No, Randy. That part's true. But your mamma has the same ideas about ex-cons that lots of people do—that they can't go straight. I went back to school when I got out. Got my degree in social work. Working with the Probation Department, I opened this gym.

"I try to keep kids like you from getting into big trouble by putting them into boxing. It was a way of putting together my talent for athletics and my new career."

Harlow waved at the wall of pictures behind his desk. "All these kids you see were in trouble when I found them. I'm proud of all of them. Some of them went on to be pretty fair fighters. Others have good jobs and are making something of their lives."

"But cops came to your house looking for me. I heard them. You told me to hide."

"I sent for them. After all, I *am* with the Probation Department, kid. I was afraid you'd run off at first—maybe go back to the neighborhood and get hurt. Yeah, I lied to you. It was to keep you in one piece.

"Besides, I saw early on that you had talent as a fighter— just like your daddy did. And what were you doing with your life, anyway? You were on your way to big trouble."

"That don't matter!" Randy shouted. "It's my life, ain't it? Who gave you the right to play God?"

"Your mamma, for one. Yeah, you're over eighteen, Randy. And I didn't much care for talking with Francie. But once I told her what my new career was, and that I was keeping you safe, she was all for it. Maybe what I did wasn't all that fair, but look at you now.

"When you came to my house, you were big and thought you were tough. But you were soft and couldn't hit the floor if you fell out of bed. I made you into a real athlete. You're even reading now, and getting better every day at it. You've done something with your life these past months. You've made yourself into a person your mamma could be proud of."

Randy's face was a mask of dark rage. He moved toward Harlow. "I ought to . . . ," he began.

Harlow held up a hand. "What are you going to do? Beat up on me? You already did that. Are you going to do something stupid, like I did, outside the ring? Or are you going to put that hot blood of yours to a good use? You're what I've been looking for all these years. You could be a champion, Randy."

"And I think I can get charges reduced because you co-operated with the police," Danni added.

"I what?"

"You gave a full statement, in your own handwriting. Your uncle saw to that. Then you stayed with him—a probation officer—until the hearing. That's coming up next month, by the way."

"But that still didn't give him the right to do what he done to me!"

"Keep you in protective custody? That's what a judge called it. Think it over, Randy," Danni said.

"I've already did that. I'm out of here!" Randy left Harlow's office and headed for the door.

"Randy!" Harlow called after him. "It's chilly out there. You don't have anything but summer clothes on. You could get sick."

"It ain't any colder than what you done to me," Randy called back. He slammed the door behind him.

Harlow looked at Danni, then leaned forward over his desk, his head in his hands. "I've lost him, Danni," he said.

"You did your best," Danni said, putting a hand on the big man's shoulder. "Why don't you shower and change? I'll start shutting down here. And you still owe me a dinner. We'll talk over some food, okay?"

Harlow nodded and went off to clean up. When he walked back to his office in street clothes, he couldn't believe his eyes. Randy was sitting in his office, talking with Danielle. The young man looked up as Harlow entered.

"Randy! You came back!" Harlow cried.

"Didn't have subway money," Randy grumbled. "Didn't even have money for a phone call. I been in your jail so long, I forgot about money."

"I gave him some money," Danni said to Harlow. "That's more you owe me."

"Then how come you're still here?" Harlow asked Randy.

"I had to ask you something. You already lied to me so much, I don't know what to believe. But did you mean it when you said I could be a champion?"

"More than anything I've ever said in my life. If you work at it as hard as you have been."

Randy looked hard at Harlow, then asked, "Can I use your phone?"

"Help yourself."

Danni and Harlow stood outside the office door while Randy dialed. Through the partly open door, Harlow could hear Randy's side of the conversation.

"Hello . . . Mamma? Yeah, it's me. . . . I'm just fine. Say listen, Mamma. Would you mind if I stayed with Uncle Harlow a while longer? No . . . I'm not sure how long. I'll send you a letter about it, Mamma. . . . Sure, in my own handwriting. What, do you think I can't? Yeah . . . I love you too, Mamma. Bye."

When Randy came out of the office, he looked at Harlow and Danni and smiled. "What's for dinner, Uncle?" he asked.

T. Ernesto Bethancourt

As the son of a Puerto Rican truck driver, T. Ernesto Bethancourt participated in the sports of *boxeo* and *beisbol*—boxing and baseball—as many Latino kids do. After absorbing enough punishment in sparring and in local matches sponsored by the New York City Police Athletic League, he decided to pursue either baseball or career diplomacy. "In those activities," he says, "it doesn't hurt, physically, if one makes mistakes."

Because his father managed fighters for a time, young Tomas spent a lot of time in the company of fighters. The theme of "Fury," he says, reflects the lives of many real-life amateur and professional fighters. The relationship between Harlow and Randy is based in part on the relationship between the famous trainer Cus D'Amato and the infamous boxer Mike Tyson.

Before becoming a writer, Mr. Bethancourt was a performer, playing blues guitar and singing in nightclubs and coffeehouses under the name Tom Paisley. He now lives in southern California, where he still plays guitar and sings on special occasions, usually when visiting schools, where he encourages kids to write their own stories.

He is the author of the popular Doris Fein mysteries, the most recent of which is *Doris Fein: Legacy of Terror,* and the novels *T.H.U.M.B.B., New York City Too Far from Tampa Blues, The Mortal Instruments, Where the Deer and the Cantaloupe Play, The Tomorrow Connection, The Me Inside of Me,* and *The Dog Days of Arthur Cane. Arthur Cane* was made into a film for ABC television that is still shown on Nickelodeon.

Viewed as a dummy by nearly everyone,
Clark has never been successful at anything. Most of all, he needs a friend.

Superboy

Chris Crutcher

Pa Kent says I ain't probly gonna ever win no prizes for smarts, but I ain't been in no contests. Long as I'm not in one, I could probly tell everone I coulda got maybe a Third or so, and who'd know?

That ain't why he says it, though. He says it cause he wants me to try to win prizes in other stuff, like he says I'm a natural born triath-a-lete, which means I can do three things just about as good as each other. The *tri* part means three. See, I ain't so dumb. I kinda wish it was just *any* three things, you know, like ridin' your BMX bike over a big ol' dirt pile an' then maybe how fast can you switch through all the TV channels, an' like a watermelon eatin' contest or somethin'. But it ain't that. You got to swim in Coeur d'Alene Lake which is about as big as the ocean, which I went to once, and then ride your ten-speed 'til the seat feels like it's stuck clear up your insides, and then you got to run all over town and even *out* of town a ways, an' you don't get to rest in between any of 'em.

So when Pa Kent first tol' me I was gonna be doin' this,

I says, "Do a lot of other dumb guys do triath-a-lons?" because I figure they gotta be perty dumb or they'd think of a way not to haf to, an' he tells me quit callin' myself dumb, which I figure it's best to get to it ahead of everybody else. That way, you're already agreein' with 'em instead of tryin' to hurt 'em for bein' ugly to you. It's hard to stay friends with smart guys if you're always tryin' to make their nose bleed. Pa Kent's a nice dad and he means good, but I been dumb long enough to be the guy that probly knows how to handle it best.

You gotta kinda look up to Pa Kent for a guy that takes perty good care of you. Like I think I musta come here pickin' my nose an' eatin' it or somethin', cause he knew right off I wasn't gonna be one of them Albert Silversteins or nothin', and he got right busy tryin' to make sure I didn't have no more hard life. It musta worked, cause I ain't had a whole lot to complain about from the time they took me out of my real house up 'til now, 'cept sometimes it feels like I miss my momma. That don't make sense cause I guess she treated me *real* bad, which is how come everbody thinks I got such a bad temper. Anyway, I might hafta groan a little about this here triath-a-lon, cause it's harder than just about anythin' I ever tried to get out of.

I get a little shivvery thinkin' about doin' it cause I done all three things by theirselves when I was a kid, an' ever time there was people got mad at me an' sometimes they fixed it so I couldn't do it no more. Like when I got on the Clark Fork Swim Team. I'd do real good in the workouts—be beatin' just about everbody as old as me, but then when a swimmin' meet would happen there'd always be somethin' to mess me up. Like I swam on this relay, which is where a whole bunch of kids swim the same race, an' I'd get too excited an' forget when it was my turn, or I'd think it was my turn when it was some other kid's, an' I'd get us this thing they called dis-qualified, an' the other kids on my team would get all pissed off at me and call me dumb. 'Course then I'd have to make one of their noses bleed. Givin' out bloody noses ain't the best way to make it so you can stay on a swim team, is what Pa Kent tol' me, but it was too late.

Or when I went to the Parks and Recreation to be in track in the summer. I was really fast but it was hard to know when you were sposed to stop an' when you were sposed to keep on runnin' an' it would be differnt ever time. That one was easier though, cause lots of times there'd be this ribbon an' when it hit you in your chest you was done. 'Cept the thing I had trouble with, was there was this gun that went off when you were sposed to go. First time it just scared me an' I ducked, an' everbody left me down on my knees on the ground while they went an' won it. But the biggest trouble with track was this kid named James that I beat almost ever time, an' once after I done that, his dad come up to Pa Kent an' said I should go to this thing called the Special Olympics so all the regular kids didn't have to get all embarrassed gettin' beat by a dummy. Next thing, Pa Kent was fixin' to make James's dad have a bloody nose an' we weren't invited to be in any more track meets.

The bike part is always good, though, 'cept for where it feels like the seat goes after you been on it too long. I take my mountain bike way out in the woods all by myself where the trees get real tall an' the road gets all skinny an' don't have no more highway on it, an' when you get far enough out there, it don't seem like you're so dumb. Sometimes I stop there cause it's the only place that feels like that.

Pa Kent ain't my foster dad's real name, just like Ma Kent ain't my foster mom's, but when I come here I guess I was perty young an' perty scared, an' I had me this Superboy doll my CPS worker—my Child Protection worker—give me cause she tol' me he was a foster kid, too. They musta been tryin' to trick me a little bit, cause they tol' me I was gettin' his very same foster parents, what with him all growed up an' Super*man* now, an' that musta seemed okay to me cause it worked, just as soon as they give me some blue p.j.s an' a red towel to pin around my neck. Plus, my name was already Clark an' even though it was my last name, we took an' made it my first one. Ma Kent says I didn't say nothin' for more than a month, which is a perty long time to be quiet, 'specially if you knew what it's like inside my head. She says I just whizzed around the livin' room makin' little grunty noises an' seemin' like I was tryin' to fly away. I guess I sweat up them Superboy p.j.s perty good. I know this is probly one thing that makes me dumb, but I still wear the red towel around my neck whenever I can, but never at school cause I tried that a long time ago an' I ended up haffin' to give out a whole bunch of bloody noses right before I ended up haffin' to go home. Ma Kent give me a bunch of Superboy comic books then, which showed how the real Clark Kent had this thing called a "secret idennity" which is where you don't let anybody know you're really Superboy. You just wear regular clothes an' act like you can't fly or give out bloody noses. Plus, the Clark Kent in the comics has glasses just like me, 'cept I don't think his are as thick as mine, cause of what my momma done to me. The secret idennity would of worked better if everbody didn't already see the red towel, which is a cape in real life, but I guess it made things better.

I don't like thinkin' back before Ma an' Pa Kent too much. First, it's hard to remember exactly, like is somethin' real or is my brain just makin' it up. Sometimes stuff jumps in my head when I'm not thinkin' about nothin', or when I'm asleep. It's bad to get too close to me when that happens cause there's no tellin' what I'll do, like I might punch you or scream so loud you'll pee. If I *try* to remember back then, it's just all dark an' bad. I heard my CPS lady tellin' Ma an' Pa Kent she ain't sure if I'm dumb cause that's how I come out, or cause of what they done to me after, but I don't see who cares cause if you're dumb you're dumb, an' it don't make no differnce how come, you're still gonna have to fight. She don't call it dumb though, she calls it "inna-lekshully challenged" but I ain't dumb, I know who all they call that, an' we get treated differnt than everbody else.

There's this guy gonna help me do this triath-a-lon. He's about my same age, which is nineteen, an' his name is Bo-re-gard Brewster. That's his real name, honest. Everbody calls him Bo though, cause if you called him all of it you'd probly forget why you was talkin' to him in the first place. Anyway, Bo's kinda famous around our school on account of he called Mr. Redmond a asshole. Mr. Redmond is the football coach and the teacher of the English class they don't let guys like me into. Really, Bo done that. Fact he done it twice, once when he was playin' football, which he don't do no more just for that very reason, and once in English class which he still does go to if he don't call Mr. Redmond that again, an' if he goes to Angry Management, which is this class that happens really early in the morning an' has mostly scary guys in it, 'cept Bo ain't one, even though everbody says he fights with his dad pretty good, too.

After he been helpin' me awhile, I ast him why he said that to Mr. Redmond, an' he said, "Settin' the record straight, Superboy. Settin' the record straight." I think that means he done it cause it's the truth. I had Redmond hollerin' at me once when I was tryin' to give this kid in the lunch room a bloody nose for callin' me "shit-for-brains"—which they ain't—an' I called him a asshole, too, but I sure didn't make it loud enough so he could hear it. If you get Redmond mad he can make bad things happen to you. I can see where he might wanna go to Angry Management hisself, but I don't think he'd really do it. Ol' Bo must have a bad enough temper on 'im that makes it so he ain't scared of Mr. Redmond, which makes us a little bit the same as each other, I think, cause sometimes I get so mad that I ain't scared of nothin'. We're differnt than each other too, though, cause I think Bo's perty smart.

Anyway Bo has lotsa extra time now since he can't play nothin' after school on account of what he called Mr. Redmond, so he makes hisself be a triath-a-lete. Man, you don't hardly ever see this guy when he ain't runnin' or swimmin' or ridin' his bike all over ever place. Pa Kent pays him money to take me with 'im sometimes when he goes trainin', an' when he goes up to the university where we both have this fake card that says we go to college there, so we can sneak into the weight room. He got one for me. Man, tell me who do you think is dumber, me, or somebody seein' a guy carryin' a red an' blue Superboy gym bag an' thinks I go to college?

So the first time Bo come over to my house to get me, I tell him right off I might not be too good at this triath-a-lon stuff cause I ain't so smart, cause you always want to tell 'em that so they don't figger it out later an' not like you, an' then you don't got a friend you thought was.

But Bo smiled an' said that was probly somethin' I had workin' *for* me. He said if I was smart I might wanna be doin' somethin' that didn't feel the same as this. An' boy was he ever right! We started runnin' an' I kep' askin' was we done yet an' he kep' smilin' an' sayin' I probly should put "done yet" outta my head, cause if you're a triath-a-lete you ain't never done, which I have to admit seemed like a perty long time so I threw up. That gets me out of a lot of stuff cause I can do it whenever I want, but Bo jus' said to not get any on my shoes, an' we kep' right on runnin'. Damn.

After that, ever time I done somethin' to try to get to quit, Bo just rubbed his hand back between my shoulders an' said I was gettin' too good an' he needed me to help him go faster, an' then he tol' Pa Kent I had this thing called a "nak," which I guess makes you go fast, an' he said he was startin' to need me just as much as I needed him. Nobody ever said that before, not nobody *ever*, an' somethin' really strange started happenin'. I started *likin'* bein' a triath-a-lete. That scared me at first, cause I thought it might mean I'm gettin' dumber, which wouldn't be good, but Bo said nope, he'd been doin' this a long time an' he got smarter ever day, couldn't I tell? I said yeah I could, but I couldn't really. See, sometimes you have to lie if it don't hurt nobody an' you think it'll make you get a friend. Plus, he wasn't gettin' dumber, an' that's all I didn't want to happen.

Bo said I needed to get me some concentratin'. That's where you think real hard about what you're doin'. I know what it is because my teachers always want me to get some, but it's easier to get when you're workin' out hard, cause you're thinkin' about stuff you can do, instead of at school where you're thinkin' about stuff you can't. Bo says the hardest part of a triath-a-lon is to keep your head in the game, which by that he means not to start thinkin' about whatever jumps in your head so you forget you're tryin' to hurry up an' win.

So we're runnin' this one day right after a bike ride an' I'm right with 'im an' everthin', an' then all of a sudden I'm "lollygaggin" like he calls it, an' so he asts me, he says, do I gots anybody I don't like, somebody like Mr. Redmond for him, an' I say you kiddin' me? cause I got more people like that than any other kind. So he tells me to pick one of 'em an' then think of what they done to make me not like 'em, an' see if it makes me go faster. Well, for some reason which I don't even know why, the one I pick is my mother—I mean my real mother, not Ma Kent—an' at first it's hard to think of why I would even pick her cause I can't hardly even see her face in my brain, but then all of a sudden I'm runnin' faster an' faster until I can hardly breathe, an everthin' goes all white, an' the next thing I'm on the ground an' Bo is shakin' me an' askin' am I okay, which I think I am definitely not. I would of started bawlin' right there, 'cept I couldn't breathe on account of I just got done runnin' so fast, so I just laid there an' felt about as awful as I ever did, an' Bo tol' me maybe I should pick somebody else.

I still couldn't breathe too good, so I just nodded my head, but I couldn't think of nobody.

So Bo sits with me there awhile, an' perty soon he asts me, he says, "What was it you remembered 'bout your mom, Superboy?" an' I says I ain't sure.

"Musta been some bad shit," he says, an' I think that's right.

Then he says, "You don' have to talk about it," an' I says I wanna talk about it, cause it's startin' to feel like I really like him, but I don' know what to say. An' he asts me was there pichers in my head or somethin', an I tell 'im it was dark at first. He wants to know was it like a blackout or like some *place* dark, an' for the first time ever, I see this here closet. An' there's me in it. An' there's somethin' else. There's this bottle that gots the pills I used to take when I had this thing called "seizures." Only even though I can see it, I can't see it, too, on account of how dark it is, an' I can't tell how much to take or when I should take it, an' all of a sudden I'm feelin' real scared right up in my throat, even though I know I'm really just sittin' here with Bo.

So Bo asts me if I wanna talk some more about it or just shut up an' run home, cause he knows this guy named Hudgie, an' when *he* gets thinkin' too much he has to go to the part of the hospital for guys with hurt brains. I ain't never thought *that* much. I know Hudge, cause he's in a bunch of my classes on account of he's a big-time dummy too, only you better not say that to him. So I tell Bo if he'll stay there with me maybe I could do just a *little* more thinkin', but he gots to promise to stop me if I get goin' too bad, an' he says okay.

So I says what should I think about, an' he says, "I don' know, maybe you should just try to see why you're in there."

Well I don't know, I tell 'im back, but I think it's cause of trouble, like why else would somebody go in a closet, an' he says he can think of a couple a other reasons.

He says, "You think somebody put you in there a lot to make you punished?" an' I tell 'im yeah, I done lotsa closet time, I think. They called it that. Mostly I think that cause I remember Ma an' Pa Kent gettin' all crazy when I stuck myself in there one time after I spilt some milk all over the kitchen table. They tol' me only reason I ever had to go in a closet ever again was to git me a coat or somethin'. I remember likin' to hear that, 'cept I didn't really believe it at first.

Bo says the reason he's askin' me all these questions is on account of he's learnin' a whole lot in his Angry Management class about what to do when things sneak up on you in your head. I ast him does that happen to him too, an' he says yup. He says if you teach yourself to remember bad stuff instead of tryin' to forget about it all the time, on account of how it makes you feel, it can't sneak up on you cause you know it's there cause you been thinkin' about it. He says it keeps him out of a lot of fights with his daddy.

So anyway, after we're done talkin' an' I'm all feelin' better an' everthin' we get back up an' start trainin' again, cause that's what you do if you do triath-a-lons. You train. But right when we first start runnin', Bo says, "Superboy, I got a idea. Maybe thinkin' about somebody you don't like to make you go fast ain't such a good idea like it is for me," an' he picks up this rock. "Know what this is?" he asts me, an' I tell 'im a rock. "Nope," he says, "this here's Kryptonite. You know about Kryptonite, right?" an' I tell him 'course I know about Kryptonite, how could I be Superboy if I didn't know that, but how come it ain't green? He tells me trust 'im, it's green on the inside. Bad guys covered it up with fake rock. Then he gets right behind me an' keeps sayin', "Better not let me touch you with this or you'll get weak an' slow," an' he gets goin' faster to touch me an' I gets goin' faster to keep him from doin' it. We got back real fast.

Bo's laughin' so hard at the end he can hardly talk, but he can a little an' he tells me when the race comes I gots to look around behind me real quick an' pick a bad guy an' pertend he's got a big ol' rock of Kryptonite an' he's comin' to touch it on me an' make me weak an' slow. I tell 'im how will I know if it's a bad guy, an' he says if he's fixin' to catch you, he's a bad guy. Now that's somethin' I can think about that'll make me get goin' I bet, 'cept when I'm swimmin', cause it's perty hard to look behind you in the water an' Bo says, "Well jus' swim fast then," an' I tell 'im okay.

One thing that makes people think somethin's wrong with me is sometimes I freak when nobody's expectin' it. I can be goin' along an' goin' along an' nothin's wrong an' then all of a sudden somethin' that shouldn't make no never minds makes me remember that dark place before Ma an' Pa Kent, an' I'll freak—maybe start screamin' an' pullin' my hair out or somethin'. Like I was runnin' along with Bo one day when the weather was gettin' better so it's almost like hot outside, an' I was sweatin' like I got automatic sprinklers in me. That don't make me no never minds cause I sweat all the time an' usually all it does is make me smell bad, but this one day it starts gettin' in my eyes, an' they start burnin' an' all of a sudden, oops. I start screamin' an' yellin' right out there on the highway, which is where we're runnin', an' before anythin', Bo is pushin' me over in the ditch an' holdin' me down, duckin' so he don't get hit. He's yellin' "Superboy! Superboy!" an' stuff—anyway that's what he tells me later, an' that's what I wake up hearin' him yellin'. He says what the hell's the matter with me an' I tell 'im I gots sweat in my eyes an' he says then wipe it the hell out. So I starts wipin' it out with my arm which has sweat all over it too, so it's like wipin' somethin' out of your eyes with whatever is already in there an' I figure out perty quick that ain't gonna work.

He says use my T-shirt but I show 'im that gots sweat all over it too an' there just ain't no answer to this an' I'm feelin' like freakin' again, but Bo gets this great idea an' he tells me if I'm truly Superboy then maybe I jus' better be wearin' my cape when we train so I can give my eyes a superwipe when shit gets in 'em an' maybe protect myself from anythin' else I'm not ready for. Now that makes me feel real good cause I ain't had no good reason to wear it for a long time an' even though the real Superboy has his "secret idennity" he still gets to wear his cape *some* of the time. When I get to feelin' a little bit calm, Bo asts me, he says, "What the hell was that all about, Superboy, cause if you're gonna be a triath-a-lete an' freak whenever sweat gets in your eyes, you're gonna be in a bad way." I tell 'im what jumped in my head was walkin' out in the livin' room at night an' seein' my mom on the couch under this guy. She went an' took this eye-dropper thing an' stuck this stuff in my eyes that made 'em burn an' burn. She said it would teach me not to be seein' things I ain't sposed to. That's how come I gots to wear these really thick glasses. Bo jus' shook his head an' said Jesus.

So then Bo gets to thinkin' maybe we oughta bring ol' Superboy back in a big way—like maybe I should wear this cape at the actual triath-a-lon to let all them other triath-a-letes know just what they got theirselves into. Put the fear of Jor-el in 'em, Bo says. We'll git you Superboy bikin' shorts an' a big red S all over the front of your runnin' shirt an' show everbody we're puttin' Smallville on the map, which is that's where the real Superboy used to live before he got to be Superman an' went to Metropolis. So I says what about when I'm swimmin'? an' Bo asts me do I know about Aquaman, an' I say uh-uh. He tells me Aquaman can do the things in the water that Superman can do in the air, which I think he means go fast in it. If there's a Aqua*man*, Bo says to me, there gots to be a Aqua*boy*, right? an' I can see how that would be. An' he says that's who I can be in the water.

Then he says he's not sure but he thinks Aquaboy has foster parents too, only probly they're dolphins, or a mermaid an' a pirate or somethin'.

• • •

When you're goin' along an' you got a friend, the first thing you want to do is not to lose him. I know it's perty easy for some guys to get theirselves friends, but that ain't me. The trouble is, a couple days after you get one, you start worryin' about that he won't be your friend very long. When I was in grade school sometimes guys would be my friend cause their mom an' dad would make 'em to help out the ones that was "less fortunate" than them, which was me. You could always tell the ones when their mom or dad made 'em do that, cause they only lasted not quite one whole day, an' you would beg 'em to stay your friend, but that would make 'em mad an' they'd end up callin' you a dummy. I really hated it when that happened an' it would usually make my head explode, which is where my temper is.

But I'm thinkin' Bo likes me cause of triath-a-lons, an' if I keep doin' it real hard he'll keep likin' me. 'Cept then it makes me think, what if he finds somebody who does 'em better than you? So I try to do everthin' faster, but it doesn't matter, the longer somebody's your friend the more scared you get. So perty soon you just have to find out.

Now I've got better at how to find out, cause if you just ast somebody will you stay bein' my friend, that usually never works, an' the second they don't answer you right back you know they won't be. An' if you beg, you lose 'em right that day ever time. But sometimes if you ask *how come* you can find out better.

So one day Bo takes me on a bike ride to the top of Mount Spokane, an' it's a long ways an' the road gets crooked-er an' crooked-er an' steeper an' steeper until you feel like your legs are burnin' inside so bad you almost wisht they'd fall off so they could hurt without you feelin' it. Bo goes in front, an' I stays right behind him all the way to the top, an' when we gets to the top he looks at his Ironman watch an' says we done it faster than he ever had of before, an' we deserve a rest, which I *always* like to hear him say that, an' he almost never does. So we get off our bikes an' take us out some Gatorade that was in our backpacks, which it made them heavier an' you wanted to throw it away back there, but you're really glad you never did.

We're sittin' there drinkin' our Gatorade an' tryin' to get back to breathin' regular an' I go ahead an' ast him how come.

He said it was cause he liked me an' cause I push him.

An' I say yeah, but would he keep bein' my friend after there wasn't no more triath-a-lon, an' he don't wait a minute or blink his eyes or cough or nothin'. He just says yes. So now my stomach's *really* feelin' all jumpy an' I can't tell why for sure, cause he said the right answer, but I gots to ast him will we always do things all the time, an' he says not *all* the time, but we'll do things, which is mostly train.

So then I ast if we could be *best* friends, cause I always wanted one of those, an' *then* he don't answer me for a second an' I'm all ready for him to make up a lie, but he just says no, probly not best friends. I hang down my head for a minute, an' just when I'm feelin' like I should probly wipe my nose with my cape, he puts his hand on me, like on my arm and he says, "But we'll still be friends, Superboy, special friends." He says *triath-a-lon* friends. I starts to pull away my arm from him, cause it feels like not a *real* friend, but he says wait, listen to him. He says, "We're not the same, Superboy. We like to do differnt things an' we gots differnt innersts." He says he'll probly go to college an' I'll go to a differnt kind of school. But he says we're the same, too. He says he gets mad jus' like me an' when he does he usually does somethin' that gets him in trouble. He says we both like to do triath-a-lons. He says even though my parents—not Ma an' Pa Kent but the for real ones—was way meaner than his daddy ever was, an' probly that asshole Redmond, too, he had plenty to be mad about hisself, an' that was kinda like me. He says we could probably teach each other stuff about that, even though I don't think I could teach anybody anythin' cause who would listen?

Then he said somethin' I didn't quite understand, but it sounded like it was true. He said 'stead of worryin' 'bout what kinda friends we *ain't,* how 'bout thinkin' 'bout what kinda friends we *are,* which what he meant by that was that we could always be friends about triath-a-lons an' parents who pissed us off an' hurt us, an' sometimes teachers too. No matter what, he tol' me, we'll always be friends about those things, an' there's probly some other things that we'll find out. He said people do triath-a-lons until they're really old, an' even if we're in differnt places, we could train together cause we could think about each other in our head.

An' then all of a sudden I don't feel scared no more,

cause I don't have to worry 'bout him goin' away from me. I know how I can keep him. I can keep Bo my friend by always trainin' for triath-a-lons, even though that seems like a long time when I'm tired, an' by talkin' to him 'bout things that we don't like, or that hurt us. Bo says that's a good way to find friends—you know, find out what's the same 'bout you, an' do some concentratin' an' talkin' on that when you're with 'em.

So I'm sittin' here today feelin' about the best a guy can feel. Soon as I get this cape pinned around my neck, an' all my stuff in Pa Kent's car, me an' Bo are goin' over to the Coeur d'Alene triath-a-lon an' pick out some bad guys what gots Kryptonite.

An' I'm not gonna tell 'im this, but 'til I find me somebody for a *best* friend, I'm gonna pertend it's Bo.

Chris Crutcher

Chris Crutcher is the highly respected author of *Running Loose, Stotan!, The Crazy Horse Electric Game, Chinese Handcuffs,* and *Staying Fat for Sarah Byrnes*. Each of those five sports-oriented novels, as well as *Athletic Shorts,* his book of short stories, was named a Best Book for Young Adults by the American Library Association. Moreover, both *Stotan!* and *Athletic Shorts* have been listed by the ALA among the 100 Best of the Best Books for Young Adults published between 1967 and 1992. Like "Superboy," each of his works provides an insightful examination of teenage struggles in a painful world, with a background of sports.

His understanding of the agony suffered by the characters in his stories is no doubt a reflection of the work he did for twelve years as a child and family therapist with the Community Mental Health Center in Spokane. His perceptions of sports, especially his insights into athletics at small schools, come from his own experiences growing up in Cascade, Idaho, where he ran track and played football and basketball. "Had to," he says, "it was a *small* school." At Eastern Washington State College he was a member of the swim team, specializing in distance freestyle and qualifying for the National Association of Intercollegiate Athletes nationals in 1967 and 1968. Now he plays "old man" basketball and is a triathlon competitor—running, biking, and swimming.

Mr. Crutcher is also the author of an exciting adult novel dealing with child abuse called *The Deep End*. His newest book for teenage readers, called *Ironman,* is about father-son power struggles, with Bo Brewster from "Superboy" as the main character.

In 1993 the Assembly on Literature for Adolescents of the National Council of Teachers of English gave Chris Crutcher its ALAN Award for his outstanding contributions to the field of young adult literature.

Overcoming Adversity

The Sultan High School wrestling team has a new coach. He's sincere but not very competent. Even though the boys try their best, they stink. Can a mascot make a difference?

If You Can't Be Lucky . . .

Carl Deuker

My name is Joey Hagstrom. I live in Sultan, Washington, with my mom and dad. Sultan is a farming community in the foothills of the Cascade Mountains about fifty miles east of Seattle. I suppose it's a great place to live. I can go hiking and skiing and fishing and hunting. But it gets boring out here with the cows and the pigs and the sheep. Every kid in Sultan—including me—would rather live in Seattle.

But this story isn't about me. It's about last year when the school district ran out of money, the athletic department fell apart, and my uncle Joe ended up as my high-school wrestling coach. It's also about his smelly dog, Cindy, and the amazing way our season ended.

My uncle Joe works at the sewage treatment plant on the Skykomish River. I'm not exactly sure what he does there. All I know is that he walks around pools of bubbling, frothy, brown water with a long pole in his hand. He wears a white suit, has a doctor's mask over his mouth, and every once in a while pokes at the water. Cindy, his big black Labrador, is always at his heels, her tongue hanging out like she's smiling. My dad says that's because dogs love anything that stinks.

I've never asked Uncle Joe what he pokes at. I've never asked why the water is bubbly, or why it's brownish, or where it goes when Uncle Joe is done with it. I'm not the only one who is squeamish about that sewage treatment plant. I've never heard anybody ask Uncle Joe anything about his work.

That doesn't keep Uncle Joe from talking about his job, though. He talks about it every chance he gets. "My philosophy is simple," he says, his face set in a fake scowl. "I look out for number one." He pokes himself on his chest for effect. "But I also look out for number two." Then he laughs, a big deep-chested laugh. "Get it? Number one and number two! You know, tinkle and poop! Ha! Ha! Ha!"

I've heard this joke at least one hundred times in my life.

"Number one and number two! Get it? Ha! Ha! Ha!"

Don't misunderstand. I like Uncle Joe. My dad runs a dairy farm for Carnation milk. By the end of the day he's too tired to do anything but lie on the sofa and read the newspaper. So if I want to go fishing or hiking, or if I want to shoot hoops or play football, it's Uncle Joe I ask. Uncle Joe is never too tired, never too busy. He always has a smile on his face. I just wish he'd come up with some new jokes and that Cindy didn't smell so bad.

• • •

I'd finished my final class one rainy afternoon last November. I was heading for home with my two best friends, Dinky Barnes and J. P. Jones, when I spotted Uncle Joe's big brown work van pulling up in front of school. I hustled over. "What's up, Uncle Joe?"

"Can't talk about it, Joey," he snapped as he strode up the pathway and into the school's main office. "Wish I could, but I can't." It was the first time in my life Uncle Joe hadn't had time to talk to me.

"What was that about?" Dinky asked me.

I shrugged. "He wouldn't say. It seems like an emergency, though."

J.P.'s eyes widened. "You don't think there's anything wrong with the school's water, do you?"

Dinky thought for a second. "I thought the water was sort of brown today, didn't you?"

"Brown?" J.P. and I said at the same time.

"Not pure brown. Sort of a yellow brown. I figured it was rust in the pipes, but now I wonder."

I almost threw up.

Uncle Joe, as usual, came breezing into our house at dinnertime that same day. "Joey, my boy! Mary, my sister!" he shouted, really excited.

My mom and I rushed out to the front room to meet him. My dad, sprawled out on our sofa, hid his head behind the newspaper.

It's hard to say how my father feels about Uncle Joe. He doesn't dislike him, but he doesn't like him either. *Tolerates* is probably the word, though *ignores* would work too.

"I got the job!" Uncle Joe shouted, and he grabbed me by the shoulders and shook me hard.

"Great!" I hollered. "What job?"

"I'm going to be your wrestling coach! That's why I was at the high school today! What I couldn't talk about!"

I smiled, not so much because Uncle Joe was my coach,

but more out of relief to learn that I hadn't spent the day sipping sewer water.

From behind his newspaper, my father grumbled. "What do you know about coaching wrestling?"

Uncle Joe looked hurt. "What do I know about wrestling? Harry, how can you ask? Once I told Mr. Popup—"

"Mr. Poppel," I interrupted.

"That's what I said, Joey. Mr. Popup, your principal. Anyway, once I told him about my experience in San Francisco, he sent the other applicants packing."

My father lowered his newspaper and actually looked at Uncle Joe. "You don't mean that crazy job you had as timekeeper for Big-Time Wrestling, do you? You can't possibly think that's experience."

"And why not?" Uncle Joe answered. "For three years I was like this"—he clasped his hands together—"with the finest wrestlers in the world. Ray Stevens, Pat Patterson, Pepper Gomez, Bobo Brazil, the Sheik, Haystack Calhoun."

My father looked from me to my mother. "Somebody tell him," he spluttered. "Mary? Joey? Tell him."

"Tell me what?" Uncle Joe demanded.

"Uncle Joe," I said softly. "High-school wrestling is different from professional wrestling."

He waved that off. "I know that, Joey. You're kids. So I won't expect the same level of professionalism. I'm not stupid. Still"—now he turned to my father—"those men taught me tricks that I can pass on to the boys." He smiled. "With me coaching, we might take the state title this year."

My father ducked his head behind the newspaper again, but I heard him chortle.

Late that night I sneaked down into the living room and turned the television to Big-Time Wrestling. The Masked Marauder was doing battle with Pretty Boy Lloyd. They pounded, punched, flipped, tripped, kicked, leg-whipped, and bit one another for ten minutes. Finally the Masked Marauder whacked Pretty Boy over the head with a folding chair, ran his head into a steel pole, body-slammed him, then flopped on top of him. "One! Two! Three!" the ref counted. The Marauder popped to his feet, gave Pretty Boy a final kick in the head, then punched the air with both fists as the crowd roared its approval.

I flicked the television off and sat in the dark trying to think of one thing I'd seen that was legal in high-school wrestling. I came up empty.

• • •

Wrestling tryouts were Monday. Uncle Joe showed up decked out in a purple Adidas warm-up outfit with a white stripe that went down the sleeve and then matched up with another stripe coming up the leg. He had on a purple headband and purple wristbands. The lettermen exchanged glances.

Uncle Joe motioned the fifty or so of us who were turning out to come close. "My name is Joe Milligan. You probably know I'm Joey's uncle. My philosophy is simple: I look out for number one." He paused, and in that second I wanted to run away and never come back. But before I could, he went on. "I also look out for number two. See, I work at the sewage plant. Get it?" he said. "Tinkle and poop! Ha! Ha! Ha!"

Amazingly, most of the guys laughed. So I laughed too. Ha! Ha! Ha! Maybe it was funny—for the first time.

Uncle Joe waved his hands. "Now, let's get to work," he said, and then he looked to me. "Joey, where's the ring?" He saw the blank look on my face. "You know, three ropes that go around four poles. You wrestle inside it." He snapped his fingers. "Come on, Joey, get with the picture!"

I didn't know what to say. "Uncle Joe, we wrestle on a mat."

"Of course you wrestle on a mat. I didn't think you wrestled on cement. But you still need a ring around the mat, don't you? How can you learn Bombs Away without ropes?"

I could feel my teammates' eyes on me—even J.P. and Dinky were staring at me. They were hoping Uncle Joe was joking, but they were afraid he was just plain nuts.

"You—You don't understand, Uncle Joe," I stammered. "There are no ropes in high-school wrestling. We just wrestle on a mat."

He was incredulous. "No ropes? No ring?"

I shook my head. "Just a mat." I pointed to the mat we were standing on. "This mat."

Uncle Joe looked down. "This mat?"

I thought for a second that he might quit on the spot, but I should have known better. Nothing keeps Uncle Joe down for long. "Well, if the school can't afford a decent ring, it can't afford a decent ring. We'll just have to get along the best we can."

He paced back and forth a few times, then cleared his throat. "Gentlemen, before we go any farther, I want to be clear about my feelings on sportsmanship." He stopped and looked us over. "I'm for it! One hundred percent! If the ref says 'Break clean!' I want to see a clean break. No punching in the throat, no poking in the eyes.

"But I'm no fool. No sirree Bob. I'm no fool. If they mess with us, we mess with them. So here is my first lesson. Come up here, Joey."

Knees wobbling, I stood and faced him.

Uncle Joe looked to the other wrestlers. "Let's say on the first break Joey here whacked you a good one in the throat. Here's what you do. On the next break, you hold your hands up all innocent until, quick as a wink"—here he grabbed my hair—"you pull straight down and pop the jerk in the forehead with your knee. Pow!"

Ty Horton, district champion at 132 pounds, jumped to his feet. "Nobody does stuff like that! The ref would disqualify you for the season!"

Uncle Joe gave him a look full of pity. "Oh, but they do, young man. They do. And refs let it go. I'm sorry to have to be the one to tell you, but it's a dog-eat-dog world out there."

Horton stared at Uncle Joe. "I won't be wrestling this year," he finally muttered, and then he walked off the mat.

Tuesday, only twenty-seven guys showed up for practice. Uncle Joe noticed. "Got some more quitters, I see. Well, good riddance to bad rubbish. Besides, with fewer guys I'll be able to teach you more—and quicker. Joey, come up here again. The rest of you, gather round.

"The great Kenji Shibuya taught me this move. First you get your opponent in a headlock." Uncle Joe squeezed my head between his ribs and his elbows. "Then—and this is the tricky part—you find the nerve below the ear that connects to the heart or the brain or somewhere. If you massage it just right . . . *poof* . . . your opponent falls asleep. Out like a baby. Then you flop on him for the easy pin!"

For the next minute Uncle Joe squeezed my head and

rubbed my neck with the thumb on his left hand. "You feeling tired, Joey?" he asked.

"A little," I mumbled.

He massaged for another minute. I thought I could smell sewage on his clothes.

"How about now?" he asked.

"I'm feeling a little queasy," I mumbled.

Uncle Joe released me. "See? It works! Just listen to your uncle Joe, boys, and we'll do great."

Wednesday he showed us how to go into a trance like the Sheik. Thursday he used a cantaloupe to demonstrate Bobo Brazil's dreaded Cocoa Butt. Friday he described the Bill Melby–Ray Stevens match.

"Talk about profiles in courage! That match was one for the ages. It was a grudge match—bad blood on both sides. We put a barbed-wire fence around the ring. Early on, Bill snatched my timekeeper's bell and banged Ray over the head with it. Bill paid for it later, though, because at the end of the match Ray raked his face over the barbed wire.

"Once the match ended, I took my girlfriend Daisy backstage." Uncle Joe stopped and pulled a white purse with dark spots on it from his equipment bag. "Bill was bleeding bad, but he still took time to autograph her purse. That's the kind of class he had. 'Best wishes, Bill,' it says right here. When we broke up, Daisy gave me this purse. She knew how much it would mean to me." Uncle Joe stared long and hard at the spotted white purse with the scrawled signature. It was the closest to tears I'd ever seen him.

By the end of that practice, we were down to ten wrestlers—all freshmen and sophomores. I think even Dinky and J.P. might have quit if they hadn't been my best friends. Uncle Joe, as usual, looked on the bright side. "With ten it will be easy to figure out tag team partners."

• • •

Saturday morning I talked to my mom. "Let's go to the library," she said. "Maybe we could find a book to give Uncle Joe. He can be a little goofy sometimes, but he's not stupid."

"He's not?" I asked.

"Not completely," she replied.

The book we found was entitled *Better Wrestling for Boys*. It explained the basic rules and had lots of pictures. When Uncle Joe stopped by for lunch that afternoon, my mother put the book on the kitchen table by his plate. He didn't notice it. He was about to leave when I sucked up my courage. "Uncle Joe," I said, holding the book out to him, "I think you should read this book."

He smiled. "A wrestling book? Joey, my boy, I don't need to read about wrestling. I've lived it."

I looked to my mother. "Please, Joe," she said. "Sit down on the sofa and read a few pages."

He shrugged. "Okay. Though I don't see why."

As he read, his lips straightened and his forehead wrinkled. After ten minutes of concentrated study, he looked up. "You really wrestle this way, Joey?"

I nodded. "Yeah, Uncle Joe, we really do."

"No sleeper holds? No Cocoa Butts? No tag teams?"

"No, Uncle Joe. And no airplane rides, no body slams, no trances either."

He went to the front door and opened it. Only then did he turn back. "Well, I'm glad I know. I'd have to find out sooner or later. But this breaks my heart, Joey. I won't deny it."

I know now how parents feel when their children discover there is no Santa Claus.

• • •

I've got to hand it to Uncle Joe: He did his homework. He started Monday's practice by explaining the double-leg takedown from the neutral position. All week he kept with it—breakdowns, tie-ups, pinning combinations, escapes, reversals. He was coaching real wrestling, and he was doing okay too.

The problem was that in Washington there are thirteen weight classifications. So with ten wrestlers we couldn't even field a full team. At every meet we'd have to forfeit three matches. Each forfeit would hand our opponents six points. We'd start out down eighteen points. That's a steep hole for any team to climb out of. And we weren't just any team. We were a lousy team.

I'd never actually wrestled in a meet. Neither had Dinky or J.P. We were the guys the good wrestlers pinned in practice. But we were all-league compared to our teammates. None of them had ever wrestled anywhere, except maybe with their moms when they were little. All the experienced wrestlers had quit.

Uncle Joe wasn't worried. The day of our first meet, he told us to think big. "Every single one of you is capable of winning!" We let out a throaty roar and charged into the wrestling room. Two hours later we silently slunk out. We hadn't won a match, let alone the meet. Monroe had clobbered us 69–0.

"Don't get discouraged!" Uncle Joe boomed the next day at practice. "We'll get better. You wait and see!"

Before the Snohomish meet Uncle Joe told us our goal was to win three-fourths of our matches. We lost 68–0.

Our goal for the Tolt meet was to win half of our matches. Tolt took us 69–0. Next our goal was to win two matches. 70–0. Then it was for someone, somehow, to manage a draw. 72–0. After that the losses piled up like homework: 70–0, 73–0, 71–0, 68–0. On and on and on. Uncle Joe never gave up, but for the rest of us the only goal left was to get through the season.

And we were almost through it, too, when the article appeared in the *Sultan News*. The headline was "A Team for the Ages." The story was supposed to be funny. The writer had discovered that no wrestling team had ever gone an entire season without scoring at least one point. With one match left in the season—and that match against the unbeaten Seattle High Roughriders—we were about to make history. *My vote goes to Joe Milligan for Coach of the Year,* the writer ended. *Think what this man has accomplished in one year!*

My father chortled as he read the article.

"It's not funny, Dad," I snapped.

"Come on, Joey," he replied. "Don't take yourself so seriously. And when I think how your uncle Joe stood right here in this room and said that with him as coach, you guys might take the state." He put the paper down and laughed so hard tears came to his eyes and he had to blow his nose.

At practice the next day Uncle Joe, his face ashen, stood before us. There was no sparkle in his eyes. "It's my fault," he said, his voice dead. "I've made you the laughingstocks of the town. I thought I could help, but . . ." He stopped and bowed his head.

It was Dinky who spoke up. "Don't blame yourself, Coach. It's not your fault we stink."

Immediately Uncle Joe's spine straightened and color

returned to his cheeks. "Don't ever put yourselves down," he snapped. "And don't ever quit." I could feel his spirit revive. "I'm not going to quit." He made his right hand into a fist. "I'll come up with something. We'll show everyone. Trust Uncle Joe."

He hardly spoke that afternoon. As we practiced, we could see him thinking. His forehead was furrowed; he bit his thumbnail; his eyes stared off into space. Then, just before practice ended, he snapped his fingers. "I've got it!" he boomed out.

"What?" we called out in one voice. "What? What? What?"

Uncle Joe smiled mysteriously. "You'll see tomorrow," he answered. "I want to surprise you."

• • •

The surprise was Cindy. When we emerged from the locker room, we saw her sitting in the center of the mat.

The guys, disappointed, looked to me. I took a deep breath. "Uncle Joe," I asked, "how is a mascot going to help us wrestle better?"

He stared at me in disbelief. "A mascot? Cindy is not a mascot. Cindy is here to teach you to become better wrestlers."

I still didn't get it. Nobody did. "How is she going to teach us, Uncle Joe?"

"You're going to wrestle against her, of course. How else could she teach you? Did you think she could talk or something?"

My face fell. "Uncle Joe, we can't wrestle a dog."

"Why not!" Uncle Joe bellowed. "Tuffy Truesdale wrestled an alligator. Willie Pappas wrestled a bear. They were better wrestlers for it. You'll learn a lot wrestling Cindy, Joey. Trust me."

So for the next three days we took turns wrestling Cindy. She turned out to be a tough customer too. She squirmed like crazy, slobbered everywhere, and growled ferociously. Whenever she was close to being pinned, she passed gas, sometimes right in your face. It was like wrestling a skunk. By the end of practice on Friday, I think we were almost looking forward to taking on Seattle High.

Saturday morning at ten the team met Uncle Joe in the Sultan High parking lot. We were going to pile into his van for the drive to Seattle. He brought Cindy, of course. "I couldn't leave my assistant coach," he joked.

Uncle Joe had us take our uniforms out of our equipment bags and lay them out on the floor in the back of the van. "I know your moms have cleaned and ironed them. They'll get wrinkled and end up smelling like your underpants if you keep them stuffed in your bags. I don't want those Seattle kids to think we're a bunch of hayseeds."

As soon as he pulled out of the parking lot, Uncle Joe started singing "Row, Row, Row Your Boat" at the top of his lungs. "Come on," he yelled out, "let's show some spirit!"

He'd driven about two minutes when Cindy spotted a cow. Immediately she jumped from the front seat to the middle seat to the backseat, barking like crazy, nose pressed against the glass, rear end in somebody's face. A smell like rotten eggs filled the van. "Cindy always passes a little gas when she gets excited," Uncle Joe called back. "You'll get used to it."

As if we weren't already!

An instant later Cindy spotted a horse. More barking,

more jumping, more gas. Then there were six cows, a dozen sheep, a little pony, two goats. Cindy bounded wildly about the van, pummeling us with her sticklike legs, barking and howling and passing more and more gas. From the front seat Uncle Joe roared: "Let's sing 'John Jacob Jingleheimer Schmidt.' "

When we reached Lake City, he pulled into a McDonald's. "My treat!" he announced. "In appreciation for all the effort you've put forth this year." As we walked to the restaurant in the cold, crisp air, Cindy put her black nose to the open crack at the top of the window and howled pitifully.

Moments later we were chowing down Big Macs, fries, and milk shakes—not exactly the recommended meal before a wrestling match, but no one complained. We talked and laughed and laughed and talked. If Uncle Joe had suggested skipping the meet entirely and going to the Space Needle instead, we would have cheered.

Too soon, Uncle Joe looked at his watch. "Anybody who needs to use the bathroom, go now. We can't keep the Roughriders waiting."

We trudged back across the parking lot with our heads down and our hands in our pockets. Uncle Joe put the key in the side door and pulled it open. The smell from inside the van was so bad guys gagged as they took their seats. "Cindy," Uncle Joe said, hugging her affectionately, "were you worried we weren't coming back?"

Back on the road we rolled down the windows. The fresh air helped a little, but only a little. For some reason the smell just wouldn't go away. And Cindy was behaving mysteriously. Instead of jumping around, she lay on the floor in front of me, her tail between her legs, a guilty look in her eyes.

When we reached Seattle High, Dinky discovered why.

"Oh no! Oh no! Oh no!" he shouted when he opened the rear door to get our uniforms.

"What is it!" Uncle Joe cried.

"Look!" Dinky yelled, stepping back. "Look!"

There were our uniforms, our spotless uniforms, strewn about. Brown paw prints covered them.

"What's that brown stuff?" J.P. asked.

Uncle Joe picked up one uniform, brought it to his nose. "It's poop," he said. "Poor Cindy had to go poop when we were at McDonald's. She must have come back here. Then she stepped in it and . . . well, the rest is history, boys."

We groaned.

"We can't wrestle now!" I said.

Uncle Joe looked aghast. "What do you mean you can't wrestle? Just because of a little number two? I take care of number two every second of every minute of every day of the week. This is nothing."

Uncle Joe borrowed sponges, towels, and a couple of buckets of hot water from the Seattle High coach. We got to work. Cindy barked encouragement. Ten minutes later our uniforms were cleaned off—sort of. Everybody had little brown splotches here and there. Dinky had a long streak down the right side of his.

"All right, boys," Uncle Joe called out. "They're as clean as they're going to get. Time to suit up!"

Pulling that uniform on was the most courageous thing I've ever done.

"Do I smell?" J.P. asked as we entered the Roughriders' gym.

"I don't smell you," I answered. "But I might not be the guy to ask."

. . .

Wrestling is never a big draw, but when you're the state champions in any sport, you get some attention. There were probably two hundred people in the Seattle High gym. We took our seats in the front row of the bleachers and waited.

The Roughriders entered the gym a couple of minutes after us. They looked awesome—every single one of them had a perfectly sculpted body of steel. They somehow managed to strut, flex their muscles for their girlfriends, and smirk at us all at once.

Dinky, all ninety-five pounds of him, was to be the first victim. As he stepped onto the mat, he reached out to shake hands. The Roughrider, scowling, slapped Dinky's hand away.

The whistle blew. Dinky's opponent, fast as lightning, executed a picture-perfect penetration step, got his head under Dinky's right arm, and was about to pull off a high-crotch, single-leg takedown when he suddenly reeled backward. The cockiness was gone; confusion was in his eyes.

Dinky, sensing his advantage, charged forward, thrust his right foot in between his opponent's legs, dropped to his knees, wrapped him up, lifted him off the ground, and took him down. Two points!

For an instant the rest of us were too stunned to do anything. Then, all at once, we found our voices. "Go, Dinky, go!" we shouted.

And Dinky went.

He chased that guy all over the mat. The Roughrider wanted no part of him. It was so bad the referee penalized him, first for stalling and then for leaving the mat. In the second period Dinky pulled off a single-leg takedown. Starting the third, Dinky was up 7–3.

Watching that third period was excruciating. Dinky had the points. He was going to win—no doubt about it—if he could just keep from getting pinned. Those 120 seconds crawled by.

Then, unbelievably, the horn sounded. Dinky had won, 10–4! We had our first points of the season! We weren't going to make the history books!

We charged the mat and carried Dinky off on our shoulders. Winning a state title couldn't have felt better.

Dinky's victory turned out to be only the beginning. After a rocky opening, Horace Humpdon chased his opponent around the mat for six minutes. The Roughrider was penalized twice for stalling. Horace won 8–3.

We won at 119 pounds and again at 126. Even when one of the Roughriders had the advantage, he didn't press it. They backed down and backed down and backed down. In the stands the Seattle High fans first grumbled and then started booing their own team. J.P. grabbed my arm. "It's Cindy! Uncle Joe was right! Wrestling her has made us better!"

I wrestle at 132, and I was so pumped up when I stepped on the mat I almost forgot to shake hands. Everything I'd always wanted to do, I did. In the first period, I pulled off a far-ankle, far-knee breakdown and got a near pin with a cross-face cradle. The Seattle High wrestler scored points for escapes, but he always seemed to be pulling away rather than coming after me. I won easily, 13–4.

I came back to the guys, grinning ear to ear. "Is this a dream?" I asked to Dinky as we watched J.P. win his match at 138 pounds.

"I don't know," Dinky answered. "But if it is, I don't want to wake up."

Right after J.P.'s victory, the Seattle High coach called the ref over to him. The coach was steamed about something. He kept pointing over at us, jabbing the air with his finger.

"What's his beef?" J.P. asked me.

"Beats me," I said.

Finally the ref came over to Uncle Joe. We all leaned in so we could hear.

The ref blew his nose loudly. "I've got an unusual complaint about your boys," he said as he put his handkerchief away.

"What *about* my boys?" Uncle Joe asked.

The ref stuck out his lower lip. "Well, Coach Garcia claims your boys stink so bad his boys don't want to wrestle. He says your boys smell like . . . well . . . like excrement, though he didn't use that word. He claims you've smeared it into your uniforms. Now I'm fighting a bad cold and I can't smell anything, but look." The ref nodded toward the empty rows of bleachers directly behind us. "Nobody seems to want to get anywhere near you. Coach Garcia's asking me to disqualify your team for poor sportsmanship."

We held our breath, wondering if our miracle was about to be taken away.

Then Uncle Joe rose to his full height. His face became majestic; his eyes gleamed. He motioned toward us as we looked up to him. "Sultan is a farm community. These are farm boys here. And they're proud to be farm boys. Me, I work for the Sewer Department. And I'm proud to work for the Sewer Department. All right, so maybe we do smell. So what? As far as I'm concerned, there's nothing wrong with the good, honest smell of poop. Where would we be if we didn't poop? Answer me that!"

The ref considered for a moment. Then slowly, a smile broke across his face. He walked back to the wrestling mat, blew his whistle, and called for the next wrestlers.

And that's how Sultan High pulled off the greatest upset in the history of high-school wrestling in Washington State. If you can't be good, be lucky. If you can't be lucky, stink.

Carl Deuker

When he was ten years old, Carl Deuker rode with his uncle Joe and his cousins Jimmy and Joseph, along with their dog, Cindy, from Philadelphia to the New Jersey coast. When they stopped for lunch they left Cindy in the car. Just as the boys did in "If You Can't Be Lucky . . . ," when they returned to their car, they found the surprise that Cindy had left for them. Years later Deuker resurrected that memory as part of this story about a losing wrestling team.

Carl Deuker was never a wrestler himself, though he says he loved watching Big-Time Wrestling on Channel 2 from San Francisco. He did, however, participate in several sports; he was good enough to make some teams but not good enough to play much. "I was a classic second-stringer," he says. "I was too slow and too short for basketball; I was too small for football, a little too chicken to hang in there against the best fastballs. So by my senior year the only sport I was still playing was golf." As an adult now living in Seattle, he plays tennis, golf, and volleyball.

Married and the father of a daughter, Marian, Mr. Deuker has been a teacher in Bothell, Washington, and is the author of two award-winning novels for young people: *On the Devil's Court* and *Heart of a Champion*, both named Best Books for

Young Adults by the American Library Association. In fact, *On the Devil's Court* appears on the ALA's list of the 100 Best of the Best Books for Young Adults published between 1967 and 1992. That novel also was named the 1992 Young Adult Book of the Year in South Carolina. It's the tension-packed story of a high-school basketball player who offers to sell his soul to the devil for one year of basketball greatness—and then is terrified that the devil might have taken him up on his offer! *Heart of a Champion,* Carl Deuker's second novel, tells the story of two friends who share a love of baseball and also struggle with alcohol abuse.

Why does Sun's dad spend more time coaching her little brother than helping her? She plays basketball too. It isn't fair. . . .

Stealing for Girls

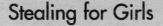
Will Weaver

It's a free country, right? I choose my clothes (sixties retro), I choose my shoes (Nikes), I choose my CDs (Hendrix and Nine Inch Nails), I choose my friends (you know who you are). If I were an adult (which I'm not—I'm a fourteen-year-old eighth-grade girl named Sun) I could vote, could choose my car, my career, whatever—like I said, a free country, right?

Wrong.

Quiz time: Please take out a number two lead pencil; *do not* open the test booklet until you're told. Seriously, my question to you is this: What's the most majorly thing in your life that you *can't* choose? The answer is as simple as the eyes and nose on your face: your parents. Your parents and your brothers or sisters. That's because no matter how free you think you are, the one thing nobody can choose for herself is her own family.

Here's another way of putting it: Being born is something like arriving at a restaurant where there are no wait-rons and no menus. Your table is set and your food is there waiting for you. It might be fresh shrimp, it might be steak, it might be macaroni hot dish, it might be all broccoli; for some kids there might be no food at all, maybe not even a table.

Me? I was fairly lucky. My parents are (1) there, and (2) at least semicool most of the time. My dad's an accountant and my mom's a college professor. Both are in their middle forties, physically fit, and usually unembarrassing in public. My gripe is the old basic one for girls: My father spends way more time on sports with my brother, Luke, than with me.

Luke is in sixth grade, is already taller than me, and can pound me at basketball. At Ping-Pong. At any sport. You name it, he crushes me. I want to say right here I'm not a klutz. I'm nearly five feet six and have at least average coordination; on our basketball team I'm third off the bench, which is not that shabby considering that our school, Hawk Bend, is a basketball power in central Minnesota. But I won't play one-on-one with Luke anymore. No way. Who likes to lose every time? It's not like he's mean or wants to humiliate me—he's actually pretty decent for a twerpy sixth-grade boy—it's just that he's a natural athlete and I'm not.

I am thinking these thoughts as I sit next to my parents watching Luke's team play Wheatville. Luke just made a nifty spin move (of course, he's the starting point guard) and drove the lane for a layup. My mother, who comes to most games, stares at Luke with her usual astounded look. She murmurs to my father, who comes to all our games, "How did he *do* that?"

"Head fake right, plant pivot foot, big swing with leading leg, and bingo—he's by," my dad whispers. A quiet but intense man with salt-and-pepper hair, he speaks from the side of his mouth, for there are always parents of other sixth-graders nearby.

"He amazes me," my mother says. She has not taken her eyes off Luke. I hate to agree, but she's right—all of which clouds further my normally "sunny" disposition. I remember Dad and Luke working last winter on that very move in the basement; I went downstairs to see what was going on, and they both looked up at me like I was an alien from the *Weekly World News*. My father soon enough bounced the ball to me, and I gave it a try, but I could never get my spin dribble to rotate quickly enough and in a straight line forward to the basket. Not like you-know-who. "Watch Luke," my father said. "He'll demonstrate."

Now, at least it's the third quarter of the game and Luke already has a lot of points and his team is ahead by twenty so the coach will take him out soon—though not quite soon enough for Wheatville, or me. At the other end of the court Luke's loose, skinny-legged body and flopping yellow hair darts forward like a stroke of heat lightning to deflect the ball.

"Go, Luke!" my father says, half rising from his seat.

Luke is already gone, gathering up the ball on a breakaway, finishing with a soft layup high off the board. People clap wildly.

I clap slowly. Briefly. Politely. My mother just shakes her head. "How does he *do* that?"

"Ask *him*," I mutter.

"Pardon, Sun?" my mom says abstractedly.

"Nothing." I check the scoreboard, then my own watch. I've seen enough. Below, at floor level, some friends are passing. "I think I'll go hang with Tara and Rochelle," I say to my parents.

"Sure," my mother says vacantly.

Dad doesn't hear me or see me leave.

As I clump down the bleachers there is more cheering, but I prefer not to look. "Sun." What a stupid name—and by the way I do not *ever* answer to "Sunny." I was allegedly born on a Sunday, on a day when the sun was particularly bright, or so my parents maintain. I seriously doubt their version (someday I'm going to look up the actual weather report on March 18, 1980). I'm sure it was a Monday; either that or I was switched at the hospital. Or maybe it was Luke—one of us, definitely, was switched.

Rochelle, actually looking once or twice at the game, says right off, "Say, wasn't that your little brother?"

"I have no brother," I mutter.

"He's a smooth little dude," Tara says, glancing over her shoulder. "Kinda cute, actually."

"Can I have some popcorn or what?" I say.

"Or what," Rochelle says, covering her bag.

They giggle hysterically. Real comediennes, these two.

"When's your next game?" Tara says to me, relenting, giving me three whole kernels.

"The last one is Tuesday night," I answer. "A makeup game with Big Falls."

"Here or away?"

"Here."

"With your record, maybe you could get your little brother to play for your team."

"Yeah—a little eye shadow, a training bra," adds Rochelle, "everyone would think he was you!"

I growl something unprintable to my friends and go buy my own bag of popcorn.

• • •

At supper that night Luke and I stare at each other during grace, our usual game—see who will blink first. Tonight it is me. I glare down at my broccoli and fish; I can feel him grinning.

"And thank you, God, for bouncing the ball our way once again," my father finishes. "Amen." If God doesn't understand sports metaphors, our family is in huge trouble.

"Well," my father says, looking at Luke expectantly.

"A deep subject," Luke says automatically, reaching for his milk, automatically.

Both of them are trying not to be the first one to talk about the game.

"How was your day, Sun?" my mother says.

"I hate it when you do that."

"Do what?" my mother says.

"It's condescending," I add.

"What is condescending?" she protests.

"Asking me about my day when the thing on everybody's mind is Luke's usual great game. Why not just say it: 'So, Luke, what were the numbers?' "

There is silence; I see Luke cast an uncertain glance toward my father.

"That's not at all what I meant," Mother says.

"And watch that tone of voice," my father warns me.

"So how many points *did* you get?" I say to Luke, clanking the broccoli spoon back into the dish, holding the dish in front of his face; he hates broccoli.

He shrugs, mumbles, "Not sure, really."

"How many?" I press.

"I dunno. Fifteen or so." But he can't help himself: He bites his lip, tries to scowl, fakes a cough, but the smile is too strong.

"How *many*?" I demand.

"Maybe it was twenty," he murmurs.

I pick up a large clump of broccoli and aim it at his head.

"Sun!" my father exclaims.

Luke's eyes widen. "Twenty-six!" he squeaks.

"There. That wasn't so difficult, was it?" I say, biting the head off the broccoli.

Luke lets out a breath, begins to eat. There is a silence for a while.

"By the way—nice steal there at the end," I say to him as I pass the fish to Father.

Luke looks up at me from the top of his eyes. "Thanks," he says warily.

"It's something I should work on," I add.

"I'll help you!" Luke says instantly and sincerely. "Right after supper!"

At this syrupy sibling exchange, my parents relax and dinner proceeds smoothly.

Later, during dessert, when my father and Luke have finally debriefed themselves—quarter by quarter, play by play—on the game, I wait for Dad's usual "Well, who's next on the schedule, Luke?" He doesn't disappoint me.

"Clearville, I think," Luke says.

"Any breakdown on them? Stats?"

"They're eight–four on the season, have that big center who puts up *numbers*, plus a smooth point guard. They beat us by six last time," Luke says. My mind skips ahead twenty years and sees Luke with his own accounting office, crunching tax returns by day and shooting hoops long into the evening.

"Big game, then, yes?" my father remarks, his fingers

beginning to drum on the table. "You'll have to box out—keep that big guy off the boards. And if their point guard penetrates, collapse inside—make him prove he can hit the jumper."

"He can't hit no jumpers," Luke says through a large bite of cake. "He shoots bricks, and I'm going to shut him down like a bike lock."

"Huh?" I say.

"What?" Luke says. "What'd I say now?"

"First off, it's 'any jumper.' And second, how do you shut someone down 'like a bike lock'?"

"Actually, it's not a bad simile," my mother says. "If this fellow is 'smooth,' so, in a way, is a bicycle—the way it rolls and turns—and a bike lock, well . . ." She trails off, looking at me.

I shrug and stare down at my fish. It has not been a good day for either of us.

"And who does *your* team play next, Sun?" my father asks dutifully.

"Big Falls. Tuesday night," I say. I look up and watch his face carefully.

"Tuesday night, isn't that? . . ." he begins.

"I'm afraid I'll miss it, honey," my mother interjects. "I have that teachers' education conference in Minneapolis, remember?"

"Sure, Mom, no problem." I keep my eyes on my father; on Luke, who's thinking. I am waiting for the light-bulb (twenty watts, maximum) to go on in his brain.

"Hey—Tuesday night is my game, too," Luke says suddenly.

"Yes, I thought so," my father murmurs. The one-on-one experts have finally put two and two together.

"What time are your games?" my mother asks.

"Seven," Luke and I say simultaneously.

My father looks to me, then to Luke. He's frowning. Suddenly his gaze lightens. "By any chance are they both at the high school? In the adjoining gyms?"

"Middle school," Luke says.

"High school," I follow.

"Damn," my father says, "they ought to take whoever schedules sporting events in this school system and—"

"I'm sure it couldn't be helped, dear," my mother interjects. "Sun's is a makeup game, after all."

"And the last one of the season," I add.

My father looks to Luke. "So is yours, right? The last one of the season?"

Luke nods. He and I look at each other. I smile. I love moral dilemmas, especially when they're not mine.

My father turns to my mother.

"Sorry," she says to him, "I'm delivering a speech in Minneapolis. There's no way I can miss it."

"Well," my father says, drumming his fingers, "I'll have to think this one through."

• • •

Amazingly, Luke keeps his promise, and after dinner we work on stealing. It is chilly outside in March, with patches of leftover snowbanks along the north side of the garage (this is Minnesota, remember), but the asphalt is clear.

"There are two main types of steals," Luke says, dribbling. "First is the most basic, 'the unprotected ball.' As your man is dribbling, he is not shielding the ball with his body, and so you go for it."

"I have part of a brain," I say, and lunge for the deflection—but Luke instantly back-dribbles, and I miss.

"It's all in the timing," he says, "all in when you start your move. Don't start when the ball is coming back up to my hand—begin your move just when the ball *leaves* my hand, just when it's released and heading downward."

I track him, waiting—then try it. This time I actually knock the ball away.

"See?" Luke says. "That gives you the maximum time for your reach-in."

We practice this a few more times.

"Be sure to reach with your outside hand," Luke cautions, "or else you might get called for a reach-in foul."

We keep working for quite a while. I start to get every third one, but I'm still not very good at it.

"It's coming," Luke says, then holds the ball. I kick away a pebble, which clatters against the garage door.

"The second type of steal is called the wraparound. It's when your man is dribbling and you reach way around behind, almost wrapping your arm around him, and knock the ball away." He flips me the ball, has me dribble, and snakes loose the ball two out of three times. Then he takes the ball back, and we work on this one for a while. I get one out of ten at best. Soon I am panting.

"The wraparound is the toughest one," Luke says. "Maybe you need longer arms or something."

From the window, my father is watching us. "Again," I say crabbily to Luke. Soon I am stumbling-tired and getting no wraparound deflections or steals at all.

"Hey—it'll come," Luke says, bouncing the ball to me. I slam the ball hard onto the cold asphalt and back into my hands.

"Yeah. Like in 2010 maybe," I say, then mutter something unprintable.

"Ah . . . I think I'll go have some more cake," Luke says.

"Fine!" I bark. He heads off.

"By the way," I call after him, "who taught you those stealing moves?" The middle-school coaches teach both the girls' and boys' teams, and I am always on the lookout for coaches who treat boys and girls differently. Nothing pisses me off more than that.

"Who taught me? Coach Dad," Luke says with an innocent smile.

I don't smile. I glare at Luke, then to the window, which is empty.

"What?" Luke says, glancing behind. "What did I say now?"

"Nothing." I turn away, take the ball, and begin to bank hard shots off the backboard, none of which fall.

• • •

That night, as my father sits at the kitchen table rattling his calculator keys and turning the pages of someone's tax return (from March through April 15 we leave him alone), I find myself rattling the dishes hard and loud as I clean up the kitchen.

"Was there something? . . ." he says irritatedly, glancing up only briefly from his papers.

"No," I say, and stomp past him upstairs to my room.

Later I hear my mother speaking softly to my father. He lets out a sigh and pushes back from the table. Soon I hear his footsteps on the stairs, and then he pops his head partway into my room, where I am reading. "Everything okay, Sun?"

"Sure," I mutter.

"Sure sure?"

I shrug.

He leans in my doorway. "So what is it?" he asks, checking his watch.

"How come you taught Luke those two types of steals and not me?" I turn to him. My eyes, disgustingly, feel glassy and spilly; they are about to dump water down my cheeks.

He stares. "Steals? Oh, you mean . . . Yes, well . . ." He trails off and stares at some empty space in front of him, thinking. Then he turns to me. "I guess I just naturally do more sports stuff with Luke because . . . because we're both boys—I mean I once was, and he's one now, that sort of thing," he finishes lamely.

"Well, I play basketball, too, dammit!" I say. I try to be hard-boiled but a large tear rolls down my cheek. "Damn," I blurt, and start crying for real.

He stares at me, then moves imperceptibly, as if to come forward either to smack me for swearing or to take me in his arms. But accountants are accountants because most of them are not good with other things—like feelings. With a confused look on his face, my father retreats from my room.

In the morning when I wake up, there is a note taped to my door. In his small, careful handwriting my father has written, "Dear Sun: There is a third type of steal. . . ."

• • •

That Saturday, when Luke is gone to hockey, my father appears in the TV room wearing his tennis shoes and sweats. " 'Stealing for Girls,' a sports clinic by yours truly, begins in fifteen minutes, garage-side."

I smile, grab the remote, and shoot the TV dead.

Before we go outside, my father sits at the kitchen table

and begins drawing neat X's and O's on graph paper. "We'll call this third type the prediction pass steal. It's something that works best with a zone defense."

"Okay," I say. On my team we have been learning the zone, and zone traps, though we haven't used them much.

"A half-court zone defense forces the team on offense to work the ball around the perimeter."

I nod as he draws lines in a large half circle.

"The faster the ball movement, the tougher it is for the defense to shift accordingly."

I nod. I know all this.

"The offensive point guard will sooner or later get into what you might call the automatic pass mode—he receives a pass from, say, his right side, and automatically turns to pass to his left."

"Yeah, sure," I murmur, for I am thinking of something that has always puzzled me.

"What is it?" my father asks with a trace of impatience.

"If you never played basketball in high school or college, how come you know so much about the game?"

He looks up straight at me. There is a long moment of silence. "I would like to have played," he says simply, "but it was a big school."

I meet his gaze, then put my hand on his shoulder.

He smiles, a small but real smile, and we both turn back to the graph paper.

"Anyway, when the point guard gets sloppy," he continues, "that's when the smart defensive man can start to think about a prediction pass steal."

"The defensive point guard?"

"No," my father says immediately. "The offensive point guard is used to that; he's been conditioned to watch out for that kind of steal. What he's not expecting is the weak-side defensive guard or even the forward to break up and across, slanting through the lane toward the key and picking off the pass. A lot of the quick but small college teams use it."

"Show me," I say, staring down at the paper.

He grabs a fresh graph. "Imagine a basic zone defense that's shifting to the ball."

I close my eyes. "Got it," I say.

"If the offense is moving the ball sharply, the defensive point guard has the toughest job. He usually can't keep up with the ball movement."

I nod. I keep my eyes closed.

"So the passes out front become 'gimmes'; they're not contested."

I nod again.

"And after a while, the offensive point guard gets sloppy. That's when one of the defensive players down low—the forward or center—can make his move. He flashes all the way up, comes out of nowhere for the steal."

My smile opens my eyes.

"Keep in mind it will only work once or twice," my father cautions, "and the timing has to be perfect—or the defense will get burned."

I look down to his drawing, see the open hole left by the steal attempt.

"Burned bad," he adds. "But if it works—bingo—he's gone for an easy layup."

I correct him: "*She's* gone."

• • •

Outside, for want of five offensive players, my father presses into service a sawhorse, three garbage cans, and my mother. "I just love my team," she says wryly.

"This won't take long," my dad says. Mom shivers; the weather is cloudy, with rain forecast.

"Sun, you're the weak-side defensive guard," he directs. I position myself, back to the basket. "Honey, you're our offensive point guard," he says to my mother.

"I've never been a point guard; I've never been a guard of any kind," she protests.

"First time for everything," my dad retorts.

Actually, I can tell that they're both having at least a little fun.

"Now," he says to my mom, "imagine you have just received a pass from the sawhorse, and in turn you'll be passing to me."

My mother, the orange ball looking very large in her hands, says, "Thanks—sawhorse," and turns and passes to my dad.

"Now—Sun!" he calls, but I break up way too late.

"Again," my father says.

This time I break up too soon, and my mother stops her pass.

"Again," my father says.

I trot back to my position and try it again. On the sixth try I time it perfectly: I catch her pass chest-high and am gone for an imaginary layup.

"Excellent!" my father calls. "Again."

We practice until we are glowing in the chilly March morning, until an icy rain starts spattering down and the ball becomes too slick to hold.

Afterward, we are sitting at the kitchen table drinking hot chocolate when outside a car door slams—Luke's ride—and then Luke thumps into the house. "Hey," he says, pointing over his shoulder, "what's with the garbage cans and the sawhorse?"

The three of us look at each other; I smile and say nothing.

• • •

For the next several days, my father and I work exactly forty-five minutes per evening on the prediction pass steal. I let Luke join us only because we need another passer. The weather remains lousy, and my mother freezes her butt off, and Luke complains about not getting to try the prediction steal himself, but my father ignores all that. He is too busy fine-tuning my timing, my breakaways.

And, suddenly, it is Tuesday morning of game day.

Both games.

"Huge day—two big games," my father says, first thing, at breakfast. He drums his fingers, glances at his briefcase, at the clock.

Luke glares at me. He is not happy about this week and his role as perpetual passer. "I guess I know which game *you're* going to," he mutters to my father.

My father says nothing.

• • •

Warming up with the team, I have the usual butterflies. The Big Falls girls look like their name—big, with huge hair tied back and bouncing like waterfalls as they do their layups. I try not to look at them, but can't help but hear their chatter, the chirp and thud of their shoes. Even their feet are huge.

I look around the gym. No family. No Dad. I miss my layup.

Just before tip-off, from my spot on the bench, I look around one last time. No family. No father. I sigh and try to focus on the game.

Which is going to be a tough one all the way. The teams are well matched at every position, and we trade basket for basket—bad news for me. I ride the pine all the way through the first quarter.

We do our "Hawk Bend Fliers!" send-off whoop to start the second quarter, and as I head back to the bench I scan the small crowd. Still no father. But it's just as well, I think gloomily as I settle onto the bench—at least at Luke's game he's seeing Luke play. Logically, if I were a parent I wouldn't come to my game, either.

Watching, chin in hands, that second quarter, with a sparse, quiet crowd giving neither team much support, I begin to think dark but true thoughts: that really, in the end, each of us is alone. That each of us, by what we choose to do, is responsible for what we achieve and how we feel about ourselves. That each of us—

"Sun. Sun!" An elbow, Jenny's, jabs me in the ribs: The coach is calling for me.

"Sun, check in for Rachel," Coach Brown says, then adds, "At forward," giving me a fleeting, get-your-head-in-the-game glance.

I have to ask Rachel who she's guarding. Tired, irritated at having to pause on her way off the floor, she looks around and finally points to a hefty, five-foot-ten forward with major pimples on her shoulders and neck. I trot up close.

"What are you staring at?" the sweaty Big Falls forward says straight off. Then she leans close to me and glares.

"There's a new soap that might clear those up," I say, letting my eyes fall to her neck and shoulders.

"Listen, you little shit—" she says, but the horn drowns out the rest.

Then the ball is in play. It comes quickly to my man,

who puts her shoulder down and drives the lane. I keep my feet planted and draw the charging foul.

"Way to go, Sun," my team calls as we head up the floor, and my mood lightens considerably.

In my two minutes of play I make one lucky basket and draw one foul—a reach-in steal attempt. I try to remember that timing is everything. I also see that our team is quicker, but Big Falls is stronger inside. Pimple Shoulders muscles me out of the way for an easy bank shot, like I was a mosquito on an alligator's back. She outweighs me by eighty pounds, minimum.

At the next time-out Rachel comes back in and I end up sitting next to the coach. I watch us get beat inside by some teeth-jarring picks and back screens; the score gradually tilts in favor of Big Falls. At the half we are down 28–21.

• • •

In the locker room the first five players lie red-faced and flat on their backs on the benches. "They're shoving underneath," Rachel complains.

"No—they're outmuscling us," Coach retorts. "Position! We've got to get position and stay planted. Like Sun did right away when she came in—get planted and draw the foul."

I play it very cool and do not change expressions.

The coach heads to the chalkboard and begins to draw X's and O's. "They might be big, but they're slow. In the third quarter I want us to run, run, run—fast-break them until their butts are dragging."

"Or ours," Rachel mutters.

"You don't want to play hard, we've got people who do!" Coach barks.

Rachel zips her lips, stares at the ceiling.

• • •

During the halftime shoot I scan the crowd. Still nobody. I feel something inside me harden further, and center itself; it's a flash of what life will be like when I go away to college, when I'll truly be on my own. Just me. No family whatsoever. Just me shlumping along through life.

On the bench as the third quarter begins, for some reason I finally get focused. I sit next to the coach; I chatter out encouragement. Our fast break begins to work. After they score or we get a rebound, Rachel rips the ball to one side or the other while Jenny, our point guard, breaks up the center. She takes the pass at the half-court line, then does her thing—either driving the lane or dishing off to the trailers. We miss some easy layups but still pull within one point.

Big Falls calls time-out. Our subs are ecstatic, but the starting five stand bent over, hands on knees, wheezing.

"Let's try to keep the fast break working through the end of this quarter," Coach Brown says, "and then we'll figure out something else."

Our starters manage a weak "Go Fliers" and trudge back onto the floor.

In the final two minutes of the third quarter I watch as Big Falls shuts down the fast break like . . . like a bicycle lock. Simple, really—just some pressure on the out-of-bounds first pass, plus coverage on the sides—and we do not score again. But I have been watching them on offense. Nearly every time down the court, Pimple Shoulders rears up inside, then looks for the pass from the point guard—who has taken very few shots from the perimeter, including zero three-point attempts.

"Zone," I say to myself. "In the fourth quarter we should go zone."

Coach Brown looks to me. Then back to the action. He strokes his chin.

At the final quarter break he kneels on the floor. "Take a load off," he commands, and the starting five slump into chairs. He points, one by one, to the next five, and we check in. Back in the huddle, Coach Brown has drawn some scrawling maps of *X*'s and *O*'s. "Zone defense," he says, with a wink to me. "Let's collapse inside and make them shoot from the perimeter. Make them prove they can hit the jumpers. But box out and get that rebound," he adds. "We've got to have the ball to score."

We fire up and trot onto the floor. For some reason I look to the middle of the bleachers—and see my father. His briefcase rests beside him and his gray suit coat is folded neatly over it.

"Zone! Box and one!" the Big Falls point guard calls out immediately, and begins to move the ball crisply side to front to side. It's clear they've had a zone thrown at them before. Still bench-stiff, we have trouble keeping up with the passes, and their point guard takes an uncontested shot from within the key—but bricks it. Wendy rips off the rebound and we move the ball cautiously upcourt. Our second-team guards have no future with the Harlem Globetrotters in terms of ballhandling, but we do know how to pick-and-roll.

I fake to the baseline, then break up and set a screen for Shanna. She rubs off her girl—who hits me, blindside, hard—as I roll to the inside. I'm looking for the ball, and suddenly, thanks to a nifty bounce pass, it's right at my chest. I clamp on it, take one dribble, brace for a hammer blow from Pimple Shoulders, and go up for the lay-in. I feel the oncoming air rush of a large-body (the image of a 747 jetliner on a crash course with a seagull flashes through my mind) but don't alter my flight path. The ball feels good off my fingertips. As my feet touch down and I open my eyes, the ball is settling through the net and Pimple Shoulders is skidding along the hardwood runway and there is major cheering from our bench. Me? I am just happy to be heading upcourt with all my feathers intact.

The Big Falls outside shooting continues to bang hard off the rim, and we continue to box out and get the rebound play and score on basic pick-and-rolls. We go up 42–38, and our bench is screaming and bouncing up and down in their chairs.

But Big Falls gets smart: They throw a zone defense at us. Not great passers, and worse outside shooters, we turn the ball over three times; barely fifty seconds later, Big Falls is up by two, 44–42, and Coach Brown is screaming for a time-out. By the time the ref stops the clock there is less than three minutes left in the game.

"Okay, good job, second team," he calls, pointing for the first team to check back in. "Stay with the zone defense, but let's run the fast break."

We all clap once, together, and send the starters back onto the floor.

"Nice work out there," the coach says to me, and motions for me to sit by him. "Stay ready."

The first team, refreshed, runs a fast break for a quick bucket and knots the score at 44 all. The teams trade baskets, then settle into solid defense, and suddenly there is less than one minute to play. Both the score and my gut are knotted. The Big Falls point guard launches a three-pointer, which goes through, but we come back with a fast break on which Rachel does some kind of wild, falling, 180-degree, dipsy-do finger-roll shot—which falls! We are down by one point, but Rachel is down, too, with a turned ankle. There are thirty seconds left.

We help her off the court. Done for the day, she cries with pain and anger.

"Sun—check in and go to forward," the coach says.

As I pause at the scorer's table, everything seems exaggeratedly clear, as if magnified: the black and white zebra stripes of the officials, the seams of the yellow wood floor, the orange rim worn to bare, shiny metal on the inside. I stare at the ball the ref is holding and can imagine its warm, tight sphere in my hands. I want that ball. For the first time in my basketball career I want the ball, bad.

The Big Falls girls are slapping high fives like the game is over; after all, they have possession with a one-point lead. The ref calls time-in, and Big Falls bounces the ball inbounds handily and pushes it quickly up the floor. There they spread the offense and begin to work the ball around the perimeter: side to front to side to front. It's too early for us to foul, so we stay with our zone defense. Their point guard, still jazzed from making the three-point basket, is loose and smart-mouthed. As she receives the ball she automatically passes it to the opposite side.

Which is when I suddenly see not Big Falls players but garbage cans and a sawhorse. To the side, on the bench, I see Coach Brown rising to signal it's time to foul, but I have been counting off another kind of time: the Big Falls passing rhythm. On the far side, away from the ball, when orange is flashing halfway to the point guard, I begin my break. Smart Mouth receives the ball, turns, and passes it. Her eyes bug out as I arrow into view; she tries to halt her pass but it's too late. I catch the ball and am gone. There is only open floor in front and sudden cheering from the sides, and, overly excited, I launch my layup at about the free throw line—but the ball goes in anyway. The Hawk Bend crowd goes crazy.

Down by one point, Big Falls calls a frantic time-out at the five-second mark. Our players are delirious, but Coach Brown is not. "Watch for the long pass, the long pass!" he rants. "They have a set play. Don't foul—especially on the three-point shot."

But we're only eighth-graders; at times we don't listen well.

Sure enough, Big Falls screens on the inbound pass, which Pimple Shoulders fires full court. There the point guard takes an off-balance shot—and is fouled by Shanna as time runs out.

Shanna looks paralyzed. She can't believe she did it.

"Three-point attempt—three foul shots!" the ref calls.

We clear off the free throw line and watch her make the first two—to tie—and miss the third. The game goes into overtime.

Back in the huddle we try to get pumped again, but I can tell it's not going to happen. We are stunned and flat. We lose in overtime by four points.

• • •

Back home we have a late supper: broccoli, fish sticks, and rice. I stare at my plate as my father finishes grace. Then he looks up. "Well," he says.

"A very deep subject," Luke replies, grabbing the bread. His team won, of course, by twenty-six points.

I just sit there, slumped and staring.

"You should have seen it," my father begins, speaking to Luke. "We're down by one and your sister is low on the weak side. The Big Falls point guard is not paying attention. . . ." Slowly I look up. I listen as my father tells the story of my one and only career steal. He re-creates it so well that Luke stops eating and his mouth drops open slightly. "Rad!" Luke says at the finish, then asks me more about my game. I shrug, but end up giving him a virtual play-by-play of the last two minutes.

When I am done, Luke lets out a breath and looks squarely at me. "Wow—I wish I could have been there!"

I stop to stare at him.

"What—what'd I say?" Luke says warily.

I just smile, and pass my little brother the broccoli.

Will Weaver

Because he has a son and a daughter, both of whom are good athletes, Will Weaver understands the need for dividing his time between them equally. But like the father in "Stealing for Girls," he admits, he sometimes finds that hard to do.

As a teenager Will Weaver played basketball and baseball and ran cross-country. He grew up on a farm in Minnesota, learning firsthand the joys and pains of the farm life he describes in *Striking Out*, his first novel for young adults. In that novel, thirteen-year-old Billy Baggs has a hard and unrewarding life until he starts playing baseball with the town team one summer, at the same time that his mother decides she needs to do more than be a farm wife. Readers can follow Billy Baggs's additional accomplishments, in sports as well as with his girlfriend Suzy, in *Farm Team* and other books Weaver is working on for future publication.

In addition to these books for teenage readers, Mr. Weaver has written two novels for adults—*A Gravestone Made of Wheat* and *Red Earth, White Earth*—and has won prizes for his writing from the McKnight Foundation and the Bush

Foundation. In 1994 *Red Earth, White Earth* was made into a CBS television movie.

Currently Will Weaver teaches creative writing at Bemidji State University in northern Minnesota, where he enjoys outdoor activities with his wife and children and, to keep in shape, "plays softball, shoots buckets, and works out."

Being a crew member in a four-hundred-pound racing canoe is part of a long Hawaiian tradition. So what does this haole—this white kid from the mainland—think he's doing?

Shark Bait

Graham Salisbury

Johnny Blas and I were lounging in the spidery shade of a coconut tree watching the haole kid from Arizona. The sparkling turquoise cove beyond winked back at us under a blue sky and burning Hawaiian sun. Johnny was eating sunflower seeds and spitting the shells on the sand.

Dad thought Johnny looked just like his father. They both had storms brewing in their eyes, he said, only Johnny still had time before his eyes grew watery and turned bloodshot and yellow like his father's. Now, at fifteen, Johnny's eyes were bright white around midnight irises. I believed he could keep them that way, but Dad said not to count on it.

To me, Johnny was more like a brother than a friend. And I thought I knew him pretty well. One thing I knew was that he didn't trust many people. But if he liked you, if he respected you, he would do anything for you. Anything. And if he didn't respect you, you'd be lucky to get the time of day.

Except if you were his father.

Mr. Blas was . . . nasty, you could say. Johnny didn't trust him, and didn't respect him. Even a blind man could've seen that. But even so, Johnny did everything for him—dragged him home from Rose's bar when he was too drunk to do it himself; skipped school to take his father's place as the maintenance man at the Kona Dolphin condos when he was sick with a hangover; did all kinds of stupid things around the house—whatever his father demanded. And even after Johnny did all that, his father still beat him up.

And Johnny never fought back.

"How come you just take it?" I asked once when he came to school with a Band-Aid over the corner of one eye. "How come you don't run? Like James?"

Johnny's icy glare shocked me. "You don't know nothing about nothing," he said, snarling the words. And I never asked him that kind of stuff again.

The kid from Arizona rolled his bike down from the road and leaned it against a coconut tree. He looked up and glanced around the beach. He saw us watching him, and for a second he stared back. Then he turned away.

He was in our class most of last year. He moved to the islands with his parents about a month after school started. They bought old man Gouveia's place down the coast by Banyans Beach. The kid disappeared from school for a few weeks in April, but showed up again in May. Johnny heard he ran away from home, hid in the engine room of a coast guard cutter, and didn't get caught until somewheres off Molokai. But that was just a rumor.

All any of us really knew about him was his name— David Ford. And that his father was an electrician who liked to drink at Rose's bar. Johnny knew about the bar because his own father had been camping out in there since caveman days. Mr. Blas had it all figured out. He told Johnny that the Ford guy was just a loudmouth bozo who moved over here to make some easy money off us Hawaiian hicks—put a couple of electrical outlets in our grass shacks and sell us TVs. But Johnny said his father was drunk when he said that.

Johnny handed me the bag of sunflower seeds and I took some. More guys showed up at the cove for practice, drifting down to the water, standing around ankle-deep, mumbling to each other. At four o'clock, Coach Freitas drove his Jeep onto the sand and parked in the small slant of shade off one side of the canoe shed. He crawled over the gearshift and got out on the passenger's side.

It was almost just like any other day, with me and Johnny and the rest of the guys in the canoe club waiting around for paddling practice to start. Yesterday was girls' day, today us. We had to alternate because we only had three practice canoes. The fiberglass kind. Our koa wood racing canoe stayed in Coach Freitas's garage until the day of the races, a four-hundred-pound, forty-three-foot speed demon called *Iwalani*.

Anyway, it was just like always, except down walks the Arizona kid pushing this old one-speed girl's bike I never knew he had. Then he sits down on the sand . . . like he was one of us. Like he was there to practice. Like he even had a chance to join Kai Opua Canoe Club. Three months already we'd been working out. We'd even had a couple of races. The state meet was only five weeks away.

And suddenly this guy David Ford shows up.

Which is why we were watching him.

"How come he don't take off his shirt?" Johnny said, spitting out shells.

"Maybe he had an operation and has a scar across his stomach."

Johnny snickered. "Or maybe got acne back."

Once at school, when the guy first showed up, Johnny made a special effort, which was unusual for him. He said "How'zit" to the kid, opening up like maybe they could be friends. And the kid ignored him. Or seemed to ignore him. He just walked past, brooding about something. But he was always like that, always deep in thought, like he was getting F's in every class. But Johnny took it personally. He squinted deadly eyes at the kid's back as he walked away. "I don't think he heard you," I said. Johnny slugged his fist into his other hand. "The punk heard, all right."

I felt sorry for the kid. I mean, to be on the wrong side of Johnny Blas.

David Ford was going into tenth grade, like we were. And he was about the same height. Five-ten, five-eleven. But that's as far as any similarities went. First of all, he had blond hair and was as white as coconut meat . . . looked out of place . . . one white face in a sea of brown paddlers. And second, he had a flattop and looked like a marine. I had to admit he had plenty of muscle, but he didn't swim, or fish, or bodysurf, like the rest of us had been doing every day of our lives since we were two. And not only that, he always wore long pants and never took off his shirt. How could you live in that heat and never take off your shirt?

The kid did go barefoot, though. Which was something.

Johnny suddenly stopped chewing, his eyes pinned on David Ford. It was kind of weird how Johnny seemed so caught up in the guy, watching everything he did, like he still carried a deep hate for getting snubbed at school.

David Ford unzipped his jeans and pulled them off, still sitting. He had red swimming shorts underneath. Then, he actually pulled his T-shirt over his head and tossed it on top of his crumpled jeans.

"Hoo, shark bait, yeah, the guy?" Johnny said.

"No kidding. Looks like a squid." The kid was white, all right. Like a tourist.

"That sun going make him sorry tomorrow," Johnny said. "How come the punk's here, anyway?"

I shrugged.

The thing about David Ford was that he didn't talk to anybody, even at school, unless a teacher asked him a question or something like that. He just went from class to class looking at the ground, like a robot. We all said, *Forget it, if he's going to be like that.*

"The guy dreaming if he thinks Coach Freitas going let 'um in Kai Opua," Johnny said.

"He's got some muscle, though. Check out his shoulders."

"Sshh . . . fricken pansy."

But later we discovered that Coach Freitas had a different opinion. Not only did he let David Ford join the club, but he put him in *our* crew, in place of Reggie Hoang, who we'd been borrowing from the fourteen-and-unders.

Johnny went crazy. "Fricken coach *stoopid*," he said after Coach Freitas walked away. "We don't need no shark bait sissy. We don't need no white man. We need somebody *big*, somebody good! *Jeez* . . . the coach got no brains. He just put another nail in the coffin, man."

I thought so, too. But who had the guts to tell Coach Freitas?

"Who cares, anyway?" Johnny said. "We ain't got no

crew . . . only you and me and Lanny. Butchie and Duck-Young not so hot. That haole punk ain't gonna make no difference."

"What's wrong with Butchie and Duck-Young? They're good."

"Yeah, but Butchie only like fool around with girls. And Duck-Young too skinny . . . tough, but skinny."

I shrugged. Johnny had to be pretty upset to start bad-mouthing his own friends. I knew he didn't mean it. Butchie was strong, and could work as hard as anyone. If he wanted to. That was the key—if he *wanted* to. I had more hope for Duck-Young. He always wanted to. He knew he had to work harder than us big guys and he was putting in the hours to prove it. He was lifting weights, and it was beginning to show. Almost every day Coach Freitas pinched his arm, flicked his eyebrows up and down, and said, "Sylvester Stallone, almost," which made Duck-Young smile.

So now Reggie Hoang was out and the haole was in.

Coach Freitas put him in the fifth seat of our six-man crew. That was a powerhouse position—seats three, four, and five were reserved for the strongest guys. And number five was supposed to help the steersman in heavy seas. But Kona never had heavy seas, and all the other positions had demands that David Ford had no experience at. So number five was probably the only choice.

In our crew, I was number one, in the front seat, the paceman. Then Duck-Young, who called the changes, was in two. Johnny, the strongest of us all, sat in three, the leader of the powerhouse. Butchie was four, middle pow-erhouse. Then David Ford. Then Lanny in six, the steers-man and the captain. Lanny was an expert at that position. Nobody was better, in any age group.

"Okay," Coach Freitas said, holding his hands above his head. "Come."

All the paddlers—five crews of older guys, us sixteen-and-unders, and a herd of fourteen-and-unders—slowly walked down to the water from our patches of shade and parked cars and trucks. Coconut trees stretched along one side of the cove, and a concrete pier angled out on the other. Behind us on the sand, our three fiberglass practice canoes sat like barracudas, noses to the sea, blue with white trim, each long and sleek with a stabilizing outrigger on the left side.

The air that day was thick and humid, making my arms sticky with sweat. I couldn't wait to get in the water and sink down into it, then slip into the canoe and break my back for Coach Freitas. I liked doing that. We all did. Paddling was inside us, part of our heritage. It made you strong. Made you *feel* strong. Made you feel like a bull.

"Who are we?" Coach Freitas yelled.

"Kai Opua!"

He started every practice that way. It was pretty dumb, but we all went along with it. Coach Freitas was a good guy. He actually liked us.

"Who?"

"Kai Opua!" we all yelled louder.

"Who can beat us?"

That was something new. Everyone mumbled, wondering what to say. We all knew Waikiki could beat us. Outrigger could beat us. And maybe Hilo. But who wanted to say that to the coach?

"Hilo," someone in back said as a joke, and everyone laughed.

Coach Freitas glared at us. "Who can beat us?" he said again.

"Nobody!" we all yelled.

"That's right. And don't forget it."

Coach Freitas got one of the men's crews going, sending them out to work on their starts. But for us, he had different plans. "You guys need to work harder than anyone," he said. "You're kind of ragged. But I know you can be good. You can even win, if you want to. But right now . . . you stink."

I stared at the sand with my arms crossed. A small, cool wave ran up and covered my feet. He was right. We did stink.

"Then why you gave us the haole?" Johnny asked. I couldn't believe he said that. I peeked over at David Ford, but if what Johnny had said bothered him, it didn't show.

"Mr. Blas," Coach Freitas said. "Are you telling me you got a problem with the way I run this club?"

"No—no," Johnny said. "I just—"

"You don't know how happy I am to hear that, Mr. Blas. Now you guys get that canoe and carry it down to the water."

The first thing he had us do was paddle our brains out with the canoe tied to a coconut tree. *Hard* to do that. Jeez. My back muscles burned and my fingers felt like corroded door hinges about to fall off. A lot of people said that wasn't a good way to train. But like always, Coach Freitas had his own opinions.

"Reach out! Pull! Come on, let's go," he yelled from shore. The canoe jumped and jerked, going nowhere. Later, Coach Freitas made us do wind sprints on the open sea. He was a slave driver.

After a half hour of sprints I felt like a car wreck. I could hear the echoing ring of the five o'clock church bell in the village. An hour still to go. I'd had it, already. I didn't know if I would even be able to *crawl* home. I prayed Dad would show up and wait around to give me a ride.

Johnny, though, when we got back to shore, got out and strutted around like he'd just taken a long, refreshing nap. But I knew that punk. He was beat. He just wasn't going to let Coach Freitas—or David Ford—see his pain. Shee. Sometimes I wondered what made him tick.

· · ·

A couple of days later, Lanny kicked up dust coming down our potholed driveway. "Hey, low rider," he said, his brown Filipino-Hawaiian muscles glistening with sweat. "Let's go already. Practice time."

I ran my hand over the smooth metallic blue paint of Dad's police Camaro, which I'd just spent two hours waxing. Dad paid me five bucks a week to keep the salt off it. "You like my car?"

"Yeah. Where is it?"

"Funny," I said, and Lanny laughed.

Beyond, the surf thumped over the reef, sending a continuous wave of salt mist inland, mist that would settle on Dad's car like microscopic termites. A mist that would make me rich.

"Hoo, hot, yeah?" Lanny said, wiping his forehead with the palm of his hand. Dad came out of the house, with Mom following him. His silver badge flashed in the sun. He kissed Mom, then stepped off the porch and walked toward us. He was shorter than me now, but still stronger. By far. He looked kind of like a bulldog in a uniform.

"Looks good, Mokes," Dad said, checking out the car. "You boys want a ride to practice?"

"Just to Johnny's house," I said. "We can walk from there."

Lanny and I squeezed into the front with Dad . . . and his radar unit, his police radio, his billy club, and his shotgun. We didn't want to sit in back and look like freshly arrested criminals.

The Blas place was an old paint-peeled shack of a house that sat back in a grove of thorny kiawe trees. The yard in front was dirt, dust, and a lawn full of weedy sleeping grass. Dad took a long, serious look around after he let us out. Then he drove away, slowly.

Johnny's father's two mental-unit dogs spotted us and charged out from under the house. "Shet," Lanny whispered.

Lanny and I froze as the dogs snarled up to us. I eased my hand out to let them smell it, to remind them that I'd been there before. Like yesterday. And a thousand times before that.

"Heyy," Johnny said. "How you punks?"

He was over near the trees with his lawn mower. I hadn't seen him there. Sometimes that guy was like a ghost. "What you doing with that thing?" I said. "You no more grass for cut."

"So. Still got weeds." Johnny kicked the lawn mower. "Stoopid thing won't start anyway."

"We got practice," Lanny said.

"I know, I know." Johnny spit on the lawn mower. "Wait, yeah? I going tell the old man, then we go." He scowled, and added, "Tst . . . he going be mad."

Johnny headed toward the house. He ducked through the front door, which was propped open with a stone. On the porch, three mangy half-wild cats lounged in the sun under Mrs. Blas's bird feeder. And beyond them, in the dirt, an old bike lay rusting its way back into the earth. James's bike. From before he ran away.

Yelling came from inside the house. An ugly sound. I felt kind of sick in my stomach, like when you're spearfishing and see a shark. When Johnny came out he looked like he wanted to kill somebody.

Lanny and I followed him out of the yard, silent as shadows. When the road curved away, and his house was out of sight, Johnny went back to being Johnny again. As far as I could tell, he wasn't afraid of his father anymore, like he used to be. Not since James left.

Now he was just angry.

James, though, had taken off. Just ran away in the middle of the night. He ended up at his uncle's place in Hilo, on the other side of the island. Dad had arrested James twice, both times for fighting. Once with an army guy from Pohakuloa, and once with his own father. Dad said James was okay, except for his explosive temper. Dad said to keep it to myself, but he was glad when he'd heard that James had run, because he was probably better off with his uncle.

But Johnny was a fighter. He was angry, sure. Just like James was. But he also wasn't the kind of guy to run away from his problems, no matter how bad they got. That's another thing I knew about Johnny: He stood up for himself.

* * *

"Eh, shahk bait," Butchie said just before we started practice. "You forgot to shave your nose. You still got shaving cream on it." Duck-Young laughed, and Butchie slapped hands with him. Lanny and I thought it was funny, too. Johnny just spit out sunflower seeds.

David touched the white sun guard on his nose, but didn't say anything. He was wearing his T-shirt again, like always. That first day without it had fried him. I felt sorry for him.

"How come you no talk, punk?" Johnny asked. "You too good for us, or what?"

David ignored him.

"Hey, I talking to you."

"Cool it, Johnny," Lanny said. "Leave 'um alone."

Johnny chewed and spit some seeds, then turned his back to David Ford.

Coach Freitas made us paddle a half-mile course at full speed. Twice. Out on the ocean, even with all that cool water, my muscles felt like they were on fire. But it felt good. The pain felt good, and the hot sun on my back. And it felt good to rest afterward as the canoe glided back into the cove. All of us, except David Ford, rolled over the side and sank down into the shallow water. David, though, hurried up to the shade, and his towel. He dried his face, then put more sunblock on his nose and cheeks. He was the only one in Kai Opua who ever brought a towel, and he stuck out like an ambulance.

One of the fourteen-and-under crews took over our canoe. "Watch those guys," Coach Freitas called out to us from the beach. "Learn something." We all gave a casual glance. For Coach Freitas. Who said we stink.

"James called last night," Johnny said. "He said the Hilo guys' sixteen-and-under crew going cream us." James, who used to paddle for Kai Opua, now paddled for Kamehameha, an enemy club in Hilo.

"How he knows that?" Butchie said. "He never seen us."

"Yeah, but I told him our time."

"But that's just practice time," Lanny said. "When we get in the race, going be different, going be better."

"Yeah," I said. "Come on, Johnny. Don't believe that. James just trying to psych you out, man. We not that bad. We still got a chance."

"We *could* have a chance, you mean. If we were a true crew . . . if we had six guys who knew what they were doing. But instead, look what we got—five guys and *that*." Johnny pointed his chin toward the beach, toward David Ford.

Nobody said anything. I didn't want to believe that we were doomed like James had said. But maybe we were, if that was Johnny's attitude. It was strange to hear him talk like that. He should have been saying, "No way no Hilo punks going take us, man . . . we going bury 'um."

"Hey, you sixteens," Coach Freitas called. "Come out of the water. I want you boys to run down to Mokes's place and back. You need to work on your endurance."

Butchie moaned and whispered, "The guy like kill us."

Lanny shoved him toward the beach. "Come on, let's go. I want to get home before midnight." We slogged out of the water, taking our time.

David Ford got up and threw his towel over his shoulder, then headed toward his bike. "Wait," Lanny called to him. "The coach said we gotta run."

David glanced back down at us, then pulled the towel off his shoulder. He bent down to pick up his bike, which had fallen over and was lying in the sand. When he started to push it toward the road, Johnny ran up and blocked him.

"Lissen, punk. If we gotta run, you gotta run."

The rest of us circled around David Ford like sharks. David studied us a moment, then started to push the bike between Johnny and Lanny. The kid had guts, I could say that about him.

"Hey!" Johnny said, poking his finger into David's chest.

David threw the bike to the side, just missing Lanny's foot. He moved up face-to-face with Johnny. "Get out of my way. I have to get home."

Johnny put a hand on David's chest. "You ain't going nowhere," he said, then shoved David back.

David Ford staggered, then fell. Instantly, he was up and charging, fists swinging, blows glancing off Johnny's shoulders, head, chest. Johnny raised his arms and ducked, trying to get out of the way. David kept coming at him, like a trapped boar. He threw himself at Johnny, and the two of them tumbled to the sand, grunting when they hit. The rest of us stepped back, gave them room. Johnny and David rolled over twice, locked together, white sand glued to their backs.

In seconds, Coach Freitas stood over them, prying them apart, shouting, "Break it up. . . . Come on, get up!"

Johnny and David let go and scrambled to their feet. Johnny's chest heaved as he gulped air. David glared at him with eyes of ice.

"Get outta here, all of you," Coach Freitas spit. "I said to run, confonnit."

Johnny didn't move.

Lanny jogged away, and the rest of us followed quickly. I glanced behind me to see what Johnny was doing and saw him jog out onto the road behind us, staying back, keeping his distance. A car passed, and we ran in the stink of its exhaust, heat waves rising from the road. When we passed Johnny's house, Johnny dropped out and went home.

• • •

A few days later, David Ford showed up at practice with an ugly swollen eye. As usual, he sat off by himself. The rest of us were standing around down by the water. We all turned and glanced up at him. He looked kind of sick.

"Look like somebody wen' slam 'um," Butchie said. "Johnny, was you?"

"Not me . . . but I wish it was."

Butchie touched his own eye, as if wondering how David's felt. "Maybe he fell off his bike."

Johnny turned and stared out to sea, hands on his hips. A fishing boat cruised by, the hum of its engine muffled by distance. Johnny watched it until it disappeared behind the pier. Then he spit and headed over toward David Ford.

We followed like fifth-graders to a sixth-grade fight.

David sat with his head resting against a tree, eyes closed. The swollen one was just a slit. Johnny stood over him with his arms crossed, watching David Ford the way you watch a dog twitching in his sleep.

"Shark bait," Johnny said.

David's eyelids popped up like toast.

"How you got that black eye?"

David closed his eyes again. "Tripped," he said.

Johnny kept staring at him. A whole minute must have passed. David opened his eyes again, peeking up. This time, he held Johnny's gaze.

"Don't lie to me, haole," Johnny said. The muscles in his jaw rippled under the skin, his eyes fixed, stone-like.

David said nothing. Didn't even glance at the rest of us. Just stared at Johnny. And Johnny stared back, some strange river of unspoken words flowing between them, some strange *thing* I didn't understand. David's hands, I noticed, were dirty, like he'd been working on a car. Thick hands, working hands. Like commercial fishermen had.

Johnny shook his head, then pulled a sunflower seed from his pocket. He chewed it and spit out the seed, which landed by David Ford's foot. David looked down at it. Johnny turned and walked away.

• • •

Just before the next practice, Johnny was acting pretty strange, didn't joke around with us like he usually did. Instead, he got a paddle from one of the canoes and took it over to David's tree. He sat down there and leaned back, just like David always did. Lanny and I wandered over. Then Butchie and Duck-Young. "How come you acting so weird, Johnny?" Lanny asked.

Johnny shook his head. "I don't know, man. . . . I got something in my brain and I can't get it out . . . about that haole punk's black eye."

"What about it?"

Johnny never answered that, because David Ford showed up just then. He looked confused when he saw us there, hanging around his spot.

"Haole boy," Johnny said.

David leaned his bike up against a tree, then untied his towel from the handlebars and threw it over his shoulder.

Johnny pushed himself up. He held the wooden paddle out in one hand. "You see this paddle? This is like your arm when you swim in the ocean. When you paddle, throw it ahead of you and bend close to the canoe, almost so your ribs touch the side. Sink 'um deep and pull. Use your back, and your legs. The power is in your whole body, haole. Not just your arms."

David watched Johnny suspiciously. His yellow eye was still puffy, but getting better.

"Hold it here . . . and here," Johnny went on. "And pull like this." Johnny demonstrated the technique, like Mr. Freitas had done so many times that you dreamed about it. When he was done, Johnny held the paddle out to David. "You try."

David pulled the towel off his shoulder and let it fall to the sand. Hesitantly, he took the paddle.

"Listen to Duck-Young," Johnny said. "He calls the switches. Mokes sets the pace. Follow those two guys . . . and listen to when Duck-Young says *hut, hut*. Follow that rhythm like it was your own heartbeat. Put your weight into the ocean and pull with everything you got. Power entry. Smooth pull. Whole body. And when you paddle, concentrate on only that. Your mind is just as important as your muscles."

David looked at the paddle like he'd never touched one before. He ran his hand along the long shaft, then gripped it the way Johnny had said.

Johnny nodded once and started to walk away, then stopped and turned back. "One more thing," he said, and David Ford looked up. "If you give up, and run . . . you lose. Are you a loser?"

Johnny drove that home with piercing eyes, and David took it in without expression. Then Johnny backed away, and David drifted over to a patch of shade.

"Something funny going on around here," Lanny whispered.

Duck-Young said, "Weird, man," and I agreed.

"I thought they was going fight," Butchie said. "But

Johnny cracking up, I think. Couple of weeks ago he was calling Mr. Freitas stupid for giving us the haole . . . now he ack-ting like Mr. Freitas right-hand man."

"Yeah, but Johnny's not stupid," I said. "He's got a reason."

Everyone mumbled in agreement.

Johnny looked up at us from down by the water. He smiled and gave us one of his royally cool Shaka signs, down by his waist, a motion that said "How'zit, you punks?" Sometimes you just went along with Johnny because you couldn't keep up with him even if you wanted to.

• • •

David Ford had drive that shamed us all. Gut-deep, and limitless.

Now, after Johnny had done that paddle thing, David Ford wasn't David Ford anymore. He was a monster. Hungry to work. *Starving* to work. Mr. Freitas scratched his head and watched him like a shocked, but pleased, father. All of us did.

Except for Johnny, who actually pushed David harder, who told him he was okay, but had a long way to go. "What? You like sleep already?" Johnny would say when David sat breathless on the sand after a hard run. Of course, David ignored him, which made Johnny smile, because Johnny knew as well as the rest of us that even an aircraft carrier couldn't have dragged that Arizona punk away from the cove.

Forget sitting in the shade. Now David came early and did push-ups while he waited for the rest of us to show up. Or sit-ups, or lifted stones like dumbbells. I figured he had to be dead tired before he even got there, because he worked—he had a job—which is more than I could say for the rest of us that summer. He worked for his father. Every now and then one of us would catch a glimpse of him, scowling in the front seat of his father's beat-up truck that had Ford Electric painted on the side.

After a while, David Ford became "Shark Bait" to us, a name that meant, in a joking kind of way, that he was dangerously white. And he never complained about it. But then, a lizard made more noise than he did.

We heard a rumor that David and his mother had been seen at the hospital the week before. All the guys made up reasons for why they were there. Butchie thought maybe Mr. Ford had had a heart attack. Lanny thought it was probably a car wreck, and that's how David got the sore eye. "Couldn't be a wreck," Butchie said. "The guy's truck no got new dents." Duck-Young said his cousin got in a wreck once.

"You guys really idiots," Johnny said, breaking in.

"What?" Butchie said.

"I said you idiots. Shuddup, already. Leave the haole alone. You don't know nothing."

"And you do?" Butchie said, puffing up to Johnny. But not too close.

Johnny laughed, which made Butchie madder.

"Come on, you guys," Lanny said, stepping between them. "We got a race coming up. We don't need to fall apart now."

"That's right," I said. "Come on, Butchie. Shake with Johnny."

After a long burning glare, Butchie stuck out his hand.

Johnny spit in his own hand and grabbed Butchie's before he could take it away.

"Confonnit," Butchie said. "Shet!"

We all laughed, and Butchie went down to scrub his hand in the ocean.

• • •

For the next two weeks we worked until we had-it, until we dropped dead, almost. Two weeks of pain—the last two weeks before the state regatta, which this year was being held in Hilo. Canoe clubs from all over the islands would be there, some of them with world-class crews, not punk kids like us sixteens. Our club, Kai Opua, was one of the top three canoe clubs in the state . . . and we, the sixteen-and-unders, were its one embarrassment. We *had* to do well.

Other than what we'd heard from Johnny's brother, we had no idea what our competition would be like. Mr. Freitas didn't believe in telling us. He wanted us not to worry about that, just develop our strength and endurance, and get our timing right. When he said *Who can beat us?* the answer always had to be *Nobody.*

I had to admit, though, we were getting better. Shark Bait was doing his share. And so were the rest of us. Butchie even gave up checking out girls for a while. Everything would have been perfect, if Johnny hadn't dislocated his middle finger punching a coconut tree . . . because of Mr. Ford.

David's father came looking for him three days before the regatta. We'd just finished a killer open-ocean workout and were sprawled half dead on the beach when he pulled up in his truck. David flinched when he heard the truck door thump. Sometimes you can do that—recognize the sound of a familiar car door slamming shut.

Mr. Ford got out and studied the pack of kids on the beach. David didn't sit up and wave at him or show him where he was. In fact, he tried to sink down into the sand. But it didn't work.

Mr. Ford spotted him and strode down to us. "Get in the car," he said. "We got a job. I need your help."

David hesitated, then said, "We—we're not finished yet," softly. "We have to go out again. . . ."

Mr. Ford's fist bunched up, like he was going to slug David or something.

David's gaze fell. Small beads of sweat glistened on his forehead, just below his hairline. "The races are in three days . . . I . . ."

"Races? What races? You ain't going to no races. Get in the car."

David picked up his towel and headed toward the truck. They gunned away, the flapping tailgate hidden in a cloud of stinking smoke. Johnny swore and punched a coconut tree.

• • •

There were thirty-eight canoe clubs at the State Championships in Hilo, but the best ones, beside Kai Opua, were Kamehameha of Hilo, the Outrigger, and the Waikiki Surf Club. If we could beat any one of those, we would be heroes.

Reggie Hoang was back in number five, more nervous than we were depressed. I felt bad for him. Johnny told him more than once that he was taking a good man's spot and that he'd better give it everything he had. Reggie said he'd try. Johnny just shook his head, and poor Reggie stared down at Hilo's dirty-gray sand, probably praying for a miracle.

And a miracle came.

One hour before our race, Shark Bait strolled up out of

nowhere and stood over Reggie. "Coach wants you," he said, and Reggie took off grinning like an idiot.

We all jumped up and slapped hands with Shark Bait, saying things like "You punk," and "You gave us a scare, man."

"I thought your father said you couldn't paddle," Johnny said.

"He changed his mind."

"How you got here?" Lanny asked.

David stuck up his thumb.

Amazing. Almost a hundred miles, and the bugger hitchhiked. And *made* it. In time to race.

• • •

There was a charged sharpness in the air over Hilo Bay. It rose from the sand, from the mud, from the soil. It shot like dry lightning over the water and over the lush, green strip of land along the waterfront. Thousands of people mingled there, and watched, cooking on small hibachis . . . miles and miles of people, and smoky barbecues . . . and canoe clubs, clumped together in their various colors, rows of folding tables checkered with half-filled paper cups of lukewarm orangeade, the empties crushed on the grass; small kids running around like goats; victorious crews from early races walking around dazed by their good fortune, peeking over the tops of leis piled so high around their necks they could hardly see; parents, girl-friends, boyfriends, strangers, all waiting with leis hanging from their arms, waiting to congratulate their loved ones, win or lose. . . .

Mr. Freitas, scowling . . . pacing . . .

At noon, our race was called. We got up, nervous as rats, and silently walked to the water.

Beyond, the ocean was calm and unusually blue for Hilo. I studied the buoy, the quarter-mile halfway point where we would turn and head back to finish. A half mile. And it would all be over. Months and months of practice to paddle one half mile.

Johnny dipped his fingers into the ocean and crossed himself. I did too, for good luck. My stomach turned when I slipped into the canoe, into my position. With slow, easy strokes, we paddled to the starting line. Nose to nose, a long line of canoes waited.

At the call, we raised our paddles and held them, poised above the water. In that moment I felt grief, and sadness . . . sadness that I had not done enough to prepare for this moment, had not worked hard enough, had not—

Pop!

Iwalani leaped ahead, shooting away from the starting line, quick as a lizard's tongue. I could see canoes on either side of me and hear paddlers grunting, fighting for position, setting a deadly pace. But our start was perfectly timed, and we shot forward with them. The question was, could we sustain it?

"Hut! Hut! Hut!" Duck-Young called behind me, his rhythm becoming the only thought, the only point of focus, our common heartbeat. The canoe lunged forward in the smooth ocean of Hilo's gigantic harbor, taking long, striding glides with each forward thrust of our six perfectly timed paddles. Reach, pull, release. Reach, pull, release. I had trouble concentrating. Shark Bait, hitchhiking, kept popping into my mind. Why did he do it? Why didn't he just get on the bus with us? Shuddup! Concentrate! *"Hut! Hut! Hut! Hut!"* Two canoes ahead of us. Only two! And one neck and neck with us, trying to creep ahead. *"Reach it out!"* Johnny yelled. *"Pull! Pull!"* My ribs touched the gunnel with each entry, white water splashing, blurring my vision. *"Fourteen! Change!"* Duck-Young called, and we all switched sides, swinging our paddles over the canoe without missing a beat. *"Hut! Hut!"* The rhythm—hypnotic, pulsing like the blood in my throat.

In minutes, it seemed, we were approaching the midpoint, the quarter-mile buoy, where we would turn and head back. Closer, closer. I could sense Lanny's steering, and paddled wide to help make the turn. Smooth. Sweet. Staying with the leaders. Turning. Turning. Still two canoes ahead of us. But not too far. Turning, heading back. Lanny steering, Lanny the pro, Lanny the best ever, gliding away from the buoy, aiming toward home. The world felt unreal, everything silent, except for the knock of paddles against the hull. The forward surge. The grunt of breath on each entry. The thrust, the pull, the rhythm, the rhythm. The fluid, silky ocean. Concentrating, thinking of nothing but the rhythm, the energy of six. Six as one.

Only two canoes now, two in my eyes. The finish ahead, closer. *"Pull!"* Johnny shouted. Butchie, Duck-Young, Lanny, Shark Bait, me. Paddles thunking. One canoe falling back. Then the cheering . . . yelling . . . the sound of winning surging through me, lifting me, filling my rubbery arms, renewing them. One canoe to beat. One, one . . .

We crossed second, inches after Waikiki, their paddles held high in two hands, the sign of victory.

Then Outrigger.

Then Hilo.

Johnny was ecstatic. Mr. Freitas ran down and called us the best sixteens he'd ever coached. He told us he was going to take us all to Huggo's Steak House when we got home. James came over and gave Johnny a bear hug and called him a cock-a-roach. Shark Bait smiled for the first time. Duck-Young and Lanny lay grinning on the beach, and Butchie puffed up like a balloon fish and walked into a pack of girls, coming back with Linda Medieros, one of his old flames from Kawaihae.

I looked around for Dad, who was supposed to have come over with Mom after work.

Johnny, as always, had brought along a couple of bags of sunflower seeds. One of them he passed around to all of us. He split the other with Shark Bait, who had never eaten them before and spent more time spitting than enjoying the salty pleasures.

Then Mr. Ford showed up, mad as a volcano.

Luckily, Dad wandered over at the same time, so Mr. Ford didn't make another stink scene. But he did drag David away.

David, we soon found out, had taken off without his father knowing it. Hitched a hundred miles. Starting before dawn. Shark Bait, who had worked his brains out to be good enough, strong enough. And had come through like diamonds.

We all walked with him to the Ford Electric truck, his father tailing us. Dad watched Mr. Ford, squinting at him. And so did Coach Freitas, who'd run over to see what was going on.

"How did he know you were here?" Butchie whispered to David.

"I left a note."

"You left a *note*? Are you crazy?"

"No," Johnny said, putting his hand on David's shoulder. "He knew exactly what he was doing."

Butchie shook his head. "You guys weird, man. Weird."

Shark Bait opened the truck door and got in, then

thumped it shut. Mr. Ford, with a face that could kill, drove off in a hurry.

As they passed, David glanced over at us, a slight smirk growing on his face. In a slow, easy motion, he raised his hand above the window and flashed us a classic Johnny Blas Shaka sign, cool as deep water.

"Just for five minutes, I'd like to get my hands on that boy's daddy," Coach Freitas said.

"Don't worry about that punk, Coach," Johnny said softly. "His daddy can't touch him."

His daddy can't touch him. . . .

Dad put his hand on my shoulder as the truck sped away. As much as I hated to admit it, Johnny was right. When it came to guys like him—and David Ford—I didn't know nothing about nothing.

How could I?

Graham Salisbury

A descendant of a Hawaiian missionary, Graham Salisbury grew up on the islands of Oahu and Hawaii, where he played soccer and was a long-distance runner on the track team, becoming MVP twice. Like the boys in "Shark Bait," he paddled. "I was the junkiest paddler in my age group," he admits, "but all my buddies were very supportive."

Mr. Salisbury is relatively new to the field of books for young adults; his second novel, *Under the Blood-Red Sun,* was published in 1994. Set in Pearl Harbor at the time of the Japanese attack, it is a story of friendship, trust, and loyalty, and family relationships are crucial to it. *Under the Blood-Red Sun* received the Scott O'Dell Award for Historical Fiction and was named an American Library Association Best Book for Young Adults, an American Library Association Notable Children's Book, an International Reading Association Teachers' Choice, and a *Booklist* Editors' Choice. It also won the *Parents' Choice* Honor Award.

Graham Salisbury's first book, *Blue Skin of the Sea,* catapulted him into the forefront of publishing for young adults. Set in Kailua-Kona, Hawaii, where he grew up, and presented as a series of short stories, *Blue Skin of the Sea* traces the growth of a boy and his relationships with friends and family members as he learns to respect the sea and understand his fisherman father's way of life. *Blue Skin of the Sea* was named an American Library Association Best Book for Young Adults and a *School Library Journal* Best Book of the Year, and received the 1992 Bank Street College Child Study Book Award, the *Parents' Choice* Award, the 1993 Oregon Book Award for Young Readers, and the Judy Lopez Book of the Year Award. Graham Salisbury was named the recipient of the PEN/Norma Klein Award as an emerging voice among American writers of fiction for children and young adults.

Educated at California State University, Northridge, and the holder of a Master of Fine Arts in writing from Vermont College of Norwich University, Mr. Salisbury has worked as a deckhand on a chartered deep-sea fishing boat, a skipper on a glass-bottom boat, a songwriter and musician in the rock group Millennium, a graphic artist, and an elementary-school teacher. Today, in addition to writing, he manages a handful of historic office buildings in Portland, Oregon, where he lives with his family. He still runs for exercise.

Competing

Jessie and Meadow have been best friends for years. Diane is a new friend of Jessie's. Perhaps a friendly game of racquetball will be a great way to get them all together.

Cutthroat

Norma Fox Mazer

"I took him home and fed him egg and milk," Jessie said. She looked out the window. Heaps of dirty snow everywhere, but it was cozy in the van. "Oh, man. You should have seen my mother's face when she walked in from work and saw that kitty sitting in my lap."

"Why doesn't she like cats?" Meadow said.

"Did I say that? He's a stray, he needs vet care, and Ma says that's like one of the most expensive things going. Anyway, she's in one of her poverty moods."

"What moods?"

"Poor. Poverty. Hello? She says we don't have any money to spare. Lots of bills and not enough bucks to go around."

Saying this, Jessie was momentarily furious, as if Meadow had forced the words out of her, as if it were a shameful thing that the Cowan family's brick house had three chimneys and four bathrooms, while Jessie, her mother, and Aunt Zis considered themselves lucky to be able to pay the heating bill on time and would think it pure heaven to have two bathrooms.

"The kitten's adorable," Jessie said, "although somewhat battered. I made him a box next to my bed. I'm soaking his injured paw. I think some jerk drove over it, or maybe it got hurt when whoever abandoned him tossed him away."

"Poor little thing," Meadow said empathically. The Cowans had three dogs and four cats, and they'd taken in strays, too. "What are you using on the paw?"

"Hot water and Epsom salts."

Meadow tossed the little blue playing ball into the air and caught it. "Better get him to the vet," she advised.

Jessie felt like pounding her best friend. Hard. Hadn't Meadow heard what she'd said about money?

"Everything okay back there, sweetie?" Mrs. Cowan called alertly from the front of the van, as if her motherly antennae had picked up Jessie's brief but sincere desire to do away with her daughter. Meadow's baby sister, Scout, was up front in the car seat, and her little brothers, Lance and Deaver, had taken over the middle. Jessie and Meadow had retreated to the back for privacy.

"Did you tell Diane what time we had the court?" Meadow put her feet up on the seat and relaced her sneakers.

"No, I didn't tell her the time. I said just come whenever you feel like it."

"So funny."

"So, do you think she's going to be on time?"

"I hope so, Meadow. We can go on and warm up if she's not."

"They get you off the court the instant your time is up. I want our full court time." She tapped her foot on the floor, as if the court time were already lost. "You said she was always late for things."

"Did I? I'm sure I didn't say that." Meeting Diane to play cutthroat had been Jessie's idea, which she was now starting to regret.

"You said it," Meadow said. "And you know her better than I do. She's your friend."

"Med, how late can she be? Relax!" Why did she keep trying to push Meadow and Diane together? It was that thing of wanting the friends you loved to love the friends you loved.

"You okay, Med?" her mother called again.

"Fine, Mommy."

"Fine, Mommy! Fine, Mommy!" Meadow's little brothers yelped.

"Shut up, you two," Meadow ordered.

"Shut up, you two," Lance and Deaver mimicked.

"Disgusting brats," Meadow said.

Jessie unzipped Meadow's sports bag to make sure Meadow had brought a racket along for her. Because she was an only child herself, the way siblings got along was a mystery to her. Sometimes Meadow was all over her little brothers, hugging and kissing, as if she couldn't get enough of them. Other times, she sounded as if she were just waiting to drop them in the nearest garbage can.

Love-hate, Jessie thought. Like their friendship?

Their relationship had started back in the misty past, when they were a couple of kindergarten kids. Meadow, slight and skinny, with tight blond braids, could do the best cartwheels, somersaults, and leaps in the class. She was also the shyest person. Jessie, not only unafraid to speak up, but eager to do so, became Meadow's voice. "Mrs. Lesesne, Meadow wants to be blackboard monitor. . . . Mrs. Lesesne, Meadow wants to carry the milk for snacks. . . . Mrs. Lesesne, Meadow has to go to the bathroom. . . ."

By now, they knew each other so well they could probably each predict what the other was going to eat for breakfast, a state that was both slightly annoying and terribly comforting to Jessie. A school psychologist had once told her she liked routine and repetition because her father had walked out on her and her mother years ago and upset the balance of her life. Okay. Maybe.

She knew people who changed their friends like they did their socks, and it was true she didn't understand that in the least. She had always assumed the Jessie-Meadow friendship would last forever. Now, though, a worm of doubt sometimes entered her mind and made her a little nauseous. She and Meadow were so far from a harmonious pair! They bickered and picked at each other like a grouchy married couple on the verge of divorce. It had never seemed to matter before. What was different now? Well . . . Diane.

Jessie had met Diane McArdle last summer at an acting class down at the Y. They'd noticed each other right away, and when the purple-haired coach had called for teams to do improv, Diane had looked at Jessie and Jessie had looked at Diane, and they'd stood up at the same moment, as if it had all been planned. They'd put their heads together and then done a sketch about two friends who couldn't agree on anything—a real natural for Jessie! The class had loved it, and Jessie and Diane had loved themselves for being funny and loud and spontaneous.

After that, they were friends, so absurdly compatible they called themselves the B&W Clones. Private joke. Diane was black, Jessie white. It amused them when people noticed them on the street. They put their arms next to each other, looked at their skin—*that's* black? *that's* white?—and laughed their heads off. Everything amused them. They made jokes and puns, teased each other. Their minds were like a couple of runners, sprinting side by side along the same track.

Jessie and Meadow, on the other hand, were more like two goats butting heads. Sure, it was affectionate, but sometimes it got real heated and they'd have a big, slam-bang fight. Still, they always made up. They had something deep between them—all those years. Jessie knew it was unfair to put her friendships on a scale and weigh them against each other, but she found it hard to resist.

• • •

"Who is he?" Meadow breathed as they walked away from the check-in desk in the clubhouse. She tipped her head back toward the blond guy with muscles behind the counter, the one who was wearing a skintight T-shirt.

"Jack Kettle," Jessie said.

"How do you know his name?"

"The universe brought it to me on the wind, Med."

"What?" Meadow said in an anguished whisper.

Jessie took pity and pointed out that parading across the skimpy T-shirt that covered those amazing pecs were ten big red letters. "J-A-C-K!" she whispered into Meadow's ear. "K-E-T—"

"Shhh! He'll hear you!" Meadow glanced back. Her normally pale skin had gone even paler, and her eyes were round and glazed, as if she were under hypnosis.

Jessie recognized the look. Meadow had just been struck by a Fatal Crush—a silly thing, in Jessie's estimation, but a silly thing she and Meadow had been through together, and more than once.

The first time this phenomenon had been noticed—and named by Jessie—had been back in fifth grade when, midway through the term, their class got a new teacher: Mr. Rivera of the bright blue eyes and dazzling smile. Poor Meadow. She hadn't been able to get a word out for the rest of the term.

"Want me to introduce you to Jack?" Jessie said.

"You don't know him!"

"I can still introduce you."

"No! No, no." Meadow held Jessie's arm in an iron grip and rushed her down the stairs to the locker room.

Diane was waiting for them, doing sit-ups. "Hi, guys." She was in powder blue sweats, her long black hair pulled up in a ponytail.

"How are you, sweetie pie baby doll?" Jessie scrubbed Diane's head.

"Just great, honey bunch piggy face."

Meadow yanked open a locker. "Jack Kettle," she mumbled.

"What's a Jack Kettle?" Diane asked.

"For most of us, Diane," Jessie said, "it's that blond bimbo with the overgrown muscles at the check-in desk. But for Meadow—"

"Shut up, Jessie," Meadow said.

"—he's a Fatal Crush."

"Is that like an Orange Crush?"

"Diane. Pu-leese! Fatal Crush, as in hopeless, impossible. As in the beloved is beyond your mortal reach."

"Beyond your *mere* mortal reach," Diane corrected.

"Meadow has had some very cool Fatal Crushes, Diane. Am I right, Med? But this time I don't think she's picked a winner." Jessie wound a bandanna around her head. "I'm afraid Jack Kettle hasn't got a single active brain cell to go with all those muscles."

"What are you talking about?" Meadow said. "How do you know anything about him, Jessie?"

"Med, guys who are obsessed with working out, guys who are always on the machines—"

"How do you know he works out? How do you know he goes on the machines? You never even saw him before today."

"Meadow, do I have to be dropped into the ocean to know it's wet? Do I have to burn my hand to know fire is hot?"

Shut up, Jessie, she told herself, as she often did. And as she often did—she didn't. "Do I have to see Jack Kettle, in the flesh, lifting weights, to know where he got those big puffy muscles?"

Meadow walked out of the locker room, slapping her racket against her leg.

"Well, let's get on the court so Meadow can beat us up," Jessie said. Now she felt bad for going on like that at Meadow's expense. Cheap shot. She'd done it to amuse Diane.

"Is Meadow a good player?" Diane asked.

Jessie laughed. "That's one way of putting it."

"She's very good?"

"Let me just say I've seen her run *up* the wall after a ball and make the point."

Diane swung her racket a few times, whipping her wrist around.

They had Court Three, one of the glass-walled courts. The first thing Meadow did was inspect the floor. She picked up a curl of dust in the corner and threw it out the door. Then she scraped the soles of her sneakers against the wall to rough them up. "Who gets first serve?"

"You," Jessie said, knowing Meadow wanted it.

Meadow took the serving box, bounced the ball five or six times, then lifted her racket and drove it down for a serve that ran so tight against the forehand wall, it would have been a miracle if Diane had returned it.

"Ace," Diane said—a trifle tensely, Jessie noticed.

"One, nothing," Meadow said, bouncing the ball. This time she served into the backhand court, Jessie's side, looping the ball up so high and so soft it seemed to hover against the ceiling like a hummingbird.

"Got it, got it!" Jessie cried as the ball slid slowly down the wall and she tried to remember all the tips Meadow had given her. *Face the side wall.... Step into the ball.... Use your wrist, don't stiff-arm it....* She barely got a piece of her racket on the ball. It was a weak return, and without even leaving the serving box, Meadow killed it against the front wall.

"Oh, shoot!" This was the first time Jessie had played racquetball with Diane. "Sorry, partner."

"We'll get her this time," Diane said.

"Come on, team," Jessie added, but she was a little taken aback to see the same nearly grim, I-play-to-win look on Diane's round face that she was used to seeing on Meadow's leaner features.

"Two, nothing," Meadow said briskly.

"Let's get her, Jessie!"

"Yeah, let's get tough." Jessie smirked at Meadow and crouched, swinging her racket like Jennifer Capriati.

On the seventh point, Diane looped the ball up into the air, forcing Meadow back, and she and Jessie made their first point. "Finally!" Diane yelled, punching her fist into the air.

"Yaaay, Diane! Yaaay, us! Yaaay for the good guys!" Jessie was determined not to be too serious about the game.

On the next point Meadow's serve came caroming off the back wall. Jessie picked it up low, something she rarely managed, and heard that thrilling sound of the racket connecting perfectly with the ball.

"Nice return," Meadow complimented her, and lofted the ball high and soft down the middle, driving Diane and Jessie to the back wall, where they collided as they both tried to take the return shot.

"Oh, now I'm mad, partner," Jessie said.

"Mad, mad, mad," Diane agreed.

"Breathing hard," Jessie said.

"Snorting fire! Watch out, Meadow!"

Meadow gave them a Tonya Harding smile, but they made the next two points. After that, though, it was Meadow's game all the way. She won, no surprise, 21–7.

In the second game, with different partners, the score was reversed. Diane, playing hard, managed to make seven points. "I should have done better," she said when they went off court for a drink of water.

"You were playing against the Jessie-Meadow team," Jessie said. "What did you expect? Oh, excuse me, I mean, it was *supposed* to be the Jessie-Meadow team. Maybe you thought you were just playing Meadow."

Meadow had been an irritating dynamo, picking up every shot Jessie was slow getting to, playing the back wall, both sides of the court, the ceiling, and up front.

"I could have brought my blankey and taken a nap," Jessie said. Meadow only smiled.

The last game, it was Jessie against Diane and Meadow. She started with some confidence—after all, she wasn't a bad, *bad* player. Besides, she had some of that I-wanna-win energy going for her right now, if only to show Meadow she could do it.

On her first serve, she stepped into the ball, used her wrist, and slammed it out of the serving box. "Ace!" she screamed. Too soon. Meadow killed it neatly against the front wall.

Unfortunately, that play was a prediction of things to come. Jessie served, Meadow killed. "This is getting monotonous," Jessie complained halfway through the game.

"Come on, Jess, go for it," Diane urged. "Get that killer instinct going."

"I have it, I have it!" Jessie cried, but the final score was a humiliating 21–3.

"Your forehand is improving, Jess," Meadow said kindly as they stepped into the showers. "Your big weakness is your backhand. You should really practice your swing at home."

Was there anything worse than being given advice you hadn't asked for? Yes. Being given advice you hadn't asked for by the person who'd just beaten you thoroughly.

"You don't always keep your eye on the ball," Meadow went on. "That's one of the most important things in any game."

"Everlasting gratitude for the arcane information," Jessie said, grabbing her towel.

"Oh, she's mad," Meadow said. "She's mad about losing."

"Hey, I am not. I love losing. It's so much fun."

"Whenever Jessie's mad, Diane," Meadow said, "she uses words no one understands. *Arcane*. Sounds dirty."

Jessie turned on the hair dryer. "Relax, sweetie, it only means 'secret.' "

"Oh, I know that," Meadow said.

"Oh, sure you do."

They were sneering at each other, but suddenly Meadow grabbed Jessie and mashed their noses together so hard Jessie grunted. "Pig! Pig! Pig!" Meadow said.

Now Jessie was supposed to say "Oink oink oink." In grade school this had been their make-up-the-fight routine.

"Pig! Pig! Pig!" Meadow repeated forcefully.

Tying her sneakers, Diane gave a snorting laugh that sounded almost as piglike as the reply Jessie was supposed to have made. "Oink oink oink," Jessie said finally, mortified that Diane was watching this.

But the truth was that, as soon as she said it, she felt much better and loved Meadow again and knew she always would. How could she not love her—they had been friends now for seven years, half her lifetime.

Yes, she would love Meadow and keep her for a friend, no matter what. Even if, she thought, she was beaten at cutthroat every week of her life, she would still love Meadow.

Norma Fox Mazer

As a teenager Norma Fox Mazer rode a bike, roller-skated, swam, and walked, but thought of herself as unathletic. Coming from a working-class family, she says, she thought of sports as something for the rich or the rare female jock—most girls then were not encouraged to take part in sports. Years later, when one of her daughters suggested it was time for her to do something besides write and wash dishes, Norma Fox Mazer took up racquetball and discovered she was well coordinated. Racquetball has become her favorite sport, and some of the details in "Cutthroat" come from her own experiences on the court.

The incidents described in "Cutthroat" appear in a somewhat different form in her newest novel—*Missing Pieces*—in which Jessie, Meadow, and Diane are characters.

Over the past twenty-four years Ms. Mazer has published nearly two dozen highly acclaimed books, including *When We First Met; Downtown; Mrs. Fish, Ape, and Me the Dump Queen; Babyface;* and *After the Rain,* which was a Newbery Honor Book. Winner of the Edgar Allan Poe Award for Best Juvenile Mystery in 1981, *Taking Terri Mueller* is the story of a girl who discovers that her mother is not, as she has been told, dead and that her father kidnapped her after her parents' divorce. That novel remains one of Ms. Mazer's most popular. Another is *Silver,* a novel about friendships and secrets, which the American Library Association identified as one of the 100 Best of the Best Books for Young Adults published between 1967 and 1992. Another of those 100 Best of the Best is *The Solid Gold Kid,* one of three novels she has coauthored with her husband, Harry.

Norma Fox Mazer's most recent award-winning novel is *Out of Control,* the story of three highly successful high-school boys who find a female classmate irritating and commit a series of petty acts against her that escalate into harassment and then into violence, changing all their lives dramatically.

Wouldn't you like your name in the *Guinness Book of World Records*? Curt and his friends are determined to achieve their goal.

The Assault on the Record

Stephen Hoffius

Roger Martell staggered around the last turn and held out the baton in a shaking hand. I grabbed it and took off. On earlier laps people had cheered when a runner came in and the chart was turned to mark another mile finished. Gathered at the high-school track had been a crowd—the nine other runners, some parents, girlfriends, buddies, even a TV camera crew. Now everyone was gone but the ten of us on the relay team, and the other guys all lay in the shade of a tree, barely noticing my progress around the track. Only Danny Daniels stood at the finish line, clapping. "All right, Curt, one more mile. You can do it! Let's go!" As soon as I was ten feet past him the cheering stopped and I had an entire lap to run in silence until I would hear his pitiful encouragement again near the finish line.

I was the eighth runner, the eighth of ten. After having run seven miles at top speed—or as close to top speed as I could drag out of my aching legs—I was already stiff, sunburned, and blistered. I ran the first four miles wearing socks inside my shoes, took them off for a couple of miles, and now had on two pairs. I started with no T-shirt, eager for people to see the great shape I was in, but for the last few miles I had covered myself up, more concerned about my flaming skin than the glances of onlookers. Besides, what onlookers were there?

Each step drove bolts of pain through my calves, but I pushed on. I had smoothed my socks when I put on my shoes, but now with each step I could feel wrinkles beneath my toes that felt like razor blades. My shirt tugged across my burned shoulders and my back like sandpaper, but I knew that if I threw it off the sun would burn deeper.

Everyone looked wasted, stretched out on lawn chairs at the edge of the track. I was the only one moving. But if I stopped, I knew my dreams—and theirs—would end. The record we were seeking would elude us. I had to keep running, despite the pain.

• • •

We were fifteen years old and anxious to be famous. Unfortunately, we had nothing going for us: There was no genius among us, no superstar athlete, no child actor, no heir to a huge family fortune. So we turned to the same thing that most people without identifiable skills think of: the *Guinness Book of World Records*. Certainly we could be the best at *something!*

Some records in the book demanded more talent than we had: doing 46,000 push-ups in a day, jumping 15 miles on a pogo stick, throwing a grape 327 feet to someone who catches it in his mouth. Those were beyond us.

So we tried to think of categories that weren't listed. For example, we would unroll cassette tapes and measure the length of an Aerosmith tape versus one of Mariah Carey's. For a couple of weeks we went on a measuring binge—toilet paper, paper towels, duct tape. . . .

Then for a while we counted: the number of raisins in Raisin Bran, chocolate chips in ice cream, Pringles in a tube, in a case, in a truckload. How many crinkles in a crinkle-cut french fry? We would go where no man had gone before. We would answer the questions that burned in everyone's mind. One weekend we pooled our money and bought a whole truckload of watermelons. How many could fit into a phone booth, into my mom's Toyota Camry, into a bathroom stall?

Maybe, we thought, we could collect our results into a book. We could write a column for a national magazine: "How Big, How Far, How Many?"

All our meetings were held at Bob Davidson's house. His mom always kept it stocked with snacks and drinks, as if this were her favorite activity. We were glad to give her the chance to fill the refrigerator again. Davidson—Bobby D was what he insisted we call him—assumed that since we met at his house, he must be the boss of our group. He always sat in the same tall-backed chair with his baseball cap pulled backward, wearing shades even in the house. Although his arms and legs looked like pipe cleaners, he tried to act macho and talked like he was in a Spike Lee movie. The only place he needed to shave was a spot on his chin, but he let that grow—a dozen greasy black hairs, half an inch long—and it made him look younger and sillier than if he had just cut them off. He shouted out directions that we ignored. He claimed we needed a name.

"We gotta have our colors," he said, tossing his closed pocket knife from hand to hand. The gesture lost some of its dangerous effect, as it was a Swiss Army knife. "Every gang got a name and colors. If we don't have 'em, people be dissing us."

"Bobby D," I said. "We're *not* a gang. We're barely even a club."

"Oh, may-an!" He shot me a glance that suggested he was embarrassed to be in the same room with me.

He proposed naming us the Counting Crows, after the band, but no one except Bobby D really liked them— their lead singer always sounded constipated—so we dropped the *r* and made it the Counting Cows, whatever that meant.

We had a name. The Counting Cows. We would be famous soon!

"This is awesome," gushed Bobby D. "The Counting Cows!" "Awesome" was his favorite word. We mocked him pretty bad whenever we left his house. "Awesome!" we'd roar about a fly buzzing around our heads. "Awesome!" for a crack in the sidewalk. He thought he was buying our friendship with chips and root beer. We let him think that.

Bobby D complained whenever he could about Danny Daniels being in the group. Danny didn't belong, he'd say; he was fat, he was gross, he wasn't as cool as Bobby D. We let Danny stay partly because it pissed off Bobby D. And it was Danny who came up with our ultimate idea. The most incredible project imaginable: a hundred-mile relay.

• • •

A mile relay was common—four guys who each ran a quarter mile. And Danny, who knew every track record ever set, gave us figures for the American record, the

Olympic record, the high-school record, the world record—every year since 1950. We had heard of four-mile relays, one runner per mile. Danny had the figures for that, too. In 1981 a hundred guys from Baltimore ran a hundred miles in a little less than eight hours. This would be more of a challenge. Much more. This would be more than anything in the *Guinness Book of World Records.* Ten miles per person, one mile at a time, a hundred miles total. Whatever we ran would be the world record, but we wanted to get as good a time as possible, so we wouldn't find out in a month that the record had been broken. We didn't want to have to do it again. This would be a record for the ages.

We wanted the fastest guys possible: Matt Feldman, the best miler on the team, even as a sophomore. Jim Luther, the best sprinter, who could run any distance. Since Daryl Wagner's accident, I was the best half-miler. Some of the guys—like Bobby D—weren't the best at anything, but they were willing to try, and we needed ten guys who would knock themselves out in hopes of getting one line of recognition in an eight-hundred-page book. We set the date for the first weekend after school let out. We called it The Assault on the Record, though it was a record that didn't yet exist.

Danny wouldn't run. He said he'd be the timer, the recorder. I thought he should run, since it was his idea, but some of the other guys were relieved, since his times would slow down our total. Bobby D, of course, made a big deal of it. "Good idea, Danny boy," he said. "You just keep your hand on the clock and leave the hard work to us. Keep that thumb loose so you can click the stopwatch, that's all you need to do. Think you can handle it?" Danny didn't pay him any mind. Bobby D was a distraction that deserved no attention and Danny gave him just what he deserved.

•   •   •

Most of us could run a mile in under six minutes. During the season, Feldman had done it in less than 4:30 in all of the meets, but we knew he couldn't continue that pace for each of ten miles. Eventually even he would slow down to six minutes, and the rest of us would be up around seven minutes or worse. We tried to figure how long this would take. Say we averaged seven minutes for a hundred miles; that would be seven hundred minutes or—we all scratched wildly on paper—more than eleven hours of running. We looked at each other anxiously.

"We could plan it so we ended at midnight when the clock strikes twelve," suggested Luther. His mother was a librarian and he sometimes got lost in all the books and stories that he read.

"What clock?" I asked. "There's no clock around here that strikes twelve. You're thinking of some Sherlock Holmes story."

"Oh, man, I got it!" shouted Bobby D. He slapped his head with both hands as if he had to hold back the brilliant ideas. "We could run all night! Start about eight at night, end right after the sun comes up in the morning. We'll light up the track with spotlights! Carry torches! It'll be like the twenty-four hours of Le Mans, like the start of the Olympics!"

"It'll be like a hospital ward," said Feldman, who was always so cautious he seemed boring. But this time he was right. There were no lights on the track, and we all knew the odds were pretty great that in the dark we would kick the inside border and stumble all over the track. Not to mention that we'd fall asleep at three A.M., waiting for our turn to run.

We'd have to do it during daylight. So we planned on starting about seven in the morning—during summer vacation, when we should have been sleeping!—and ending about six P.M. People could come and cheer for us throughout the day, we'd make the evening news, and we'd get home in time for dinner. It would achieve the maximum audience. The time was set.

"I'll check with the Guinness people," said Danny, "to be sure no one has a previous record." He took out a sheet and began plotting the order of runners. Feldman would be the anchor.

"I'll be the leadoff," announced Bobby D.

Danny didn't even look up. "No, we should save you for a later spot," he said, penciling him in for the number nine position. "Between Curt and Feldman. We need you there for a strong finish."

"Well, anyway, you need me," agreed Bobby D. He had the refrigerator open and was handing out cans of pop. "As long as you remember that. You need me."

• • •

The day of the race, I got to the track half an hour early, but lots of the guys had already arrived. Andy Berlinsky was the first runner, and he was already stretching. I saw Bruce Hecht, a junior wrestler who really wasn't much of a runner but who wanted in on a world record, and Roger Martell, the number two quarter-miler, a rich guy who wanted you to know he had money. We weren't all best friends, but for this goal we'd work together. There were about a half dozen parents. People had brought lawn chairs, coolers, a sign with hooks to hang numbers on for each mile finished, and, of course, a red, white, and blue ribbon to hang across the finish line for the end. The night before, we had met at Bobby D's to paint a sheet:

"The Assault on the Record"
100 MILE RELAY
By the Counting Cows

We had each signed it in marker, ten runners and Danny.

Bobby D saw me as soon as I started to walk up. "My man! My man!" he shouted, like a big-city hipster. "Now The Assault can begin!" He held out his fists for me to slap.

"How you doing, Bobby D?" I asked. "You got all the media here?"

We had given him that job, and he and his dad, who ran a restaurant in town and knew lots of reporters, had spent days on the phone. I doubted anyone would come. I mean, we were only ten high-school kids running around a track. It couldn't be *that* slow a news day, could it?

He nodded with his usual smug look. "At least two TV stations, and the paper is sending a photographer." A wide grin split his face.

"No CNN, huh?" I shook my head. "I'm disappointed, Bobby D. Disappointed."

"Some damn summit in Geneva," he said. "I don't know what the big deal is. But, you know, I wonder if we did this like a walkathon—you know, pledge so many dollars for each mile, raise money for starving kids or homeless shelters or some other crap—I think we could get them. I thought about delaying the whole thing a week, but then I thought, ah, the guys are ready; I don't want to let them down. Besides, my dad's gonna videotape a lot of it. He'll be able to sell the tape to CNN for millions. You know how much that guy got for taping that beating in L.A.? We could all go to college, thanks to this."

I patted him on the shoulder. "Good, Bobby D. Get me a dorm room with cable and a view." I walked away. I wondered how much of his hype was real. TV camera crews? For us?

Luther arrived with three pairs of shoes—long spikes, short spikes, and sneakers. Feldman was rubbing sunscreen on his legs and arms. Danny was lecturing to a group on the closest comparable races that he had discovered. He had posted a notice on an Internet bulletin board and people everywhere were now aware of it.

I pulled Danny aside. "Why'd you announce our race like that," I asked, "before we even do it? What if someone sets the record before we do?"

He looked up at me and smiled. "No one would set this record but you, Curt," he said. "No one's crazy enough!"

Danny had a starter's gun in a leather bag. It looked like the real thing. He pulled it out of the bag, slipped in the blanks, and held it down as if it were loaded with slugs. Everyone gathered around the starting line. Andy was ready, with a big paper "1" pinned to the front of his running jersey. A picture of a cow cut out of a magazine peeked around the side of his number. Andy scowled for the video cameras four of the parents held, but redheads with freckles have a hard time looking tough.

"Are you ready for the start of The Assault on the Record?" shouted Danny. "The World's Record Hundred-Mile Relay?" Everyone but Andy cheered. He tried to look as serious as if he were starting the Olympics 1500 finals. Danny held up his arm with the blank gun. "Runner, take your mark." He had a huge grin on his face, like he was doing just what he had wanted to do for years. "Get set." Andy leaned out over the line, his fingers curled so his thumbs touched his middle fingers. "Go!" The gun went off and Andy sprinted away. Everyone cheered. Bobby D punched the air, as if he had just won a championship ring, though he hadn't done anything yet.

Luther and I sprinted across the field to meet Andy at the 220 mark and play rabbit for him for twenty or thirty yards. We had to hurry. He wasn't jogging slowly, he was giving his all. We got there right when he did, stayed with him to the curve, and then let him go. Everyone else was lined up at the homestretch—runners and parents, and finally some girls had arrived. "Assault on the Record!" they chanted. "Assault on the Record!" Andy picked it up for the stretch, then eased up a bit at the turn. He'd get a good time, starting us out right. And Feldman, our fastest runner, would anchor it, so we'd end right, too. In between were some weak links. I just hoped I wouldn't be one of them.

Luther and I ran back to the 220 mark to lead Andy around again on his second lap. "How you feeling?" we asked when he got to us. "Good, good, only nine miles to go after this," he puffed. "This won't be so bad." His face was becoming streaked with red.

We ran with him to the curve and let him go. The fans were gathered again at the homestretch. Then Luther remembered that he was the third runner and had to do some more stretching. I still had about half an hour before my turn, but I decided to start loosening up, too.

• • •

Our first ten miles, one for each of us, went smoothly —good times and cheers for everyone (though I noticed that the crowd at the homestretch was pretty thin after the first four runners). Girls arrived in groups of three or four. They talked with the guys who lounged in lawn chairs, and they rubbed our shoulders. Most of us— not Feldman, of course—had our shirts off. We were ready to catch some eyes, turn brown in the sun, maybe line up some dates for the summer. I had been disappointed when Mariella told me she'd be out of town the day of the relay, but that meant she couldn't complain if I was friendly with some of the other girls. As he started the final lap of his first mile, Luther threw off his Tigers baseball cap. We all cheered for that. "Kip Keino," we chanted, "Kip Keino." Danny had explained that a long time ago a Kenyan miler of that name had tossed off his cap as he started his final laps. I think he set a world's record doing that.

My first mile was a pretty decent 5:05. As I handed off the baton to Bobby D, everyone was lined up with their hands raised for me to high-five. "Looking good, looking good," they shouted. Danny pointed to the mileage marker. "You get to turn it over, Curt," he said. Then he turned back to the track. He had two stopwatches, one with my time to be recorded, one for Bobby D. He was directing things like a general, a strange role for a fat kid who was usually picked on by some of the other kids, but everyone knew they couldn't match his knowledge of track history and details. I looked over as he marked my time on a huge chart, his pale puffy white legs sticking out of his shorts, and I smiled. At last other people were realizing he wasn't just a tub.

• • •

My time turned out to be second best on the team, after Feldman's unbelievable 4:25. Hecht was almost seven minutes, even for his first mile, but we had expected that. The big surprise was that Bobby D—an okay athlete, though he hadn't even gone out for the track team—turned in the third-best time, just ten seconds slower than mine.

Danny aimed the chart out at the street so passersby could see how we'd done. Hecht, whose time was slowest, thought that was a dumb idea. Andy Berlinsky, whose name was first on the list, thought it was great. Bobby D thought the names should be listed in order of times, not running position, so he would be third instead of ninth.

My second mile was 5:15, ten seconds slower than my first, but still a good time. Feldman was still way under five minutes. Somehow Bobby D kept up the pace, this time with a 5:30. I went up to him afterward and asked how he could run such strong times. Had he been working out? Running distance in the spring without telling anyone? He turned away from me and faced the other guys on the team as they sprawled in the lawn chairs, trying to chill out. "Hey, guys, listen to this! Curt's getting nervous! He knows who the power in this race will be! Check out Feldman—he looks a little tense, too. The mighty Bobby D is running up their backs and they don't like it one bit!"

Everyone laughed. I turned away. I was just trying to be friendly, pay him a simple compliment, and he had to grandstand with it. I realized my fists were clenched. Danny came up and leaned his head toward mine. "Don't worry," he said softly. "I think he'll take care of himself."

I looked at him closely, but he turned back to the track, where Luther was coming in for the second lap of his third mile.

· · ·

Each mile my time slowed. Everyone's did. Some guys' times went up a lot, like Hecht's, which rose twenty or thirty seconds each mile. Feldman's times hovered below five minutes, then climbed to 5:10 on the sixth mile. I added about ten seconds each mile, though twice I went up twenty seconds.

Around noon we had a big crowd. My folks brought a cooler of juice and candy bars—"Quick energy," said my dad with a smile. A TV station came by and shot some film of us. We tried to get the cameraman to stay for Feldman's turn, so we'd look as good as possible, but he shot Hecht instead as he struggled around the track. He talked with Bobby D (who did the interviews with his shades on and his shirt off, his muscles flexed the whole time) and left. We just shook our heads. This was our chance for fame, but on TV we'd look slow and arrogant.

We figured out that we could eat or drink during the laps of the first two runners after our turn. That would leave us about an hour to digest stuff before we had to run again. About the fifty-mile mark most of us realized our skin was being burned to a crisp, and we finally covered up. It was too late.

During the eighth mile I wondered if we could finish at all. Each step my feet and calves throbbed and I had to make up mind games to keep going. Seven miles done, I realized—more than half of my goal. After this there would be only two more miles. And I had already run half a lap. How many yards would that leave me? It would be easier to figure with a calculator or computer, but I couldn't see myself lugging a laptop around the track with me.

Three and a half laps to go, 440 yards for each lap, that was 880, 1,320, and a half lap more would add 220—1,540 yards until I could rest. But just in adding that up I had run 110 yards—what would that make it?

Drivers on the street alongside the track looked over and waved. During the first few miles I had waved back to each one. Then I had merely nodded. Now I didn't bother. Who cared?

After I passed Danny, I'd have three laps to go—440, 880, 1,320 yards until I finished my eighth mile of ten. All of us together would have done seventy-eight miles—only twenty-two to go until we set the world's record. Who cared about the record anymore? But we had started out for the record, it had seemed so important, and I wouldn't be the one to quit.

When I finally handed off to Bobby D, I realized he looked even worse than I felt. About the fifth mile his times had gone through the roof, increasing about thirty seconds each mile. His sixth-mile time had been fifth best of all the guys; his seventh mile placed him eighth. His times were getting to be like those of Hecht, who chugged through, grumbling that he hadn't realized what he was getting into. Seconds after Bobby D took the baton, I wondered if he was running at all. My momentum took me past him, but he didn't race past the way I had expected. I turned to see where he was. His legs were moving, his knees came up, but there was no forward speed. "Bobby D, you okay?" I asked. He didn't answer, and finally he passed me and continued around the track.

Danny came over to show me my time. "You're still

second or third best," he explained. "Luther beat you on two miles."

I nodded toward Bobby D. "What about him?" I asked.

Danny smiled big. "What'd you expect?" he said. "He couldn't keep up with the times he had at the beginning. He was between you and Feldman and was determined to keep up with you both. No way he could continue that."

"So why'd you put him there if you knew he couldn't keep up?"

He shrugged. "Somebody had to bring him down to size," he said. "And this way he does it to himself." It was the first time I'd ever noticed Danny looking devious.

He turned to the scoreboard and wrote my time in big numbers. I flipped the mileage marker to 78. Bobby D was still only halfway around the track.

When he came by at the end of the lap, the guys started to cheer for him. "All right, Bobby D. You can do it!" He looked over and snarled. Everyone shut up. His teeth were bared, his face squinched with pain—you could see he was working as hard as he could, but his legs were moving in slow motion. When he finally ended his mile— 8:30, one of the slowest yet—he came over to the chairs and collapsed, his baseball cap pulled low over his face. "So how'd it feel, Bobby D?" asked Roger. There was no answer. "Just two more to go," added Andy. Nothing. "Bobby, you okay?" asked Roger. He slapped him lightly on the leg and Bobby D shot upright. "Don't touch me!" he bellowed, swinging his fists in a circle around him. We suggested that he remove his shoes while he wasn't running, but he shook his head and said he would never be able to get them back on. Then he fell back on the chair and pulled a towel over his head and shoulders. A few minutes later he was snoring.

The guys could barely wake him up for his next turn. Danny said he expected Bobby D to lash out at the people around him—"Why didn't you get me up earlier?"— or to snap at them with his usual sarcasm: "You guys are so lame I can't even count on you to wake me up!" Instead, he rose silently, stretched stiffly for about a minute, and then hobbled over to the starting line. "Let's get in a good one, Bobby D," announced Danny as he took the stopwatches in his hands. Bobby nodded, looking almost meek, took the baton from me, and staggered away.

Danny came back to the lounge chairs, smiling widely.

• • •

During our ninth miles, the crowd returned. All the parents arrived with their cameras, the girls came back, and even Coach Kirby stopped over, probably looking for new runners for the team next year. With fans watching, our times leveled off. I thought they might improve for the last mile, if only because of adrenaline, but only Feldman's did. We couldn't ignore our blistered feet, cramped legs, and burned shoulders. But at least our times didn't continue to soar. Except for Bobby D's. His ninth mile was ten minutes, his final one almost twelve.

With a crowd around us, we started joking again—teasing each other, showing off. Not Bobby D. He pulled a lounge chair away from the others, fell onto it as soon as he finished his laps and got a drink of juice, and didn't move until we dragged him out for his last turn. He didn't say a word and hobbled with each step. He seemed like a different person from the swaggering show-off who had always made fun of everyone else.

• • •

The important thing was that we finished, with a total time of twelve hours, seven minutes, and thirty-six seconds. We posed for photos, everyone in a line behind the mileage marker that finally said "100." We all put our arms around each other's red shoulders, then cringed at the pain. That night I soaked in a cold-water bathtub with baking soda for almost an hour, then lay on my bed with a thick coating of aloe vera cream that my mom rubbed on my shoulders and back. The next day we got a two-paragraph article on the third page of the sports section. Everyone's name was mentioned, so we did achieve a small amount of fame, but that was the final activity for the Counting Cows. We never wrote our newspaper columns or compiled a book. Danny Daniels put out the word on the Internet about our accomplishment, and some guys in Oregon broke our record that August. Bobby D said he wanted nothing more to do with a group that would attempt such stupid projects. Without the availability of his refrigerator, we all went off to other things. I didn't see Bobby D again until school started. He was still quiet, still limping.

Stephen Hoffius

Stephen Hoffius, a half-mile runner in high school, recently entered the field of publishing for young adults with the award-winning *Winners and Losers*, which the American Library Association named in 1994 a Recommended Book for Reluctant Young Adult Readers. It's about parental pressure, competition between two friends on a track team, and what happens after one boy's heart stops during a race.

Many of the characters in *Winners and Losers* appear in "The Assault on the Record," a story that had its beginnings in Stephen Hoffius's own high-school days. During the summer after his sophomore year, Steve and nine friends (who, he says, "like me, had more energy than sense") ran a 100-mile relay, one mile at a time. They needed a week to recover, he admits. But they got a little smarter as they got older. The following year he and nine friends ran another 100-mile relay, this time with each runner completing twenty half miles. "A tip for those who would try it: The half miles were easier." For all Mr. Hoffius knows, they still hold the record for this distance, though he can't remember their times.

Stephen Hoffius was born in Grand Rapids, Michigan, and lives in Charleston, South Carolina, with his wife, Susan Dunn (an attorney), and their two children, Anna and Jacob. He is the director of publications for the South Carolina Historical Society and managing editor of *South Carolina Historical Magazine*. He is also a freelance journalist who covered the Olympic track-and-field trials in Eugene, Oregon, in 1980 and whose articles have appeared in a variety of newspapers and magazines, including *The New York Times, The Christian Science Monitor,* the *Detroit Free Press, The Progressive, Swiss Air Gazette,* and *Southern Exposure.*

Mr. Hoffius's next novel is about three teenage girls in Charleston and how their lives are affected when a hurricane hits South Carolina. He expects to call it *Hurricane Coming!*

He has been one of the best competitors in the galaxy, No. 1 on the Power Thought Team entered in the Interscholastic Galactic Finals. But is he good enough to handle the Challenger from the Unified High School of the Barren Planets?

The Defender

Robert Lipsyte

The Interscholastic Galactic Defender was licked awake by ice blue energy rays. Coach gently rocked his floating sleep slab. "Perfect day for the match, No. 1. Low humidity, no sunspots."

Coach tipped the slab and the Defender slid to the floor. He stepped out of his paper pajamas and onto the cleansing pedestal. A million beams refreshed his body, scraped his teeth, washed his hair, shaved his chin. The Defender then wrapped himself in a tunic of blue and gold, the school colors.

The Varsity was already at the training table. The Defender felt their admiration and envy as he took the empty seat at the head of the table.

He felt calm. His last high-school match. Across the table, his best friend, No. 2, winked. Good old No. 2, strong and steady. They had worked their way up the rankings ladder together since Basic School, rivals and teammates and buddies. It was almost over and he should have felt sad, but he didn't. One more match and he could be free to—

No. 4 caught his eye. He sensed that her feelings were the same. One more match and they wouldn't be numbers anymore, they would be Sophia and José, and they wouldn't have to guard their thoughts, or worse, turn them into darts and bombs.

Coach lifted a blue and gold competition thought helmet out of its recharging box and eased it down over the Defender's head. He fastened the chin strap, lengthened the antennae, and spun the dial to the lowest reception and projection power, just strong enough for noncompetitive thought in a small room.

For a moment, the Defender's mind was filled with a quivering crosscurrent of thought waves. There was a nasty pinprick from No. 7, only a sophomore but one of the toughest competitors in the galaxy, a star someday if he didn't burn himself out. There was a soothing velvet compress from No. 4, a hearty shoulder-banger from old No. 2.

The Defender cleared his mind for Coach, who was pacing the room. Psych talk time.

"As you know, the competition today, the Unified High School of the Barren Planets, is the first non-Earth team to ever reach the Galactic Finals. It wasn't expected and our scouting reports are incomplete."

No. 7 thought a blue and gold fireball wrecking the barren planets.

"Overconfidence can beat you," snapped Coach. "These guys are tough—kids from the orphan ships, the prison planets, the pioneer systems. They've lived through things you've only screened."

The freshperson substitute, No. 8, thought, "What about their Greenie No. 1?"

"We don't use the word 'Greenie,'" said Coach. "It's a bias word."

"A Greenie?" sneered No. 7. "'A hairy little round Greenie?"

"Don't judge a mind by its body," snapped No. 4, blushing when she saw the Defender's approving blinks.

No. 7 leaned back and flashed an image of himself wearing hairy green bedroom slippers. Only No. 8 laughed.

Coach said, "We respect the Challenger. It wouldn't be here if it wasn't good."

"'It'?" asked No. 2. "Male or female? Or a mixed gender?"

"We don't know anything about it," said Coach. "Except it's beaten everybody."

In silence, they drank their pregame meal—liquid fish protein and supercomplex carbs.

Back on his slab, the Defender allowed his mind to wander. He usually spent his prematch meditation period reviewing the personality of his opponent—the character flaws, the gaps in understanding that would leave one vulnerable to a lightning thought jab, a volley of powerful images. But he knew nothing about today's opponent and little about Homo Vulgaris, mutant humans who had been treated badly ever since they began to appear after a nuclear accident. They were supposed to be stupid and unstable, one step above space ape. That one of them could actually have become No. 1 on the Power Thought Team of a major galactic high school was truly amazing. Either this one was very special, the Defender thought, or Earthlings hadn't heard the truth about these people.

He closed his eyes. He had thought he would be sentimental on the day of his last match, trying to remember every little detail. But he wished it were already over.

The wall-lights glowed yellow and he rose, dialing his helmet up to the warm-up level. He slipped into his competition robe. He began to flex his mind—logic exercises, picture bursts—as the elevator rose up through the Mental Athletics Department. When he waved to the chess team they stopped the clock to pound their kings on their boards in salute. The cyberspellers hand-signed cheers at him.

Officials were in the locker room running brain scans. The slightest trace of smart pills would mean instant disqualification. Everyone passed.

The Defender sat down next to No. 2. "We're almost there, Tombo." He flashed an image of the two of them lying in a meadow, smelling flowers.

Tombo laughed and bounced the image back, adding Sophia and his own girlfriend, Annie, to the meadow scene.

"Think sharp!" shouted Coach, and they lined up behind him in numerical order, keeping their minds blank as they trotted out into the roaring stadium. The Defender tipped his antennae toward his mother and father. He shook the Principal's hand.

"This is the most important moment of your life, No. 1. For the good of humanity, don't let those Unified mongrels outthink you."

The varsity teams from the Physical Athletics Department paraded by, four-hundred-pound football players and eight-foot basketball players and soccer players who moved on all fours. Some fans laughed at youngsters who needed to use their bodies to play. The Defender was always amazed at his grandfather's stories of the old days when the captain of the football team was a school hero.

It was in his father's time that cameras were invented to pick up brain waves and project them onto video screens for hundreds of thousand of fans in the arenas and millions more at home. Suddenly, kids who could think hard became more popular than kids who could hit hard.

"Let's go," roared Coach, and the first doubles team moved down into the Brain Pit.

The first match didn't last long. No. 7 and No. 4, even though they rarely spoke off the field, had been winning partners for three years. No. 7 swaggered to the midline of the court, arrogantly spinning his antennae, while No. 4 pressed her frail shoulders against the back wall. The Unified backcourter was a human female, but the front-courter was a transspecies, a part-human lab creature ten feet tall and round as a cylinder.

The Defender sensed the steely tension in the Unified backcourter's mind; she was set for a hellfire smash. He was proud of No. 4's first serve, a soft, curling thought of autumn smoke and hushed country lanes, an ancient thought filled with breeze-riffled lily ponds and the smell of fresh-cut hay.

Off-balance, the backcourter sent it back weakly, and No. 7 filled the lovely image with the stench of backpack rockets, war gases, and kill zone wastes and fireballed it back. The Unified brainies were still wrestling with the image when the ref tapped the screamer. Too long. One point for the home team.

As usual, No. 7 lost points for unnecessary roughness—too much death and destruction without a logical lead-up to it—but as the fans cheered wildly he and No. 4 easily won. Their minds had hardly been stretched; the Psycho-

Chem Docs in the Relaxant Room would need little tranquilspray to calm them down. Good, thought the Defender; No. 4 would be out in time for his match.

Except for thinking about her, the Defender began to lose interest in the day. How many times had he waited to go down into a Pit and attack another mind? It had seemed exciting four years ago when Coach had pulled him out of a freshperson mental gym class and asked him to try out for the team. His tests had shown mental agility, vivid imagery, and, most important, telepathic potential.

It was the first thing he had ever been really good at. After he won a few matches, the popular kids began talking to him in the halls. Teachers asked him about the team. Letters began arriving at home from colleges owned by major corporations. His parents were so proud. He would be set for life.

But now it seemed like such a waste—fighting with thoughts instead of creating with them. Maybe he was just tired at the end of a long, tough season of defending his title. He thought about the meadow, with Sophia and Tombo and Annie. Instead of thoughts, they would throw an ancient toy around. It was called something like frisbill. Frisboo? Frisbee!

Coach tapped his helmet. "Pay attention."

No. 5 and No. 6 were staggering under a vicious barrage. They lost, and the standings at the end of the doubles were even, 1–1.

The crowd fell silent as No. 3 lost her singles match and the scoreboard blinked Visitors 2, Home 1. As No. 2 lumbered down to the Pit, the Defender sent an image of a victory wreath to him.

Good old No. 2, steady and even-tempered and sure

of himself. Mentally tough. He might have been No. 1 on any other high-school team, but he never showed resentment. For a moment, the Defender almost wished that No. 2 would lose; then the score would be 3–1 and nothing No. 1 could do would be able to salvage the team match. No pressure—he could play the game just for himself. If he won, great, he'd be the first player in history to win the championship twice. If he lost he would only disappoint himself; he wouldn't be letting his team and his school—and humanity, according to the Principal—down.

But No. 2 won and the score was tied and it was up to him.

The No. 1 player for the Unified High School of the Barren Planets, the Interscholastic Galactic Challenger, was waiting for him in the Pit.

He (she? it?) looked like a green teddy bear. The Defender had never seen one in the flesh. He forced his mind to think of the creature only as an opponent.

The Defender served first, a probing serve to test the quickness of the Challenger. He used an image, from a poet who had written in the dying language called English, of a youth gliding over a hilltop at night to catch a star falling from a shower of milk-white light.

The Challenger slapped it right back; the star was nothing but a burnt-out children's sparkler made from fuel wastes. The youth on the hilltop was left with a sticky purple mess.

The Defender was surprised at how long he struggled with the sadness of the thought. A Judge hit the screamer. Unified led, 1–0.

Coach called time-out.

The falling-star image had been one of his best serves,

a frequent ace. No one had ever handled it so well, turning the beautiful vision of humanity's quest for immortality into an ugly image of self-destruction.

They decided to switch tactics—to serve a fireball, No. 7 style. The Defender hurled a blazing tornado of searing gases and immeasurable heat. The Challenger's mind scooped it up like a hockey puck and plopped it into an ocean filled with icebergs.

Off-balance, the Defender tried to give himself time by thinking steaming vapors from the ocean, but the Challenger turned the vapors into great fleecy clouds that shaped themselves into mocking caricatures of famous Earthlings.

Desperately, the Defender answered with another fireball, and a Judge hit the screamer, calling it a Non Sequitur—the thought had not logically followed the Challenger's thought.

Unified led, 2–0.

The Defender served a complex image of universal peace: white-robed choruses in sweet harmony, endless vials of nutrient liquids flowing through galaxies aglow with life-giving stars, and hands—white, brown, green, orange, blue, black, red, and yellow—clasped.

The Challenger slashed back with mineral dredges that drowned out the singing, lasers that poisoned the vials, and a dark night created by monster Earth shields that were purposely blocking the sunlight of a small planet. The clasping hands tightened until they crushed each other to bloody pulp.

The Defender was gasping at the bitter overload when he heard the screamer. He was down, 3–0. He had never lost his serve before.

The Challenger's first serve was vividly simple: black

Earthling trooper boots stomping on thousands of green forms like itself.

Screamer.

The Judge called "Foul" and explained that the thought was too political—the Galactic League was still debating whether Earth colonists had trampled the rights of the hairy green offspring of the accident victims.

The Challenger's second serve was an image of black-gloved Earthling hands pulling apart Greenie families and shoving parents and children into separate cages.

Foul screamer.

The third serve was an image of Earth rocket exhausts aimed to burn down Greenie houses.

Foul screamer.

Tie score, 3–3. The Judge called an official time-out.

Coach's strong thumbs were working under the Defender's helmet. "Register a protest, right now. Don't let that little fur ball make a farce of the game."

"He's allowed to think freely," said the Defender. He wondered if the Challenger was a "he." Did it matter?

"He's using the game just to further his cause."

"Maybe he has a just cause."

"Doesn't matter," said Coach. "This is a game."

"I'll get him next period," said the Defender, trying to sound more confident than he was.

The second period was a repeat of the first. The Defender's best serves were deflected, twisted, sent back in bewildering patterns while the Challenger fouled on three more images of Earthling inhumanity. As the scoreboard glowed 6–6, the crowd buzzed angrily.

Coach said, "I order you to register a protest or you will never play for this high school again."

"It's my last game here."

"I'll see you don't get a college scholarship."

"I'm not sure I ever want to play this game again."

"Look, José"—Coach's voice became soft, whee-dling—"you are the best high-school player who ever—"

"Not anymore," said the Defender.

His helmet had never felt so tight—it was crushing his mind numb—as he trudged out for the last regulation period.

His three serves were weak, random flashes of thought that barely registered on the video screens. The Challenger easily re-created them into bursting thoughts that made the Defender's head spin. The Challenger's three serves were cluster bombs of cruelty and greed, horrible images of his people trapped in starvation and hopelessness because of Earth. They were all called foul.

It was 9–9 going into sudden-death overtime.

The Principal was waiting for No. 1 at the edge of the Pit. With him was the Chief Judge, the Superintendent of Earth High Schools, the Commissioner of the Mental Athletics Association, the Secretary-General of the Galactic League, and other important-looking faces he recognized from telepathé-news.

They all nodded as the Principal said, "You are the Defender. You have a responsibility to your school, your people, the planet. I order you to register a protest. We cannot be beaten by a foul little malcontent Greenie."

"It's only a game," said the Defender.

"Maybe to you," snapped the Superintendent.

He strode back into the Pit.

The Challenger had never left; the Defender suddenly realized the little creature had no coach or friends. He had come up alone to stand and fight for himself and his people.

The warning buzzer sounded. Seconds to serve. Sudden death. The Defender would go first. He thought of his all-time best serves, the ones he saved for desperate situations, because coming up with them was so exhausting, so mind-bending that if they failed he was lost. He thought of the end of the world, of sucking black holes, of nightmares beyond hope.

Suddenly he knew what to do.

He served an image of a dry and dusty field on a lonely colony planet. The land was scarred and barren, filled with thousands of round green creatures standing hopelessly beyond barbed wire as a harsh wind ruffled their dry fur.

For the first time, the Challenger took the full five seconds to return serve. He was obviously puzzled. His return was his weakest so far, merely widening the image to include a ring of Earthlings, healthy and happy, pointing and laughing at the Greenies. It was just what the Defender had expected.

He took his full five, then sent a soft, slow image of two Earthlings leaving the circle to walk among the Greenies until they picked one whose hands they held.

They led it skipping into a golden meadow under a sunny blue sky. The Earthlings were José and Sophia, and the Greenie who danced and sang with them was the Challenger.

In the shocked silence of the arena, the Challenger took the thought as if it were a knockout punch, his mind wobbling.

He was unable to deal with the thought, the kindness in it, the fellowship.

He can't handle love, thought the Defender. What a way to win.

The Challenger was still struggling to answer when the screamer sounded.

The match was over, 10–9. The crowd was roaring, the Principal was dancing on his chair, the video screens were filled with the face of José Nuñez, the first ever to win the galactic championship twice.

They swarmed around him now, the important faces, calling his name, slapping at his helmet, but he pushed through, shutting out their congratulations, the screams of the crowd, the exploding scoreboard.

He made his way through to the Challenger, alone and quivering in the middle of the Pit. I don't even know its name, thought the Defender. "It"?

Sophia and Tombo were running toward them. They knew what José was thinking.

It was only a game.

But it might be a start.

Robert Lipsyte

A former prizewinning sports reporter for *The New York Times,* Robert Lipsyte entered the world of young adult books in 1967 with *The Contender,* the story of a young African American boxer trying to be somebody. Besides receiving other awards, in 1994 the book was named by the American Library Association one of the 100 Best of the Best Books for Young Adults published in the previous twenty-five years. Alfred Brooks, the contender in that first novel, has appeared more recently in *The Brave* and *The Chief* as a police officer who attempts to help a young Native American boxer become a challenger.

Mr. Lipsyte is also the author of two nonfiction books for teens, *Assignment: Sports* and *Free to Be Muhammad Ali.*

Years of covering boxing and other sports, and of thinking about how important it is to "psych out" an opponent, led him to create the world of mental competition portrayed in "The Defender."

In addition to writing novels for young people, Mr. Lipsyte was a reporter and interviewer for the CBS television program *Sunday Morning with Charles Kuralt* and then the host of his own program, *The Eleventh Hour*, on New York City's public television station, for which he received an Emmy Award.

He has most recently written lively biographies of Jim Thorpe, Joe Louis, Michael Jordan, and Arnold Schwarzenegger as part of the Superstar Lineup series, while developing a television documentary about sports.

One might think that with a reputation as a sports reporter and a writer of books featuring real and fictional athletes, Robert Lipsyte would have been a very athletic teenager. Instead, he reports, "I was a varsity writer as a kid." The character of Bobby Marks in his *One Fat Summer* and its sequels, *Summer Rules* and *A Summer Boy*, more accurately reflects Mr. Lipsyte as a teenager. He now jogs, plays tennis, and does yoga.

Dealing with the Unexpected

The Moose is an outstanding left tackle.
But he longs for the chance to be in the
backfield, to dazzle the crowd in the
stands, to carry the ball. . . .

Just Once

Thomas J. Dygard

Everybody liked the Moose. To his father and mother he was Bryan—as in Bryan Jefferson Crawford—but to everyone at Bedford City High he was the Moose. He was large and strong, as you might imagine from his nickname, and he was pretty fast on his feet—sort of nimble, you might say—considering his size. He didn't have a pretty face but he had a quick and easy smile—"sweet," some of the teachers called it; "nice," others said.

But on the football field, the Moose was neither sweet nor nice. He was just strong and fast and a little bit devastating as the left tackle of the Bedford City Bears. When the Moose blocked somebody, he stayed blocked. When the Moose was called on to open a hole in the line for one of the Bears' runners, the hole more often than not resembled an open garage door.

Now in his senior season, the Moose had twice been named to the all-conference team and was considered a cinch for all-state. He spent a lot of his spare time, when he wasn't in a classroom or on the football field, reading letters from colleges eager to have the Moose pursue higher education—and football—at their institution.

But the Moose had a hang-up.

He didn't go public with his hang-up until the sixth game of the season. But, looking back, most of his teammates agreed that probably the Moose had been nurturing the hang-up secretly for two years or more.

The Moose wanted to carry the ball.

For sure, the Moose was not the first interior lineman in the history of football, or even the history of Bedford City High, who banged heads up front and wore bruises like badges of honor—and dreamed of racing down the field with the ball to the end zone while everybody in the bleachers screamed his name.

But most linemen, it seems, are able to stifle the urge. The idea may pop into their minds from time to time, but in their hearts they know they can't run fast enough, they know they can't do that fancy dancing to elude tacklers, they know they aren't trained to read blocks. They know that their strengths and talents are best utilized in the line. Football is, after all, a team sport, and everyone plays the position where he most helps the team. And so these linemen, or most of them, go back to banging heads without saying the first word about the dream that flickered through their minds.

Not so with the Moose.

That sixth game, when the Moose's hang-up first came into public view, had ended with the Moose truly in all his glory as the Bears' left tackle. Yes, glory—but uncheered and sort of anonymous. The Bears were trailing 21–17 and had the ball on Mitchell High's five-yard line, fourth down, with time running out. The rule in such a situation is simple—the best back carries the ball behind the best blocker—and it is a rule seldom violated by those in control of their faculties. The Bears, of course, followed the rule. That meant Jerry Dixon running behind the Moose's blocking. With the snap of the ball, the Moose knocked down one lineman, bumped another one aside, and charged forward to flatten an approaching linebacker. Jerry did a little jig behind the Moose and then ran into the end zone, virtually untouched, to win the game.

After circling in the end zone a moment while the cheers echoed through the night, Jerry did run across and hug the Moose, that's true. Jerry knew who had made the touchdown possible.

But it wasn't the Moose's name that everybody was shouting. The fans in the bleachers were cheering Jerry Dixon.

It was probably at that precise moment that the Moose decided to go public.

In the dressing room, Coach Buford Williams was making his rounds among the cheering players and came to a halt in front of the Moose. "It was your great blocking that did it," he said.

"I want to carry the ball," the Moose said.

Coach Williams was already turning away and taking a step toward the next player due an accolade when his brain registered the fact that the Moose had said something strange. He was expecting the Moose to say, "Aw, gee, thanks, Coach." That was what the Moose always said when the coach issued a compliment. But the Moose had said something else. The coach turned back to the Moose, a look of disbelief on his face. "What did you say?"

"I want to carry the ball."

Coach Williams was good at quick recoveries, as any

high-school football coach had better be. He gave a tolerant smile and a little nod and said, "You keep right on blocking, son."

This time Coach Williams made good on his turn and moved away from the Moose.

The following week's practice and the next Friday's game passed without further incident. After all, the game was a road game over at Cartwright High, thirty-five miles away. The Moose wanted to carry the ball in front of the Bedford City fans.

Then the Moose went to work.

He caught up with the coach on the way to the practice field on Wednesday. "Remember," he said, leaning forward and down a little to get his face in the coach's face, "I said I want to carry the ball."

Coach Williams must have been thinking about something else because it took him a minute to look up into the Moose's face, and even then he didn't say anything.

"I meant it," the Moose said.

"Meant what?"

"I want to run the ball."

"Oh," Coach Williams said. Yes, he remembered. "Son, you're a great left tackle, a great blocker. Let's leave it that way."

The Moose let the remaining days of the practice week and then the game on Friday night against Edgewood High pass while he reviewed strategies. The review led him to Dan Blevins, the Bears' quarterback. If the signal-caller would join in, maybe Coach Williams would listen.

"Yeah, I heard," Dan said. "But, look, what about Joe Wright at guard, Bill Slocum at right tackle, even Herbie Watson at center. They might all want to carry the ball.

What are we going to do—take turns? It doesn't work that way."

So much for Dan Blevins.

The Moose found that most of the players in the backfield agreed with Dan. They couldn't see any reason why the Moose should carry the ball, especially in place of themselves. Even Jerry Dixon, who owed a lot of his glory to the Moose's blocking, gaped in disbelief at the Moose's idea. The Moose, however, got some support from his fellow linemen. Maybe they had dreams of their own, and saw value in a precedent.

As the days went by, the word spread—not just on the practice field and in the corridors of Bedford City High, but all around town. The players by now were openly taking sides. Some thought it a jolly good idea that the Moose carry the ball. Others, like Dan Blevins, held to the purist line—a left tackle plays left tackle, a ballcarrier carries the ball, and that's it.

Around town, the vote wasn't even close. Everyone wanted the Moose to carry the ball.

"Look, son," Coach Williams said to the Moose on the practice field the Thursday before the Benton Heights game, "this has gone far enough. Fun is fun. A joke is a joke. But let's drop it."

"Just once," the Moose pleaded.

Coach Williams looked at the Moose and didn't answer.

The Moose didn't know what that meant.

The Benton Heights Tigers were duck soup for the Bears, as everyone knew they would be. The Bears scored in their first three possessions and led 28–0 at the half. The hapless Tigers had yet to cross the fifty-yard line under their own steam.

All the Bears, of course, were enjoying the way the game was going, as were the Bedford City fans jamming the bleachers.

Coach Williams looked irritated when the crowd on a couple of occasions broke into a chant: "Give the Moose the ball! Give the Moose the ball!"

On the field, the Moose did not know whether to grin at hearing his name shouted by the crowd or to frown because the sound of his name was irritating the coach. Was the crowd going to talk Coach Williams into putting the Moose in the backfield? Probably not; Coach Williams didn't bow to that kind of pressure. Was the coach going to refuse to give the ball to the Moose just to show the crowd—and the Moose and the rest of the players—who was boss? The Moose feared so.

In his time on the sideline, when the defensive unit was on the field, the Moose, of course, said nothing to Coach Williams. He knew better than to break the coach's concentration during a game—even a runaway victory—with a comment on any subject at all, much less his desire to carry the ball. As a matter of fact, the Moose was careful to stay out of the coach's line of vision, especially when the crowd was chanting "Give the Moose the ball!"

By the end of the third quarter the Bears were leading 42–0.

Coach Williams had been feeding substitutes into the game since halftime, but the Bears kept marching on. And now, in the opening minutes of the fourth quarter, the Moose and his teammates were standing on the Tigers' five-yard line, about to pile on another touchdown.

The Moose saw his substitute, Larry Hinden, getting a slap on the behind and then running onto the field. The Moose turned to leave.

Then he heard Larry tell the referee, "Hinden for Holbrook."

Holbrook? Chad Holbrook, the fullback?

Chad gave the coach a funny look and jogged off the field.

Larry joined the huddle and said, "Coach says the Moose at fullback and give him the ball."

Dan Blevins said, "Really?"

"Really."

The Moose was giving his grin—"sweet," some of the teachers called it; "nice," others said.

"I want to do an end run," the Moose said.

Dan looked at the sky a moment, then said, "What does it matter?"

The quarterback took the snap from center, moved back and to his right while turning, and extended the ball to the Moose.

The Moose took the ball and cradled it in his right hand. So far, so good. He hadn't fumbled. Probably both Coach Williams and Dan were surprised.

He ran a couple of steps and looked out in front and said aloud, "Whoa!"

Where had all those tacklers come from?

The whole world seemed to be peopled with players in red jerseys—the red of the Benton Heights Tigers. They all were looking straight at the Moose and advancing toward him. They looked very determined, and not friendly at all. And there were so many of them. The Moose had faced tough guys in the line, but usually one at a time, or maybe two. But this—five or six. And all of them heading for him.

The Moose screeched to a halt, whirled, and ran the other way.

Dan Blevins blocked somebody in a red jersey breaking through the middle of the line, and the Moose wanted to stop running and thank him. But he kept going.

His reverse had caught the Tigers' defenders going the wrong way, and the field in front of the Moose looked open. But his blockers were going the wrong way, too. Maybe that was why the field looked so open. What did it matter, though, with the field clear in front of him? This was going to be a cakewalk; the Moose was going to score a touchdown.

Then, again—"Whoa!"

Players with red jerseys were beginning to fill the empty space—a lot of them. And they were all running toward the Moose. They were kind of low, with their arms spread, as if they wanted to hit him hard and then grab him.

A picture of Jerry Dixon dancing his little jig and wriggling between tacklers flashed through the Moose's mind. How did Jerry do that? Well, no time to ponder that one right now.

The Moose lowered his shoulder and thundered ahead, into the cloud of red jerseys. Something hit his left thigh. It hurt. Then something pounded his hip, then his shoulder. They both hurt. Somebody was hanging on to him and was a terrible drag. How could he run with somebody hanging on to him? He knew he was going down, but maybe he was across the goal. He hit the ground hard, with somebody coming down on top of him, right on the small of his back.

The Moose couldn't move. They had him pinned. Wasn't the referee supposed to get these guys off?

Finally the load was gone and the Moose, still holding the ball, got to his knees and one hand, then stood.

He heard the screaming of the crowd, and he saw the scoreboard blinking.

He had scored.

His teammates were slapping him on the shoulder pads and laughing and shouting.

The Moose grinned, but he had a strange and distant look in his eyes.

He jogged to the sideline, the roars of the crowd still ringing in his ears.

"Okay, son?" Coach Williams asked.

The Moose was puffing. He took a couple of deep breaths. He relived for a moment the first sight of a half dozen players in red jerseys, all with one target—him. He saw again the menacing horde of red jerseys that had risen up just when he'd thought he had clear sailing to the goal. They all zeroed in on him, the Moose, alone.

The Moose glanced at the coach, took another deep breath, and said, "Never again."

Thomas J. Dygard

Thomas Dygard began writing about sports for the *Arkansas Gazette* (now the *Democrat-Gazette*) in his hometown of Little Rock when he was a senior in high school, and then covered sports for the Associated Press in Little Rock, Detroit, New Orleans, and Birmingham. He later served as chief of the AP bureaus in Little Rock, Indianapolis, Chicago, and Tokyo. He and his wife have always enjoyed foreign travel and have visited twenty-nine countries in Europe, Asia, and North Africa. They now live in Evansville, Indiana, near their two married children and four grandchildren.

In 1977 Mr. Dygard published his first work of fiction, a novel about a football quarterback with a strong fear of being injured, appropriately titled *Running Scared*. Writing fiction on weekends, usually in the mornings, Mr. Dygard produced more than a dozen sports novels before he retired from the AP in 1993. The most popular of these books are *Halfback Tough* and *Quarterback Walk-On*. His most recent novels are *The Rebounder*, a story about an outstanding high-school basketball player who injures another player and the difficulties he faces as a result, and *Infield Hit*, a story about the problems a high-school baseball player encounters in comparing himself with the father he hardly knows, who was a major-league star.

The event depicted in "Just Once" is based on an incident described to Mr. Dygard by a lineman friend, who told him how scary it was to have everyone on the field trying to knock him down.

It began as something different for Patrice and her father to do. Nobody expected it to change the way she viewed the world.

Brownian Motion

Virginia Euwer Wolff

Patrice

The whole adventure began as a diversion, a simple intermission between high school and college. My dad asked me to take a scuba diving class with him. It was the first novel thing that had come along in quite a while. For a couple of years I'd thought about going to medical school, either that or doing physics research, but all those plans had begun to look like an awful lot of effort. Coming very close to the end of high school, I was having senior burnout. I'd already been accepted at the university, with a pretty big scholarship, so my next four years were planned. Scuba looked like a wonderful interruption.

As it turned out, there was far more to it than that.

Jim

February was nothing but rain and snow and slush, cars needing jump starts in the morning, people out of the office with the flu. The exercise bike wasn't as much fun as it had been when I bought it. I needed something different, and scuba diving caught my attention one day, in a window display I saw from the bus, which I was riding because the car had been buried by the snowplow. The display had colorful fish like in a Jacques Cousteau film, and a scuba diving guy and girl with bubbles coming up from them. The sign said, SCUBA DIVING—THE ANSWER TO THE WINTER BLAHS!!!

I signed up as soon as I could, and the woman in the store asked me if I'd be bringing my own buddy to the classes at the Y. My wife, Susannah, wasn't especially interested, and Sandy's only eleven. My older daughter, Patrice, would be the perfect buddy, I said to myself. She's strong and agile, and she's a science nut, which I figured would be helpful in scuba. And frankly, she looked like she could use a break from her studies. About the time the fourth storm of the season put a foot of clean snow on top of two feet of dirty, the idea seemed better every day.

Susannah

With the entire night shift at the hospital ready to quit if the policy didn't change immediately, I was in no position to do anything as frivolous as go underwater and breathe from a tank. It was a perfect time for Patrice to take classes with her dad before going off to college next year.

Sandy

I wish it had been me. I'm old enough in my mind, just not in their rules. They wouldn't know I was only eleven if my dad didn't tell them.

Patrice

With three essays due by the end of March and the physics tutorial I ran twice a week and the knowledge that I was setting myself up for another decade of study after high school—I was ready for a change. Nothing at school was very exciting. My friends and I had agreed that the boys in our class were too immature even to bother dating anymore. Worse still, our bunch of girls was beginning to be tired of each other.

Shifting my schedule around gave me eight Wednesday nights free to meet my dad at the Y and learn to dive.

Susannah

Jim and Patrice began to approach Wednesday evenings like a couple of children who'd formed a new club.

Patrice

The first time we were supposed to clear our masks underwater I did it, and the self-confidence felt great. Add to that the familiarity of Boyle's law, Charles's law, Dalton's law, and Henry's law—which are pretty basic physics stuff—and Wednesday nights were pure fun. Even in the pool at the Y, where the underwater sights are extremely dull.

The self-contained underwater breathing apparatus, or scuba, pioneered by Jacques Cousteau himself, is one of those simple-but-complex things that make the difference between what human beings can do by themselves and what they can do with an imaginative device. The tank and regulator make breathing underwater as comfortable as breathing in air. Fins provide sleek mobility, the snorkel and the buoyancy compensator (BC) are there for safety, and with some knowledge of the hazards and of how to keep from dying of air embolism and other terrible things, off you go.

In fact, the course was mainly a set of lessons in safety. Kind of like driver's ed. Getting in a car and starting it are pretty simple things; the crucial part is knowing what to do with all that power.

Jim

Well, on Saturday mornings I started hanging around the dive shop where I'd first seen the window display. I'd go in there and plan which regulator I'd buy, and I'd read diving magazines, and I'd compare different kinds of BCs, and I'd talk with the divers. I was learning the lingo: "First rule of diving: Never, never, never hold your breath." "Plan your dive and dive your plan." "There are old divers and there are bold divers. But there ain't no old, bold divers." "S.A.F.E. means Slowly Ascend From Every dive." They tell you to ascend sixty feet per minute to keep your lungs from exploding. I even filled out a ticket to win a diving trip to the Caribbean and dropped it in the little treasure trunk sitting there on the counter. I began to daydream about going to a tropical island. Me, who'd never been to one.

Patrice

For my dad, converting Fahrenheit to Centigrade and vice versa was a little bit tricky, but what really stumped him was the gas laws. He understood the nitrogen-oxygen-carbon dioxide relationships, but I had to keep reminding him of the decreased volume–increased density connection. I gave him sample exercises to do after class, as we sat at the kitchen table drinking the banana milk shakes I had been making all winter long. He passed every one of the quizzes. We were good diving buddies; the water exercises were designed to equip us to cope with various kinds of emergencies, and we learned buddy breathing and BC use and decompression rates.

Susannah

The phone call came while Jim and Patrice were away for an entire Saturday doing their open-water checkout dive. Neither Sandy nor I had any idea that Jim had even *tried* to win a trip to the Caribbean, let alone filled out the lucky ticket. We had six hours to plan, to get the suitcases out and put them in the dining room, to go out and buy ourselves snorkels and fins, and to decide just exactly how we'd announce it when they got home.

Patrice

The bay was cold and murky. We wore full wet suits with hoods, we could barely see our diving instructor, and the old cans, rusty anchor chains, and mossy boat hulls were genuinely disappointing. For this I spent eight Wednesday nights of my life?

Jim

We passed the open-water checkout dive, Patrice and me, and we came out with our certification cards. It wasn't the kind of diving I'd been reading about in the magazines at the shop, but we were in the water and we were breathing, and we checked out. We walked in the door ready to show our brand-new cards and take Susannah and Sandy out for pizza.

Sandy

I got to watch for them out the window and call Mommy when I saw the car. We had our bathing suits on under our clothes and we stripped off our clothes fast and put on our snorkels and fins and stood in the dining room shivering when they walked in the door. Mommy pretended to sound mad. She said, "Jim, something has happened. We've had to change our plans. Something has come up." She was trying to go on like this, all upset, and Daddy and Patrice were holding little cards in the air and looking shocked at how Mommy and I were all undressed for the beach in the dining room, and

Mommy's upset voice collapsed and she started laughing and we both told.

"First time I ever won anything in my life! This is not a dream! We are going to the tropics to dive the reef!" Daddy was so excited he was like a kid and I was like the parent because I knew hours before he did and I wasn't all bug-eyed in surprise.

Susannah

We made our plans for the girls' spring break. I took one of the several weeks of vacation time I had coming. Let the nursing staff tend to their own unrest without my coddling them and soothing their feelings for a week. I was off to the Caribbean. Just like that.

Jim's boyishness has given me a lot of treats over the years, I'll admit. I was overjoyed to think about a week of snorkeling and reading and resting in the shade of a palm tree.

Patrice

From senior burnout to a week in the tropics was an easy switch to make. I put my schoolbooks and winter clothes out of my mind. Sandy and I bought new bathing suits in the Cruise Department. We each tried on about a dozen suits and came home giddy in the pouring rain, wearing our new sunglasses and smiling at everybody on the slushy street.

My friends were delirious with envy, of course. I promised to send postcards.

Sandy

At the dive shop where I went with my dad they said there would be plenty enough to see with snorkel and fins, and Daddy bought me a plastic fishwatching book. It has pictures of hundreds of colorful reef fish in it, and it's waterproof so it can go underwater. I would get to be the one to hold the book when we would go out in the boat to the reef and Daddy and Patrice would go diving down deep. At the store the man showed me in the book twenty different fish I'd be able to see just with a snorkel if I could hold my breath pretty long. I proved to him I could hold it a long time.

Patrice

Looking out the window of the airplane, I understood the word "aquamarine." The Caribbean is aquamarine. The most placid shade imaginable—and yet so exciting. Real scuba diving in real water in the real world.

Susannah

The hibiscus were wonderful, big and rich in the tropical sun. And the coconuts. And the sea grape trees. And the water! I never was in such water in my life. Clear, warm, gentle, buoyant, with black, spiny urchins and glowing, pink conchs close to shore, and an entire school of squid that lived just under the dock of the hotel.

Jim

I went down there and had to laugh at what we'd had for our checkout dive. Here, the visibility was forty, fifty feet in front of us, with sunlight. And the varieties of fish and other wildlife were too many to count, all swimming back and forth right in front of our eyes.

As we went around down there I got to thinking about my life. I spent my childhood walking to the outhouse and back. When the car broke down we walked till we could afford to get it fixed. I saw a lot of the side of the road. It was a world with rules, and I learned how they worked. The big guys ate the little guys, and if you were a little guy you hustled to try to keep ahead of the big guys. I never went outside the county I was born in till I was eighteen, and then I joined up. And I saw that world too, and it has its rules and I know how they work. The big guys eat the little guys and the little guys hustle. When I got out, I went to work, and it was the same thing.

On the outside, if you're just looking in, it all looks pretty. Underneath, there's all that eating and hustling going on.

And that's the way it is down under the water in the tropics. It's beautiful, I'll say that for it. It takes your breath away. It lets you be a little kid, wandering around staring and playing. You can gawk all day long at this peaceful-looking scene. It's a panorama, that's what it is. You have to look close to notice the predators and the prey, but they're right in front of you.

Patrice

It was heaven. From my first sight of a three-inch purple and orange fairy basslet slipping in and out of lacy little coral windows, I was hooked.

A young yellowtail damselfish with jewels for spots on its electric blue sides hovered in front of me; I went close up, staring through my mask, and the fish slid past my face, a silky breeze of fins—a miracle of a meeting in the bright sunlit Caribbean afternoon.

Jellyfish. Some are built like bells and maybe they even ring, in voices only they can hear. When they lose pieces of themselves, they replace them. Their cells can reconstitute a whole new body amazingly fast. Researchers use hydra and hydroid jellyfish to study growth and regeneration.

Even the sponges. They grow on the reef in forms like vases, urns, bowls. And the tubeworms. Just to look at them living on the coral is better than any of the museum trips my art class ever took. These amazing pieces of life have formed themselves—are forming themselves—and we can just lie suspended in the water and watch them at it. We can touch them, feel their textures. Some of them have heads like morning glories.

Underwater, the entire system is in a graceful, continually evolving equilibrium. The reef itself is a live thing, being built constantly by the coral polyps. They're tiny animals that build limestone cups to live in, the limestone itself coming directly from the water.

Our native diving guide, Sydney, has been in the water since he was a child. He wears shiny jewelry and speaks in rolling melodies. "Watch the sea fans waving—they will show you how the current is going." "Will you be pleased to go to another part of the reef tomorrow, Miss Patrice? Mr. Jim? There I can show you some more different corals, and you will like it, I think."

Yes, yes, and yes. Sydney the Black Beauty can take me to any part of the reef he wants. I'll just go finning along beside him, feeling graceful, noticing how elegant the world is in its intricate details. It's the closest I've ever come to pure, uncomplicated happiness.

Jim

That diving guide, Sydney, knows what he's doing. He led a barracuda alongside us and away, just by holding his hand solid near its side as it swam. Never saw anything like it. I'd never expected to get so close to one of those ugly faces, with their underjaw all stuck out in aggression. Looked like a killer, all right. I take my hat off to that Sydney.

Sandy

They feed us squid and shark, and even barracuda, and stew made of conch meat, and they feed us breadfruit, and they put the salad on top of sea grape leaves from the tree just outside our bedroom. And we ate grouper one dinner and sea turtle soup. And we have bananas in everything, in pancakes and in dessert and with coconut for lunch.

Susannah

Everything is so soft here. Even the voices.

Sandy

While we're outside playing, somebody comes in and sweeps the sand out of our room, Patrice's and mine. And they make our beds.

Patrice

I sent postcards to my friends by putting them in the handwoven basket on the hotel's desk. One evening I noticed somebody listening to a shortwave radio there. Communication with the rest of the world seems to be casual and optional.

We dove to thirty feet, to forty-five feet, to sixty feet and beyond. As the depth increases, the color intensity decreases. First the reds fade from mere human sight, then the oranges, the yellows, the greens. In the order of the spectrum, in fact. Completely logical. At ninety feet, all that is left is the blue.

Another physics principle is at work down there, too, invisible to the naked eye. The molecules in water are constantly colliding, in a hugely complicated pattern. Each water molecule has around 10^{15} collisions per second—that's ten, with fifteen zeros following it. It's called Brownian motion, named for the Scottish botanist who discovered it. Water looks clear because the collisions average out to a uniform whole. It's just one more bit of evidence that nothing is as simple as it looks.

Susannah

Our job here is simply to enjoy ourselves. What an unimaginable thing. All we're supposed to do is have a good time. Fill up the day with pleasure. Go walking, go snorkeling, pick up shells, read, rest, eat. Amazing.

Patrice

This morning when we were getting our gear ready to go diving, along the dock came a beautiful little shining girl, her dress waving and her bare feet padding on the wooden boards, with hardly enough weight to make the dock vibrate. Black Beauty, who was bent over a pile of weight belts, stopped what he was doing and walked back along the dock to meet her. I watched while they had a short conversation and nodded their heads to each other. Then they hugged and she ran back to shore and he returned to finish gathering the diving equipment. "She is my little sister," he explained. "Some question she had of me."

"How old is she?" I asked.

"Oh, she is nine, she is a big girl now."

"And she goes to school?"

"Well, no, not now," he said in his voice that always sounds like singing. "Her schoolteacher went away and now they have no school for her."

"No school? Don't you have laws? I mean, don't you have to go to school till a certain age?"

"Well, yes," he said, slowly as always. "But if there is no teacher, there is no school. Here on this side of the island only four children have been in the school in the one room. To get a teacher to come across the island for only four little ones, this is hard."

"You mean her education will just stop?"

"Oh, sometimes she can go to the school on the other side. Sometimes when I go across the island for business. Then she can ride along. Or my mother teaches her at home."

"What's your sister's name?"

"Celestine."

"What does your mother teach her? At home?"

"Oh"—and with this he carefully placed two air tanks in the stern of the boat—"they sew; my mother teaches her about sewing. And embroidery."

My stomach got a horrible feeling, like a house collapsing in it. A beautiful nine-year-old girl whose education stops because there's no teacher.

Susannah

The patois the islanders speak is so gracious. It's restful. The human voice at ease with itself.

Patrice

When Black Beauty's hand with its gleaming ring pointed downward to my left I looked in time to see the top side of a vast flat something, dark with gold spots, as it fluttered out of the sand and soared over our heads looking like a waving velvet blanket, white on the underside. Its wingspan was enormous. Sydney imitated its wavy motion with his hand and I imitated his. A real underwater conversation. Later, back in the boat, he showed it to me in Sandy's fishwatching book. "This is the ray, this spotted eagle ray. That was a big one down there, near two meters across the wings." Most beautiful English I ever heard in my life.

Sandy

On day 1, I went out in the boat with the divers and snorkeled. I watched Daddy and Patrice heading down with Sydney and the other grownups. For a while I could follow them completely by their streams of bubbles, which got bigger in coming up toward the top. Then the clusters of bubbles all crowded together and I lost track of them, so I snorkeled around carrying the waterproof fish book with me. One grownup from the boat wasn't scuba diving, so we went around together. We saw sea fans and brain coral and little fish in all gypsy colors. Day 2, I had a different grownup with me, and we counted 11 kinds of fish, including three rock beauties that look like yellow and black Volkswagens. Day 3, I couldn't go because I was sunburned and I had to stay behind, wearing a T-shirt. A girl named Celestine was here and she went for a long walk on the beach with my mother and me for 4 miles. We saw 2 dead sea urchins drying out on the sand. Celestine showed me how to pull the dead needles out and have a beautiful shell left over, all decorated with dots in patterns of 5's. It stinks from being dead, and she showed me where to take it to the kitchen so they would clean it up for me to take back home. Celestine lives here all the time, the whole year, ever since she was born. She is only 9. Day 4, I got to go snorkeling out at the reef again but with a T-shirt on. I dove down way deep just holding my breath and Sydney told me afterward I went down 2 and a half fathoms. I saw the MOST AMAZING fish which is a Queen angelfish of all gold and blue, more than 1 foot long and it is flirty-smily just like a queen. I got stung by fire coral on my leg the same day Patrice had the same thing happen to her. Day 5, it still itched. We all got my mother to come snorkeling out at the reef with us and you should have seen her face when she found out how deep down Daddy and Patrice go. She was scared for a while and climbed back in the boat, but I was convincing to her because we were going home the next day. She got back down the ladder and I was her snorkeling guide, sometimes I even held her hand and we saw a complete school of blue tangs which I showed her the name of in the fish book. Their young ones are bright yellow. Tangs are some of the many fish that are tall like a bicycle wheel and very thin. We also saw a trumpetfish who stands on its head.

Susannah

Oh, oh, oh, oh, oh. I have never seen such wonders all at once. I don't know of anything in human experience to equal this underwater world, the neighborhood of staghorn coral and sea fans waving to and fro, the community of elegant fish, graceful fish, cute fish, funny fish. Huge fish, tiny fish. Fast fish, slow fish. And colors. Enough colors to keep anybody happy. Not since childbirth have I had such a sense of miracle.

Jim

It's too bad we have to leave this place. This is what you might call a perfect spot on earth.

Patrice

When we'd had our last dive, I walked back along the dock with Sydney and a tangle of regulators and tanks. I tried to thank him for the most fun I could remember ever having. "I just never saw anything like this. All that life going on down there on the reef. Thanks for a great adventure," I said.

"It is my pleasure, surely. Will you come back?"

"Oh, yes. Oh, yes." My mind made a leap. "*Some*body has to teach in that one-room school."

He smiled his radiant smile. "You will do that?"

The idea had surprised me, coming out like that. "Maybe," I said.

"We would like that," he said. "If you come back here, we will dive again; the reef is very large."

Sandy

I wrapped my cleaned-up sea urchin shell in 2 socks to take home with me. And I'm taking 2 conch shells and a whole collection of smaller shells. I wonder if all my friends have gone to the ice skating rink every single day of vacation like they said they would. There's no radio here. There might be whole new songs by the time we get back, and I won't know any of them.

Patrice

We had to let twenty-four hours elapse between our last dive and getting on the airplane. The reason is in physics. When we're underwater, pressure from the water above us causes us to breathe in more nitrogen than we would up top. The nitrogen goes into all of our body cells. If you come off a dive and then get on an airplane, when you enter reduced air pressure as the plane rises, the nitrogen wants to come out of the body cells fast, and can become bubbles in the bloodstream. Waiting twenty-four hours allows the lungs to expel the extra nitrogen more slowly. In scuba, the rules are all based on physics. They make sense. How many things in life can you say that about?

So, on our last afternoon on the island I watched Black Beauty take a boat full of people and equipment out to the reef, and I snorkeled alone and thought about my life.

And this is the way it looked:

The way I lived back home, the laborious, repetitive, stifling sameness of it, suddenly revealed itself. Keep getting an education so you can get a job so you can pay your bills and keep busy till you get old and die.

I like physics and I like research and I like to help people, so I've spent lots of time in high school competing for scholarships to college. I would do the same for medical school or another graduate school. Even if I didn't end up in medical school, I'd work and study nearly seven days a week, year after year, to qualify to compete with other highly qualified people for research fellowships. By the time I'm thirty, I might be getting to do the work I want to do.

For what? For a world that's so corrupt that even the

people in charge stand around scratching their heads wondering how to manage us?

In a whole week on the island I haven't seen television, heard a telephone, seen a headline or a computer, tasted junk food, seen or heard or smelled a car, or thought about a movie.

No wonder my body and mind have felt so at ease.

I finned the length of the dock slowly, watched the school of little squid that lived underneath it, finned my leisurely way east, parallel to the shore.

I suddenly thought about the possibility that I'd never see another gleaming butterfly fish in my whole life. It brought tears to my eyes.

At home, my dad begins his day on the exercise machine and ends it at the computer. My mom puts on her makeup on her way to work, while she drives the car. We have two cars so that both Mom and Dad can go to their jobs. In our home we have four phones, two TV sets with remote controls, one VCR, one computer, one microwave, two toasters, a food processor, a blender, a dishwasher, a clothes washer and dryer, an oil furnace, three blow-dryers. And those are just the things on the surface.

I feel perfectly fine without the clutter of things that were daily custom a week ago. We all feel fine. I haven't see Mom and Dad so relaxed since I can remember. They've been late to breakfast three times.

The exquisite balance of the reef is one of the most compelling things. The fish, the coral, the food chain, the age of it. The stability. For more than 500 million years it's been building, and it's one thing the human species hasn't destroyed yet. The island, too. Not spoiled.

I turned over on my back and floated, legs and arms outstretched.

The whole discombobulated, noisy world we left a week ago has stopped mattering to me. As if it had just slipped away. I could walk away from it and not miss a thing. My friends and family could come and visit me for vacations, to get themselves back to normal.

My first choice would be not to go back at all, but I'm opting for my second choice: Go back home, graduate, pack up my things, and let the university know I want to delay entrance, maybe for a year or two. Come back to the island as soon as I can, with my savings to get started on.

I'll bet they'd hire me to be the tutor at the one-room school. They just couldn't call me an official teacher. Four children. Reading, writing, math, science, field trips. I could do it.

I'll write to the university: "I don't feel that I could sustain my focus at the university, and so with regret I am returning"—No, "declining"—No, "refusing"—"I feel that the university's trust in me would be misplaced at this time, and I am returning the"—"I don't want the scholarship, I don't want to go to college. Instead, I want to scuba dive and teach four children in a one-room school so their education doesn't stop before they're ten years old." What if I just came out and said it like that?

Susannah

I should have known this was too good to be true. Patrice has lost her mind. She wants to throw away her university scholarship and live on this island somehow, doing something, existing in some way that I just utterly don't understand. She seems to have an idealized view of a tropical paradise that's going to make life perfect, or something. I can't comprehend any of it.

I sit here on the terrace, under the thatched roof, looking out at the water, and wondering how in the world I'm supposed to know how to cope with this one. Nobody ever teaches you how to be a mother.

Sandy

Patrice wants to come and live on this island and she says it's because she wants to be the tutor to Celestine in the one-room school. But it's really because she wants Sydney to be her boyfriend. When they were talking on the dock beside the whole bunch of Scuba tanks I saw the way she was. She was all ooey-gooey-looking, not her normal-looking face. Her whole body was standing different, with a mermaidy girlfriend look.

But they didn't touch. I was watching the whole complete conversation.

Jim

It's one thing to enjoy a vacation, to forget your troubles and have a great time. It's another thing to go completely off your rocker and want to throw your normal life away. I said that and Patrice answers back, "You think the way we live at home is *nor*mal? That's not normal, that's crazy. It's a treadmill. We're like mice in a lab and somebody's watching how long we'll endure the stress before we tear our own flesh apart."

Now, that is not normal thinking.

"The sun's gotten to you, Patrice. You're not thinking."

"Not thinking? I'm thinking more clearly than I have in a long time. This is the real me thinking."

The conversation went on in that zigzag kind of way, the way it is when everybody wants something so bad, and everybody gets off-balance.

Patrice

I said to my parents, "But if I go to college now, I'll just be vague about it. I'll *sort of* want to be there. If I come back to live on the island, I'll be completely focused because I'll be doing what I want to do, not just waiting to do it. Not just sort of vaguely getting ready to do it."

"And what is that exactly?" Dad asked. "Just run it by us again so we can be sure."

"I want to dive, and teach—well, tutor—in the one-room school on this end of the island. Those little kids don't have any school at all now."

"What are you going to live on?"

"Why couldn't I be a jellyfish collector? Or a something-else collector? It would be simple. Research labs need specimens; I can easily find someplace that needs something collected. That's the easy part."

"Do you really think living on this island is going to be the way it's been for us for a week? Think again," said my father. "We've had luxury—it's not like that for the year-rounders. You won't have maid service."

"Dad, this is me, your daughter. Have you ever, *ever* seen me expect maid service?"

"Daddy's right. You'll be appalled at the difference," Mom said.

"That's it. A difference. I want to make a difference," I said. "Now. I want to do it now—not wait ten years till I've logged enough lab hours to drive me batty—"

"Look at it this way, Patrice," interrupted my father. "If it's the lab hours you don't want to put in, try another field, something without lab hours. There are all kinds of great possibilities for you out there in the real world."

"You think *that* world is real?" I said.

"You think this one is?" he said.

"Doesn't that depend on what you mean by 'reality'?"

"Reality is what you wake up to every morning," said my father.

"No. Reality is what you make out of your potential and your ideals. People make their own reality," I said.

Dad got in his stubborn voice. "Well, I didn't get to take honors this and honors that in school, and I don't understand all that. It sounds like some kind of excuse-making to me. It sounds like some kind of philosophy, I don't know what name they have for it this week."

My father is completely rational and sane, up to a point. When you hit that point it's a dead end, and you have to go back and try another route.

Jim

When Patrice got over people making their own reality, she asked me, "Didn't we come here because you wanted to get out of a rut?"

I told her, "Yes. Sure we did. But the whole point is we

get in ruts because in ruts is where we get work done." I was trying to defend something that ordinarily doesn't need defending—a way of life. "Remember the scuba rule: Plan your dive and dive your plan."

"Dad! That's exactly what I'm talking about. A scuba plan is there because it's for safety. A life plan is a whole different thing. I think a life plan can get to be a life *rut* just because people are afraid to change."

"And I think you're seventeen years old," I said.

If I'd gone to college instead of the army, I might be a vice president by now. We might have a vacation home on an island like this. It's my dream to see her with a college degree.

And I know if she delays for a year, then another year, and another one, college might look too hard. She might end up settling for less than she deserves. I've seen it happen. Lots of kids have big plans and then they end up settling for a life that eventually disappoints them, just because the other way was too much work.

When I was a kid I didn't have the choice she has.

I took a walk down the beach.

Susannah

Only Patrice and I were left on the terrace. We sat looking away from each other. I said toward the sunset, "Life is bland and dull one moment and utterly shocking the next."

"Are you making a point?" she asked my back.

"No, I'm telling you how I feel."

"How do you feel?" She sounded tight-lipped.

"Confused."

"Do you want me to apologize for confusing you?" she asked.

I didn't answer for a while. No, I didn't want her apology, I wanted her to be the way she was before. And I can't expect my daughters to be the way they were before. That was before.

"No. I just want you to be safe."

She was quiet, not making a move behind me. I could imagine her staring up the beach, watching the waving grasses and the little ripples of the water, wrinkling the inside ends of her eyebrows up just slightly.

"You can't keep me safe, Mom. Life isn't safe."

That turned me around. "That's what I'm afraid of," I said.

A look passed between us, a look of wanting. I was yearning for her to come into my arms and be my old familiar firstborn again, whose heartbeat I knew so well. She was aching to be free of that very thing, her mother's protective embrace. We looked at each other in the quiet, as the sun sank and the terrace turned grayish with night.

Patrice

The older people get, the fewer chances they're willing to take. It's a law of inverse proportion.

Sandy

I ran to catch up with Daddy going down the beach. He put his hand in my hair. "Sandy with sand in her hair," he said. I reached his fingers out of my hair and we held hands walking along the sand. There was a tiny little warm breeze from the water. "You all packed?" he asked. I told him yes and I figured out I could walk 3 steps and kick a piece of dried-out coral, 3 steps and kick a shell, 3 steps and kick a twig or stick, going all down the beach.

"You turned into a champion snorkeler," he said. I told him I knew it.

We walked and I kicked for a while. Then I told him a thing nobody even mentioned before. "What if a barracuda bites her?"

Daddy looked at me and took a mosquito out of my hair. "Right, Sandy," he said. "That's right. What if a barracuda bites her?"

"That'd be too scary. What would happen to her?" I said.

"We won't let that happen," said Daddy.

How could we not let that happen if she comes to live here without us?

Jim

When Sandy and I came back onto the porch, Susannah was saying, "There's no guarantee that you'd even be *liked* here, Patrice. Just because of your color. You might be so uncomfortable . . . so uncomfortable."

Patrice said, "I don't expect to go through my life being comfortable. That's not the point of being alive."

I have to admit I was proud she said that. But I didn't say so. "Patrice," I said, and I lowered my voice. It was nearly dark, and the mosquitoes were biting, but still there might be others near enough to hear our private family conversation. "Patrice, this island has poverty, backwardness, racism—Did you have any services performed for you by anybody white?"

"No," she said.

"How do you feel being called 'Miss Patrice'?" In the dark, of course, we are all the same color. If somebody else had stepped onto the porch just then, we wouldn't have known what color they were till they began to speak.

"I feel terrible. Guilty. But I didn't ask to be called Miss Patrice—"

"You look like Miss Charming when Sydney calls you that," said Sandy.

Patrice

There wasn't even a moment of silence to mourn the depths this conversation had sunk to.

"Ooohhh!" said my mother. "Oh!" said my father. "*That's* what you—" said my mother. "Now I see," said my father.

There was nothing at all cute about Sandy at that moment. She was a small-minded, petty, vicious, gossipy child.

Susannah

Patrice said, very slowly, into the darkness, "Do you actually believe I'd be moronic enough to let a crush on my diving guide take me thousands of miles from home and cause me to rearrange my life? Not quite, thank you. I'm more mature than that." Something in me wanted to agree with her.

Jim

I have to admit I felt a fatherly protection. I said, "He's a real nice fellow, Patrice, but . . . Well, this is all getting too complicated—It's so . . . All I know is—Oh, I don't know anything anymore. Anybody have a solution to this thing?"

Everybody was silent and just a mosquito buzzed in my ear.

Susannah

And then Patrice said, "I just feel good here. I feel balanced. This place just feels right. How can you argue with that?"

I told her lots of things feel good that aren't necessarily good *for* you.

She said, "I didn't say it feels *good*, I said it feels *right*. You're not *lis*tening to me." I heard what I heard. I was listening to her.

It sounded so familiar, her saying that. *This place feels right*. What am I trying to remember?

We sat in the dark, four loving people who couldn't speak.

'Trice's Cool. That's it. She was . . . what? Four. She must have been four. She disappeared from nursery school one morning and the teachers were frantic, nearly crazy with fright. The assistant teacher found her in a room down the hall, all by herself, with a stuffed duck and a book. She was reading to the duck. She was having her own school, and she called it 'Trice's Cool. She let herself be taken back to the room where nursery school was in session, and she explained to me, later, when she showed me her private schoolroom, "This place feels wight."

Even then, she wanted her own learning place, not the regular school. 'Trice's Cool.

Patrice

I wanted to make my own choice, to explore the possibilities of being alive. My parents wanted me to be comfortable and safe. Sandy wanted everything to be smooth and familiar; she can't see beyond her own view of anything. We all love each other. We were all making each other afraid. Next morning we got on the airplane. The island sailed away underneath us.

Molecules in water collide roughly 10^{15} times per second. The path of a single molecule is chaotic, complicated, ragged. On the outside, the water looks serene.

Jim

I'm sure that was only Round One. In fact, I'll bet on it.

Patrice

Nothing is as simple as it looks. When you go down deep you find things you'd never even thought to wonder about in your whole life.

Virginia Euwer Wolff

Like Patrice in "Brownian Motion," Virginia Euwer Wolff says, she "adores being in the water." She loved swimming as a teenager, was a lifeguard, and taught swimming before trying scuba diving. "My scuba diving experiences have been some of the high points of my life," she declares.

Although the teenagers in her three award-winning novels are not involved in sports, they are competitive and determined. *The Mozart Season,* an American Library Association Notable Book and winner of an Anti-Defamation League Award, is the story of one summer in the life of a twelve-year-old violinist preparing to play in a competition. In *Probably Still Nick Swansen,* the main character is a special-education student who must deal with repeated rejections, as well as his guilt over the death of his sister. Besides winning several other awards, that novel was voted one of the 100 Best of the Best Books for Young Adults published between 1967 and 1992 by the American Library Association.

The recent *Make Lemonade* focuses on two young women trying to find a hopeful future—a poor teenage mother and the girl who baby-sits for her two children. That novel has earned Virginia Euwer Wolff, among other honors, the Golden Kite Award from the Society of Children's Book Writers and Illustrators, the Oregon Book Award for Young Readers, and the Bank Street Child Study Book Award. In addition, it was selected as *Booklist*'s Top of the List winner for 1993.

A native Oregonian, Virginia Euwer Wolff has lived in New York, Ohio, Pennsylvania, Massachusetts, Connecticut, and Washington, D.C., and currently lives in Oregon City. Besides writing, swimming, playing the violin, and rooting for the Portland Trail Blazers, Ms. Wolff teaches English at Mount Hood Academy, a high school on the slopes of Mount Hood for skiers who are aiming toward the Olympics. She has a grown son, Tony, who is a professional jazz guitarist; a daughter, Juliet, who is a psychotherapist; and a grandson named Max.

There is plenty of action in the video arcade. But outside, in the shallow turquoise waters along the Florida coast, something even more exciting awaits Max and Andrew.

Bones

Todd Strasser

The sun is high and hot. The sky is that amazing shade of endless blue you rarely see up north. Not a deep blue, but a blue with depth, a blue you could disappear into as if it were a thick, foggy thing. It's strange then that the air feels almost lifelessly thin. But it's just the heat.

Around the pool the adults lie motionless on chaises—iguanas soaking up the sun. The kids scream and splash like birds bathing in a puddle. I must be the only person in sight wearing chinos and a long-sleeve white shirt with a brown eyeglass case clipped to the pocket. As I pass a pair of cute girls lying on chaises, brown skin glistening with oil, one turns to the other and whispers something with a smile. They probably think I'm a dork. I mind, but only a little. This is my last day here; I'll probably never see them again.

Past the pool I pull open a glass door and feel the chill. The temperature drops at least twenty degrees inside this dim room. The door swings closed behind me and my ears are bombarded with booms, crashes, sirens, and grunts. Welcome to the video arcade.

Andrew is frozen in front of Suicide Pact, standing in a puddle where his baggy orange bathing trunks have dripped. His damp black hair falls into his eyes as his hands flick over the buttons faster than a telegraph operator from the old West. On the screen two steroid-fed cartoon gladiators bash each other into unrecognizably bloody blobs.

I tap his shoulder. "Time, dude."

"I'm gonna crush this mother." Andrew hasn't quite heard.

"Crush him later. Vic's gonna be here any second."

"Vic can wait." Andrew doesn't budge from the machine. "Watch this."

One gladiator bludgeons the other. Blood spurts from his head; an eyeball bounces to the ground and rolls away.

"Great, Andrew. Can we go now?"

"Go without me." Andrew hasn't taken his eyes from the screen.

I knew this was a possibility. "I don't have enough money. You know that."

"Crap!" Andrew shouts. One gladiator raises his bulging arms in triumph while the other, now headless, lies on his back jerking spasmodically. Large red numbers flash on the screen, counting down from ten. Andrew jams his hand into the pocket of his trunks for another quarter to keep the carnage going.

"No way." I grab his hand.

Andrew squints angrily at me. "What?"

"We're going fishing, remember?"

The numbers run down to 0. GAME OVER. Andrew rolls his eyes.

"Great, Max, thanks." He stares at my clothes. "What is this?"

"Sun protection."

He smirks. "At least I'll get to work on my tan."

He has to go get the money from his old man. I suggest he bring sunglasses and a hat as well, but who knows if he's listening.

At the dock, waiting for Vic. The sun is beginning its afternoon descent. Three pelicans glide overhead like miniature pterodactyls. They come in smooth fifty yards away in the turquoise shallows of the inlet. Today is my last shot at a bone.

That's why Andrew's coming. I've already been out twice with Vic this vacation, but the winds and tides were wrong. So now I've begged and borrowed for one last shot. I've barely got half of Vic's fee. Andrew's the other half. I know him from previous trips to this resort. Our families come back every year at Easter. He's okay. Not someone I'd be friends with at home, but good for hacking around with one week out of the year.

A small white skiff comes around the bend and slows. There's Vic under the faded red baseball cap and Polaroids, wearing a white polo shirt and khaki shorts, nose coated white with zinc oxide.

"Hey, Max." He smiles slightly as he throws a rope around a dock cleat. "Ready?"

"Soon as my friend gets here." I look back across the pool. No sign of Andrew, of course. I'm starting to regret this.

Vic busies himself with the boat, stirring the shrimp in the live well while I strain my eyes for a glimpse of Andrew through the chaises and white umbrella tables.

"Maybe I better go look." The words are hardly out of

my mouth when Andrew comes strolling toward the dock, taking his time, in black T-shirt, orange trunks, and untied high-top sneakers.

He stops, looks down, and frowns. "That's a *fishing* boat?"

Vic looks up. I can't read his expression behind the Polaroids, but I know what he's thinking: that's a *fisherman?*

"Cool engine," Andrew says, nodding at the big black Merc. "This thing must fly."

"Get in and you'll see."

Andrew and I climb down and sit in the two white swivel chairs in the bow. Vic stands behind the console. With a roar, the skiff guns out of the inlet, the acceleration pushing us back in our seats.

Caught by surprise, Andrew grabs for the gunwale. Then he grins. "Boss!"

The wind rushes into our faces as the boat roars down the buoy-lined channel. I swivel my seat back to Vic and shout, "How's it look?"

Vic gazes out at the water for a long time. "Hard to say," he shouts back. "Tide's a bit strange. Could use a little more breeze. Not the best conditions."

"Maybe we shouldn't go," Andrew yells, hair whipping in his eyes.

"Vic's just foaming the runway."

"Huh?"

"He always says it's not great. That way he looks like a hero when you get fish."

"What's that got to do with foaming runways?" Andrew asks.

"Think about it."

Out of the channel, Vic hooks a right and the skiff tilts

hard, leaving a long, curving white wake in the blue-green water.

"Whoa!" Andrew shouts, and grabs the gunwale again. "Where's the fire?"

"He wants to get to the fish."

"So let's fish," Andrew says.

"Not here."

"Then where?"

"He knows."

I suspect Andrew must feel the way I did the first time, when we raced for nearly half an hour to a small mangrove island that looked exactly like every other mangrove island we'd passed along the way. But since then I'd learned that few fish are more mysterious and unpredictable than bones, and few people are better at unraveling the mystery than Vic.

"What do we catch them with?" Andrew yells over the roar.

I point at the thin spinning rods stowed along the gunwales.

Andrew makes a face. "Must be pretty wimpy fish. We pole-vaulting?" He points at the straight aluminum push pole that rests along the gunwale of the skiff.

"You'll see."

The run today is short. Vic throttles down and kills the Merc. The small skiff rises over the backwash, then settles down. An electric whine follows as the big engine tilts forward, angling the prop out of the water. Meanwhile, we're gliding softly over the glassy surface. Suddenly it's become very, very quiet.

Vic baits the hooks with live, kicking shrimp. His eyes slowly scan the water for two hundred yards in every direction. Andrew leans over the gunwale and looks down.

"Wait a minute, I can see the bottom," he says. "How deep is this?"

"About a foot," Vic replies, staring straight off the bow. He already sees something, but no matter how hard I try, I can't see what it is.

"A foot?" Andrew asks. "What are we gonna catch, minnows?"

"Shhh . . ." Vic picks up the push pole and climbs to the carpeted platform over the Merc. He plants the pole in the water and begins to push the skiff forward.

"See it?" he whispers.

Seventy yards ahead to the left a dorsal fin cuts through the flat water. The fin is the size of a playing card and nearly transparent. The sight sends a thrill up my spine. I hold my breath. I've waited a year for this.

"See what?" Andrew asks, a little too loud.

"Shhh. Seventy yards at eleven o'clock, coming across the bow."

"He's moving," I whisper.

"Something's bothering him." Vic leans into the pole and pushes the skiff ahead. "Maybe he'll turn this way. Get ready."

I stay seated, every muscle tense and my eyes straining to keep the fin in view as I grip the butt of the rod and pray Vic can bring me into range for a cast.

Then, just like that, it's gone. Nothing there but a slight ripple. Vic eases up on the pole.

"What happened?" Andrew asks.

"Something spooked him."

Andrew looks suspiciously at me. "This is a joke, right? Fishing in a foot of water for fish you can't see? My old man's gonna be thrilled he paid for this."

There's no point in trying to explain. I scan the broad,

flat, blue surface. Here and there a plant or a piece of coral sticks out of the water. About a hundred yards away a large white egret stands motionless, waiting for unsuspecting prey to cross its path. The sun beats down, and I wonder how Andrew's taking it. It's so quiet it doesn't seem possible that we're still on the planet.

I catch a glimpse of a fin moving thirty yards to the left and my arm shoots out, pointing.

"Shark," Vic says quietly.

"Where?" Andrew gasps. "Let's get it!"

"Shhh." Vic begins poling to the right, away from the shark. Fifty yards away two sets of fins move slowly through the water. "Get ready."

Once again I grip the rod. Vic poles the skiff swiftly and silently toward the fish. Suddenly I'm in range. It seems like a miracle they haven't spooked and run.

"About eight feet to the right," Vic whispers.

I rise slowly in the boat and cast. *Plop!* The shrimp hits the water and sinks. Almost at that exact moment, both fish veer to the left, away from the bait.

"Bring it in," Vic whispers. "They know something's up."

He starts to pole after them. I reel in and sit frozen in my seat, watching the tails swish gently back and forth twenty yards ahead.

"How come they don't just disappear like the last one?" Andrew asks.

"They're not sure."

Suddenly the fish turn sharply left, almost coming back toward the boat. "Ten feet ahead of them," Vic whispers with a new urgency.

I rise carefully and deliver the bait. The fish don't turn away. They're right over it! A tail fin pops out of the water as one of the bones pokes his nose down at the shrimp.

"He's got it," Vic whispers.

Line is whipping off my open bail. One . . . two . . . three . . . I crank the reel, setting the hook.

Eeeeeiiinnnnn! the reel's drag begins to scream. Line peels away. I lift the rod and it arcs like a crescent moon. The fish is running like an express train! This is what I've been—

Plip! The line suddenly goes slack. The rod straightens. It's over. I flop back into my chair in disappointment, consoled only by the fact that I'm pretty sure it wasn't my fault.

"What happened?" Andrew asked.

"Needlefish; coral," Vic says, offering the two most likely explanations.

"Needlefish?"

"They look like little barracudas. They see the line cutting through the water and think it's something to eat."

"Bummer."

Vic starts poling again. I notice that Andrew, for the first time, is hunched over, peering out at the vast plateau of glassy water. Some green mangrove islands dot the distance, and here and there a white egret stands in the shallows, waiting.

"There!" Andrew points. Two fins rhythmically break the surface, disappear, break the surface again.

"Ray," Vic replies without looking. He's already seen it.

"*Sting*ray? Cool."

Vic poles, we wait. The sun's lower; some cottony clouds have appeared out of nowhere. High above, a tiny glimmering silver jet leaves a silent vapor trail across the blue.

Down here, there is no sign, or sound, of civilization anywhere.

"This is like a safari," Andrew whispers.

"Ten o'clock," Vic whispers.

A lone fin moseys along fifty yards away. Andrew glances at me quizzically.

"Your turn," I whisper.

Andrew starts to rise.

"Sit!" Vic poles the skiff closer.

The bone and the skiff are on a collision course. Suddenly the fish turns right.

"Ten feet in front of him," Vic whispers.

Andrew casts. His bait lands twenty feet behind the bone.

"Crap!" He starts to reel it back in.

"Leave it."

The bone decides to turn right again. Vic poles the skiff hard, dragging Andrew's shrimp across the bottom. It doesn't seem possible . . . but then the bone does what we least expect—it turns one more time.

Suddenly it's right over the bait. Its tail fin rises.

"He's taking it."

Line starts whipping off Andrew's rod.

"Reel!"

Instead of reeling, Andrew jerks the rod sideways, trying to set the hook.

"Get the tip up!"

Eeeeeiiiinnnnn! the reel screams. The rod bends like a horseshoe. Vic reaches over and pushes the rod tip up as Andrew starts to reel crazily.

"Jeez, what is this?" he gasps.

"A bonefish," Vic replies, chagrined. He doesn't think Andrew deserves this. "Stop reeling!"

"But he'll take all the line!"

"Maybe."

"Can't you do anything?"

"Keep your rod tip up and your line tight."

A hundred yards from the boat, leaving a visible wake, the bone shows no intention of slowing its desperate run for freedom.

"I can't believe this thing!" Andrew cries as the reel continues to scream. "Can't you stop it?"

"No. Keep the tip high."

Another twenty . . . forty . . . sixty yards of line comes off the reel. There's hardly anything left on the spool.

Then the screaming ends.

"He stopped!"

"Reel!"

Andrew starts to reel. The line goes completely slack. The rod straightens. Andrew's shoulders sag. He stops reeling. "He's gone. I lost him."

"Reel!"

"But he's gone," Andrew argues. "There's nothing there."

"There won't be if you don't reel."

Andrew gives me a questioning look.

"Do what he says."

Andrew starts to reel. "What's going on?"

"He's coming back toward us."

"Huh? Why?"

"Because he's a bonefish. Reel faster!"

Andrew reels like a maniac. Suddenly the line goes tight again.

Vic smiles. "There he is."

This time the bone takes off across the bow, the thin

monofilament line kicking up a spray as it cuts through the water.

Eeeeeeiiinnnn! the reel starts to scream again. Andrew turns the crank.

"Stop reeling. Let him run."

The rod arcs as the fish shoots through the water.

"That's not a fish, it's a torpedo!" Andrew cries.

"Tip up."

The bone's second run isn't quite as long as the first. Andrew reels again.

"Man, my arms hurt. This thing must be a giant!"

"Eight to ten pounds."

"No way!"

Andrew gets the bone within thirty feet of the boat when it turns and races off again. *Eeeeeeiiinnnn!*

"I can't believe this!" he gasps.

I share a look with Vic that turns into a smile.

The bone has two more runs. Andrew holds on to the thin rod, babbling like a little kid at the circus for the first time. Short of jumping off the boat and trying to run across the flat, he's done almost everything wrong.

And yet the fish is still there, now exhausted, floating on its side next to the boat. Grabbing the line, Vic brings the bone close without taking it out of the water. The silvery fish has dark stripes. Its eyes are blank and defeated. Vic gently removes the hook, sloshes the fish back and forth in the water to get its gills working, then lets it go.

Slumped in his seat, his arms hanging helplessly at his sides, Andrew shakes his head. "Unreal . . ."

"Ready to go home?"

"No way. I want to catch another."

The afternoon winds down. Andrew and I hook four more bones; manage to land two.

Now the sun is a deep orange ball hovering on the liquid horizon. The cottony clouds above are streaked crimson and pink. The whole sky is a huge dome of gradually shifting pastel hues. The water has turned the color of slate. The air is silent, profoundly still.

The fishing's over. It's hard to see the transparent fins in this light, but we sit for a moment before heading back. The skiff rocks gently; no one speaks. The sunset is a vast panorama of color. We might as well be a thousand miles away, a million years in the past, or on another planet altogether.

"Time to go, gentlemen."

We race home over the smooth water, the wind in our faces, the sky turning dark in the east. Feeling tired but satisfied, I hope the people who make beer commercials never get their hands on this.

Andrew's been strangely quiet.

Back at the dock, it's dark. We thank Vic and pay him. He turns the skiff around and heads off into the inky shadows with his red and green running lights on. For him it was just another day's work.

Andrew and I stand under the bare lightbulb at the end of the dock, watching the red and green lights gradually disappear into the dark. Vic's wake sloshes against the pilings under the pier. Bugs and moths flit around us, crazed by the lightbulb. The kids are still in the pool, screaming.

Andrew turns toward me. "Next year?"

I slap his hand. "Yeah. Save those quarters."

Todd Strasser

Todd Strasser has written several award-winning novels for teenagers, among them *Angel Dust Blues, Friends Till the End,*

A Very Touchy Subject, Workin' for Peanuts, The Complete Computer Popularity Program, and *Beyond the Reef,* along with a trilogy about a musical group *(Rock 'n' Roll Nights, Turn It Up!,* and *Wildlife),* a horror series *(Nightmare Inn),* and a romance series *(The Lifeguard).* Among his most popular books are *The Accident,* a mystery about a teenage drunk-driving accident, and *Help! I'm Trapped in My Teacher's Body,* a humorous story about what happens when a boy and a male teacher switch bodies. Jake Sherman, the main character in that novel, returns in *Help! I'm Trapped in the First Day of School,* in which he discovers he can't get to the second day of school without making some serious changes. Another recent novel by Todd Strasser is *How I Changed My Life,* the story of a shy young actress and an injured football player trying to discover whether they are meant for each other.

Mr. Strasser has also gained notoriety for his novelizations of popular movies, including *Ferris Bueller's Day-Off, The Wave, Home Alone,* and *Free Willy. US* magazine called him "the most prolific writer" of this kind of book.

When he isn't writing at his home in Westchester County, New York, or conducting writing workshops for young people in schools across the country, Todd Strasser likes to play tennis, ski, and fly down to the Florida Keys to fish for bones.

Nineteen-year-old Kirsty Fleming knew how to sail. But she wasn't quite ready for the adventure that awaited her on the *Dolphin*.

Sea Changes

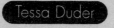

Tessa Duder

"If" is such a funny little word, isn't it? A conjunction, we learned in class, joining two clauses, but really, joining whole worlds of what might have been, or better, what here and now *is*. Let me start my story by adding up the ifs:

—If I hadn't grown up with a father who took me, his daughter, sailing on the Norfolk Broads because he had a wife who gets seasick just looking at a boat . . .

—If I hadn't done that Italian cookery course when I was only fifteen because my mother wanted me to do something "civilizing" . . .

—If I hadn't gone backpacking to New Zealand when I was sixteen . . .

—If I hadn't had a letter of introduction to that mad family in Auckland . . .

—If I hadn't stepped foot on a yacht called the *Dolphin* . . .

Then I wouldn't be settling down to talk to a tape recorder. I wouldn't be back in my parents' Elizabethan cottage just outside of Oxford, England, with a letter on the oak desk offering me ten thousand pounds for my story in five thousand words.

That's right, you heard—ten thousand pounds. The figure leaped out at me, about the only thing I could understand of four pages of small legal jargon signed by someone called Penelope Higgins, Publisher. First, actually, she rang, wanting a reporter to come and do an "in-depth" interview. My father said, don't consent to a bit of it, in-depth or otherwise. He's an academic, a child psychologist who writes books on things like child abuse and is always being misquoted. "They always get it wrong," he said. "Do it yourself, girl."

So here I am, doing it myself, the talking. After that they will have my tape transcribed onto paper and they will help me edit it down to five thousand words. I've not the foggiest notion what five thousand words looks like.

"Just talk for a couple of hours, my dear," Penelope said on the phone. "Just tell your story." If she isn't the Duchess of something she ought to be. My father, who knows about book contracts and editing, insisted that my letter back say something about my retaining final approval.

So, here I am, a contract signed, feeling a bit of an idiot, but I guess that's a small price to pay for ten thousand pounds. I'm lying on my patchwork quilt. Bess (she's my Labrador) is snoring at my feet; the diamond-shaped panes of my attic bedroom windows want cleaning. I can smell old dust, old lavender, Mother's Benson & Hedges, seawater in my wet-weather gear hanging behind the door, my own Benetton perfume. The scene is pretty, cozy—and doesn't move. Outside June is bustin' out all over. Bluebells, jonquils, the copper beech, the apple trees, Mother's white roses, striped just-mown lawns.

Oh, it's all a long long way from the rolling sapphire seas of the South Pacific. . . .

Perhaps I'd better explain that these days I'm a professional yachtsperson. Kirsty Fleming, aged nineteen, from Oxford, England. I've just been chosen for the British challenge in the Whitbread round-the-world yacht race, the only woman on an otherwise all-male crew. I've just sailed round the Pacific, the only woman on an otherwise all-male crew, and I wasn't chosen for my cooking. Well, in a sort of way I was, but I was *not* the bottom sheet, despite what you may be thinking. On that trip I had a different sort of training, and it was mostly in stamina.

Stamina, I hear you say?

You need more than stamina to race around the world. You need to know about spinnaker poles and knots and rigging and halyards and sheets and guys and splicing and jibs and genoas and navigation and sextants and weather and signals and flags and lights and buoys and rules of the road and medical emergencies and how to sleep in two inches of black water with the boat on the verge of a capsize and an unseen iceberg lurking two miles ahead.

What's something nebulous and unskilled like stamina got to do with it?

I can't do this cold—talking to a machine?

Are you listening, in there?

I'm going to call you Martin.

I once had a friend called Martin. He was my first boyfriend, me aged fourteen, him fifteen. But he didn't like my mother or my father's demands, too early in our friendship, that he come sailing, make up a threesome on the eighteen-foot day boat we keep on the Norfolk Broads. Martin hated sailing. He came only once and got seasick, and then puked over the wrong side of the boat and the wind blew it all back. So our romance went nowhere. But he was a sweet boy, gentle, nonmacho, and we kept talking. He listened to all my ravings for a year or so. I felt safe with him. He's at Cambridge now, reading English. He graduates next year.

So listen, Martin.

What? Oh, you want some ground rules. No sailing jargon; no poops and stanchions and heaving to and all the rest of it. All right, I agree with that. Most stories about the sea are so full of sailing jargon you need a nautical dictionary to get past the first page. Ever tried to read Joseph Conrad? As a kid I couldn't even cope with Arthur Ransome! So I'll talk about the sharp end, the blunt end, the kitchen, my bed, ropes. Okay, mate?—as they say in New Zealand.

Oh yes, New Zealand, where it all started. You remember I ran away to New Zealand when I was sixteen? Well, it wasn't quite running away, not an act of teenage defiance and rebellion, a daughter-goes-missing, headlines-in-the-*Daily Mail* sort of thing. I just told my parents I was flying to New Zealand next week because it was the middle of winter and I couldn't stand the snow and school one moment longer and it was either an airplane or a bottle of pills.

I meant it.

I said I'd booked my fare and could they please loan me a thousand pounds for the ticket, a new backpack, and spending money until I got a job in New Zealand. Mother had an attack of the vapors about me being far too young and not finishing my A-levels and the dangers of young girls going hitchhiking, but Dad knew what I was on about.

He signed a check and gave me this letter of introduction to some old friends in Auckland. He'd been at university, Yale or Duke or somewhere, with the wife. Mother bought a money bag to put around my waist and a whistle to blow if/when I got raped. She helped me pack so that I didn't start off already overweight. Dad lifted my bulging purple backpack into the car. They both cried at the airport. Then there was a five-hour delay while we waited for a blizzard to blow itself out. I wanted them to go, leave me, but they wouldn't.

Remember, Martin, I rang you the night before I left?

You couldn't or wouldn't understand. Why New Zealand, *New Zealand* for God's sake? Because it's as far away as I can possibly get, I said, unless I sign up for space travel, and after watching Christa McAuliffe's spacecraft fly to pieces on the telly five minutes after takeoff, I wasn't so keen on that. Jumbo jets to New Zealand don't often go down in flames. They usually arrive.

Auckland's a hole, you said. It wasn't like you, Martin, that comment, not you at all. You've never been there, how could you know? I said, Missing me already? Desperately, you said. Come with me, I said. Take a trip. The slight pause at the other end of the phone made me think you just might. Come with me.

But you didn't and Auckland wasn't a hole. It was a Monday in January. Coming nonstop from Los Angeles, we flew in from the north, which meant over the Hauraki Gulf and the Waitamata Harbor. The pilot was a Kiwi who liked talking to his passengers, so we heard all about the famous cruising grounds, and Rangitoto, which is the circular volcanic island at the entrance to the harbor, and the anniversary regatta. This regatta, he explained, was why there were so many yachts out sailing: over a thousand, celebrating the founding of the city in . . . I think he said 1840. It was the oldest and largest one-day regatta in the world. Yawn. He apologized for the low cloud. Air traffic control had told him that occasional rain squalls were giving the yachts a hard time down there on the water. Just get this airplane down safely on the tarmac, I thought. I couldn't see much anyway, just low green hills, white-speckled sea, drifting gray clouds. I was sitting between a fat businessman who had asked for (and got) two meals each mealtime and a very ugly baby attached to a young mother in leather jeans. Neither of them was going to tell me much about Auckland's cheapest backpackers' hostels, were they? We landed in the pouring rain at six at night. Actually, Martin, I was scared stiff.

I shall pass with dignity over the airport, where they made me empty out my backpack to the last pair of panty hose, and the bus trip into town, where I got off at the Hilton by mistake, instead of the Hylton Backpackers, and my first night in a dorm with two German lesbians who seemed to think I was one of them. I speak enough German to understand something of what they were saying. Eight o'clock next morning I got on the phone to Dad's friends and by that night I was one of the family.

Now, to understand why I'm now a famous round-the-world yachtsperson, Martin, you've got to understand something about Auckland. The place is sailing-mad. In Britain we might think Cowes is something special, and over in America they've got Newport, Rhode Island, and Chesapeake Bay and Miami and San Diego, but in Auckland you don't have to be rich to own a boat. *Everybody* sails something, or drives something flashy with a big engine, or small with a little outboard, or goes windsurfing or surfing or fishing or canoeing or rowing or just swimming. They're sea-mad.

The family I stayed with weren't rich, but they owned about five boats: a keelboat, three sailing dinghies, and a runabout with an outboard, and two Windsurfers. The keelboat was seventy years old, vintage wooden; the sailing dinghies were between ten and fifty years old; the Windsurfers were brand-new, and they kept them all in a scruffy tumbledown boat shed on the edge of the harbor. Perhaps "scruffy" isn't quite the right word. "Messy," "chaotic," "a shambles,"—totally fascinating. You wanted it, some bolt, or block, or brass screw or length of rope or scrap of sail, Pete would find it for you, somewhere, like an archaeologist digging in a scrap heap.

They don't really come into this story much—Pete and his boats and his mad, messy, chaotic, and fascinating family: the wife who went to Yale, five teenagers, four cars, five boats, two dogs, and a pet seagull—except as links in the chain that led me to be turning over the tape for side two.

Are you still listening, Martin?

Where was I? Oh yes, Pete the teacher. If I thought my father was slightly obsessed with his little day boat on the Norfolk Broads, I hadn't then met Pete, or other equally boat-mad Aucklanders. Various members of the family and friends thereof sailed most weekends and all the summer holidays. They painted other weekends. They read yachting magazines at night and talked races and designs and sailing gossip round the dinner table. The house was full of sailing ship watercolors and wet life jackets.

When the Whitbread round-the-world yachts came to Auckland every four years, they hosted a crew, which meant providing dry stationary beds and iced beer for fifteen randy young men and doing great piles of their stinking laundry. One year they all took Spanish lessons because they were to be hosting a Spanish yacht. Next time it was the Russians. Pete taught science and maritime studies at a high school, "the wife" taught clinical psychology at the Auckland medical school, and the five kids were all students, from university down to primary school.

Now, I didn't freeload, Martin. I really liked Mrs. Pete and Fanny, the daughter, same age as me, and I didn't mind being teased about my Pommy accent and pale skin. During the two weeks I was there I pulled my weight with housework and shopping and odd jobs on the boats. All the schoolkids were going back to school at the start of their new year in February. I lay on the beach down by the boat shed, below the house, and stupidly got blistered quite badly on my shoulders. They'd warned me about New Zealand's ultraviolet sun and holes in the ozone layer, but after Oxford's snow I just couldn't resist basking. I began to see Auckland as the beautiful city it is, between two harbors, with its little green hills that are dormant volcanoes. Not dead, note: dormant. They say one of them will pop sooner or later. You can climb up and see the old craters, shaped into deep and sinister cones.

Mid-February is lazy time in New Zealand. The kids are all back at school and university, but the country still feels like it's on holiday. I had started to make halfhearted attempts to find a cheap apartment and get waitressing work when Pete suggested I meet some youngish bluewater yachting friends of his who were looking for crew.

The next if.

The silly thing is that I wasn't then an athletic type, far from it. Yes, I'd done some sailing with Dad at home. I knew how to steer a boat and put the sails up, but I wasn't really hooked on sailing as "my sport." I didn't particularly see the need to have a sport at all. I liked going to films, cooking things like sauces for pasta and especially rich Italian cheesecakes, just being with my friends. I loathed any exercise, but especially the team games we did at school, hockey and such. I was hopeless with a tennis racket, and no one swims much in England, though technically speaking I could stay afloat with a sort of breaststroke. I was a bit plump. Let's say, being truthful, very plump. I smoked quite a bit to avoid becoming plumper. I wore very baggy clothes, of dark and obscuring colors. I was a bit of a blob, really.

So I don't suppose I looked like very promising crew material when I stepped aboard the *Dolphin,* which was tied up at a city marina, for the first time. And frankly, the thought of three months at sea at various strange angles, being frozen, bored, or sunburned to death, didn't appeal to me much. I didn't know if I'd get seasick out on the wide ocean, did I, as opposed to the sedate Norfolk Broads. And the first sight of Barry and Harry Wildblood (cousins, and their real names, no kidding) didn't do much for me.

If I was on the plump side, they were both as skinny as rakes, with hard muscles stretched taut over long bones, like scarecrows. Hair cut ferociously short, three days' stubble, eyes wrinkled up, ice blue; the searching eyes of mad scientists you see in that *National Geographic* magazine with the yellow cover. They'd met Pete when they came to Auckland to avoid the Pacific hurricane season and do some work on the boat. Aged about thirty, give or take five years either side. It's difficult to tell. They looked like ex-cops, actually, tough and mean. But Barry had very red lips at the center of his stubble, and a voice like silk. He laughed a lot. Harry was quieter, with tattoos of sailing ships on his arms. Their accents were vaguely English—hard to tell, though they told me they had New Zealand passports. They wore very short shorts, gold chains, Rolex Oyster watches, the best French sunglasses, and that was all. They both smelled nice, though French toiletries for men didn't quite fit on a yacht.

I wasn't too impressed. But the yacht was impressive. They took me on a tour. It was forty feet long, a steel ketch, New Zealand–built, their home for the past six years. On deck were lots of color-coded ropes, new sails in bright blue bags, and shining chrome. Below, a huge galley—sorry, kitchen—lots of varnished wood, Italian-looking cushions, two bunk rooms; everything tidy, clean. Electronic gear. Charts. Fresh flowers. They grew herbs. I noticed lots of books, CDs, tape cassettes. It all felt rather luxurious. I wondered what they did for money.

Now, Martin, and my eventual readers, you're probably thinking, What was this nice sixteen-year-old English girl thinking of, going sailing with these mean-looking but mysteriously smiling rogues? They had welcomed me politely enough. I heard that they planned to write a book about their coming Pacific trip. They were going to study seabirds and Polynesian methods of navigation along the way, heading for Tahiti, Hawaii across to Vanuatu, the Solomons, many of the islands in between, and finally back to Auckland. We sat on the deck in the sunshine, drinking chardonnay, crunching macadamia and pine nuts. They asked me about my family, about England, about the sailing I'd done on the Norfolk Broads, but I got the distinct impression that I hadn't passed the potential-crew test. Too young, too plump, too inexperi-

enced—right on all counts. I told you I was a bit of a
blob.

So I wasn't thinking of vast Pacific oceans when I accepted their invitation to go sailing for a weekend around
the inner Hauraki Gulf. A shakedown cruise, said Barry. I
thought, why not, just for a bit of a laugh; these were Ki-
wis being kind to the young English visitor. Safety in
numbers. Just bring enough gear for two nights. No food.
They'd been provisioning the boat for the long voyage,
due to start shortly, just as soon as the hurricane season
was over. Bring wet-weather gear, swim togs, sunblock, a
hat. Bring yourself.

They were friends of Pete's, weren't they? And Pete was
a friend of my father's. How naive can you get?

I honestly think they really did intend—at first—to
drop me off back in Auckland before they headed off into
the wild blue yonder. That's another if . . . if I had not
cooked dinner on that Friday night. But I'd looked in the
food lockers and seen wonderful fresh provisions and offered to cook a pasta and make a salad. Harry produced
extra-virgin olive oil, balsamic vinegar, pine nuts, fat
cloves of garlic, capers, homemade fresh pasta, Gorgonzola.

That's another thing about New Zealand, or Auckland,
at any rate. For someone who loves good food, it's Mecca.
It was the capsicum season, the apple season, the peach,
apricot, nectarine, raspberry, courgette, and tomato season. The city is surrounded by orchards and gardens. Perhaps it's coming from England, where fruit and veggies
are all wilted or frozen or horrendously expensive, but
I'd never seen anything like the fresh stuff Pete's wife
brought on her way home from work every second day,
nor what was loaded on that yacht.

So, when we came to anchor in a green bay fringed with trees, I made an Italian salad with basil and capers, and a pasta with Gorgonzola and pine nut sauce, and a frothy zabaglione with marsala and raspberries. Over a fire Barry built ashore with smooth stones, we butter-basted and grilled the three small snapper we'd caught with a line out over the side. It was a good meal, a wonderful meal. Barry and Harry loved it. That meal, I was shortly to realize, was my big mistake.

Now it's wrong to say I was kidnapped, or abducted, or hijacked, or captured, or taken hostage, or any other legal word that a whole lot of horrified adults used when I finally reappeared in this world two years and seven months later. I just wasn't allowed to get off, that's all.

Hey, wait a minute, I hear you say. Not *allowed*? A sixteen-year-old, forced against her will to go blue-water sailing and heaven knows what else besides? That's *dreadful*. Find these Wildblood cousins, charge them with all sorts of crimes, expose them to the world as child-stealers, exploiters, molesters, or worse. Who are these young men with so much money and so few morals that they can swan around the Pacific on a forty-foot yacht with a sixteen-year-old girl as their hijacked cook and bottle washer, and no doubt sexual object and slave? Feminists of the world unite against these scoundrels, these . . . these . . . *men*.

There won't be any charges, Martin and readers. No recriminations. Just a sort of love, thanks for making me what I am. How can I convince you that it was the best thing that ever happened to me?

The night I cooked my fateful meal we lay on the beach and watched the stars come out. As we rowed out to the boat, phosphorescence swirled like a million Tinker Bells around my fingers and the blades of the oars. We had a

glittering silver swim, and later that night I saw phospho-
rescent dolphins as we sailed out into the gulf. I was utterly at peace.

It wasn't until I woke, until next morning, that I first
thought something odd was going on. It wasn't until I'd
seen no land at all for three days that Barry admitted we
were bound for the vast expanse of the Pacific. We were
already well east of North Cape, New Zealand's north-
ernmost point. "We've passed the point of no return,
sweetie," said Harry with a disarming smile. "You are such
a superb cook, we just had to keep you."

Now this is where you might think me quite odd.

Barry and Harry, didn't they expect—Martin and readers, aren't *you* expecting—that I would be throwing
tantrums, mounting a one-woman mutiny, demanding to
tell the VHF radio that the yacht *Dolphin* had a kidnapped, helpless sixteen-year-old English girl aboard and
would they please send a helicopter or a frigate from the
Royal New Zealand Navy to get me off?

Wasn't I terrified, terrorized, alone on the ocean with
two strange and dubious men?

Didn't I want my mum?

And of course I didn't have a passport, traveler's
checks, enough gear, or two years' supply of tampons and
decent shampoo and sunblock and other girlish necessi-
ties.

At the very least, surely I would be refusing to go anywhere near the kitchen.

I worried about none of those things.

I decided to outwit Barry and Harry, for however long
it took.

I allowed them to send a radio message to Pete, and
therefore to my parents, that my plans had changed but I

was perfectly okay. I determined that I would not complain—and I didn't. I would not get seasick—and I didn't. I would not allow myself to be touched or in any way sexually approached by Barry or Harry—and I didn't. I would cook—and I did, superbly. I would enjoy the cooking—and I did. I would take the opportunity to learn everything I could from Barry and Harry about the sea, seamanship, the boat, all those things I listed earlier—and I did. I would always sleep watchfully—and I did. I would lose weight and become fit and strong and capable—and I did. I would become a woman—and I did.

Too good to be true, you are saying. No teenager could have that sort of self-control, that sort of stamina for two and a half years, especially in the cheek-by-jowl living of a forty-foot yacht with only two cabins. Come *on*.

But you are forgetting one thing: Barry and Harry were not child molesters or rapists or murderers. They were decent people whose weakness for good food led them to convince themselves that they'd just played a little joke on me, and they'd let me get off at Fiji or somewhere. But by the time we called at Papeete in Tahiti for food and fuel, we'd become rather good friends. Without a passport or money, I joined in the elaborate precautions through which I escaped detection by any customs officer of the island ports we visited for that whole two years.

They never asked for any money from me. I shared their clothes, and found out how few clothes you actually need; how little washing when the rain is free and you let the oils in your skin do their work; how you *can* manage without tampons and shampoo and a choice of twenty-five varieties of deodorant.

It wasn't that holier-than-thou back-to-nature stuff, it was just simple living with two together people in a small space with the right supplies aboard. We were in harmony with the sea and the elements. You looked after everything carefully, from brass screws to olive oil to every last inch of rope to every last squeeze of toothpaste, simply because you knew there wasn't another supermarket just beyond the horizon.

When we were scudding along in the sunshine and I sensed they needed some privacy without having to shut themselves in their cabin, I would go and sit up by the bow (sorry, Martin, the sharp end), watching the froth of the bow wave swirling off the glistening arrowhead of the yacht for hours on end. Or I would steer while they lay on the foredeck, hidden from my view by the cabin top. Barry sang a lot—songs from the seventies, songs from shows, songs he wrote himself. He taught me sea chanteys and to play a ukulele, poker, five hundred, Chinese patience, and mah-jongg. I learned to navigate with a sextant, while Barry practiced his navigation, Polynesian style. Together we studied French and Maori. Harry spent a lot of time keeping a log and writing in a large notebook. Barry wrote his songs down too.

Occasionally, in calm, settled seas and with a good forecast by the electronic nagivation equipment, two of us, in strict rotation, would blissfully share a joint while the third sailed the boat. Otherwise, neither of them assumed the role of skipper. Nor did they scrap or bicker or argue, as most parents do. We laughed a lot. I was a sort of daughter/friend/able seaman. And they didn't need me for any sort of sexual adventure, because they had each other. That is why they went sailing, why they had escaped even from the nineties when such things are supposed to be okay. They didn't have AIDS. They just loved each other and had decided on a different sort of life. I tried to respect that. Most people wouldn't call it a marriage, but I would.

Of all people, you, Martin, will understand.

I'm not going to bore you with details of that long Pacific journey. Thirty-one months I was at sea. Yachting magazines and whole books are full of long accounts of visits to the Galápagos, the Canaries, Alaska, or the Antarctic, but when it's all boiled down, seafarers all have much the same sort of experiences, don't they? They have gales and disasters and they hit things, and the ones who survive write tedious books about their adventures.

But we had our adventures, oh yes. We survived storms, lightning, two freak waves, and another, bigger still, which pitchpoled us. We sloshed around in flat calms and reveled in trade winds and ran terrified before gales and put out sea anchors. I've seen icebergs. I've changed sails with snow on the deck, ice on the rigging. I've seen flying fish, whales, albatrosses, and rare dolphins and slept on the deck under the stars when it was too hot to sleep below. We hit a whale off Tonga and a container between Tahiti and Hawaii. On that long passage, one night, we also lost Barry over the side. Because he was a good seaman, he was wearing a lifeline, and Harry and I hauled him back on board, trembling and shocked and half drowned. Once is enough for that sort of exercise. We had weekly person-overboard and fire drills.

Harry tended me when I got tropical fevers and rope burns, as gentle as any nurse. He dug fishhooks out of my hands and foreign bodies from my eyes. I learned to cook all kinds of exotic fishes in coconut cream and banana leaves and pineapple juice. We attended village feasts in the Cooks. Our eggshell-thin dugout canoe got nudged by a twelve-foot shark in a lagoon. We sailed past that dangerous, rocky landing place on Pitcairn Island where Fletcher Christian's mutineers found another sort of escape and refuge. Barry studied his birds and his navigation and wrote his songs and Harry wrote his book. I learned to splice and mend sails and carve dolphins on bone. I was very happy. I returned to Auckland a different person and knowing what I want out of life.

And that is the end of the tape, and where I hope I've totted up my five thousand words and earned my ten thousand pounds.

It's got quite dark, making Mother's bed of white roses below my window glow, almost as though touched by phosphorescence. I have Harry's book of stories and Barry's book of songs beside me on my bed. I haven't yet decided what to do with them.

They returned me safely to Auckland, without having to explain anything to any customs or immigration officer. I'd just been on rather a long holiday around the Hauraki Gulf, that's all. Quite an undercover operation it was, with Pete sailing his keelboat out into the Pacific fifty miles east of Great Barrier Island and a dawn meeting between two small yachts making sure no one else was snooping around. Pete took food and fuel too, but the cousins wouldn't or couldn't tell us what their plans were, just that they were heading north into the sunshine again.

It was only when I got back to Pete's house that I found the two books in my pack. Harry's was written by hand, of course, but it wasn't a book about birds or navigation. It was a book of short stories, all about different sorts of love, but especially their sort of love. And Barry's was a book of music—song words with melodies and guitar chords.

I haven't read them properly yet, because I need some

space between my dawn memory of the *Dolphin* sailing away from Pete's yacht and the news item a month later that a yacht had been lost on remote reefs south of Tonga. They never properly identified the pieces of the yacht or found any bodies, but there was speculation that it might have been a yacht called the *Dolphin* owned by two thirty-something cousins, New Zealand citizens but believed to be British-born. They were such careful, meticulous navigators. I can't . . . I'd rather believe they are still sailing round the Pacific somewhere, or beyond, westward to the Indian Ocean or the Mediterranean.

From them I learned everything I know about seamanship, about the sea, about living, about enduring, about love, and about myself. I got aboard the crew for the Whitbread race next month because, though I could not produce a written curriculum vitae to tell them my true story, I was confident enough to persuade the skipper to take me for a trial sail.

We were somewhere south of Land's End when a fearful storm blew up in the English Channel, one that wasn't forecast. It was nearly as bad as that terrible gale that flattened southeast England at the end of 1987. Apart from the skipper, I was the only one who wasn't seasick, who could help get the sails down and the sea anchor, the storm jib, and lifelines rigged in the storm's initial fury. I took continual cups of tea and dry bread to all the others who were horizontal on their bunks, and cleaned up their vomit. We had to run before the storm into the Atlantic. The skipper and I sat up three nights without sleep, sharing the helming and the cooking.

One day, after the race, we might share a life too.

So, Martin, there's my whole story, or nearly whole story. Not bad, is it? The earlier part will earn me ten thousand pounds, enough to buy a small yacht of my own or travel again. That earlier part must be about five thousand words, what I have recorded for Penelope's magazine.

I decided to tell the story because I want girls to know that you can take risks when you are traveling and find you've trusted your instinct and it's okay. Not every risk turns out to be a horror story about white slavery and girls ending up in Thai jails convicted of being drug couriers, despite what my mother still thinks.

But one detail I'm not telling anyone, not even you, Martin, not yet, anyway. Not for instant fame like Priscilla Presley or John Lennon's girl Yoko Ono; not if every woman's magazine in the world offered me thousands of dollars or Hollywood wanted the rights to make a horrible, dishonest film about a girl abducted by a couple of gays sailing round the Pacific. I'm not greedy, and I made a promise.

I'll tell my bear instead. He sits on my bed and has heard all my ramblings so far as the sun dropped behind the birch trees and the sky turned twilight pink. The roses are still glowing white and Mother is calling me for supper.

Remember, bear, I wondered what Barry and Harry did for money?

They had a beautiful, well-appointed yacht, everything on board new and carefully chosen, the best German wines, the best Jamaican rum you can buy. There was always money in the bank, whatever port we visited. They bought me mementos I treasure: a collection of silver dolphins, some French jewelry in Tahiti—real gold; a pearl ring; an uncut sapphire, the color of Pacific waves, for a ring when I meet the man I shall marry.

Remember I said Barry sang a lot?

Remember a certain teenage pop star of the late seventies who disappeared mysteriously about five years ago . . . the beautiful English boy with long limbs, a beard, long tawny hair, the flower child idolized by millions of girls, and boys too . . . who wrote all his own songs—another Bob Dylan, they called him? He was just about to make the big time in Hollywood. He'd have been another David Bowie or Sting. There was a lot of publicity and speculation at the time—about murder, about the drug underside of the music industry. He just vanished.

Well, he showed me photos one night, and apart from Harry and a lawyer in London I'm apparently the only person in the whole world who knows the real and famous name of Barry Wildblood.

Now *there* would be a story. And I have a manuscript book of his last songs.

Tessa Duder

Educated as a journalist, Tessa Duder has been a professional writer for fifteen years. Her seventeen books have brought her six major awards, several fellowships, and travel to international conferences from her home in Auckland, New Zealand.

She is known best by teenage readers for her novel *Alex*, published in the United States as *In Lane Three, Alex Archer*. The novel, which is about a teenage girl's efforts to make the New Zealand swim team for the 1960 Olympic Games in Rome, was a best-seller in New Zealand and was made into a feature film called *Alex*. Ms. Duder followed that success with three more novels about the competitive swimmer: *Alex in Winter, Alex in Rome,* and *Songs for Alex*. The Alex books were later published together as *The Alex Quartet*. Ms. Duder's most recent book for teenagers is an anthology called

Nearly Seventeen, which includes her short play "The Runaway," about an incident in the life of Joan of Arc.

Although she played tennis, field hockey, and cricket as a teenager, Tessa Duder's main sport, like that of the main character in her Alex books, was swimming. She was the first woman in New Zealand to compete seriously in the butterfly stroke, and in 1958, at age seventeen, she represented New Zealand in the Empire Games in Cardiff, Wales, where she won the silver medal in the 100-yard butterfly event.

Her sporting life now, more than twenty-five years later, is limited mainly to yachting and fitness workouts. She has sailed as a watch officer on both of New Zealand's sail-training ships, *Spirit of Adventure* and *Spirit of New Zealand.* Ms. Duder reports that she has met several young female British travelers like the girl in "Sea Changes" and has been on a yacht that was the home of a gay couple who seemed to be spending their life cruising around the Pacific without worrying about money. The mysterious past of one of the characters in this story, however, is entirely her invention.

Jennifer has a mysterious past and won't talk about the future. But she and Andrew play winning tennis together, so he doesn't ask too many questions. Still, what is she hiding?

The Gospel According to Krenzwinkle

David Klass

Never develop a crush on your mixed-doubles partner.

She had a ridiculous last name, Krenzwinkle. It sounded like a cartoon character, but her first name was Jennifer and there was nothing remotely cartoonlike about her bright blue eyes or her blond hair or the way her long legs flashed beneath her white tennis dress.

The Krenzwinkles had just moved to our town during Christmas vacation, so no one in our high school knew very much about Jennifer. When she came out for the tennis squad and Coach Nutterman paired the two of us up as the varsity second mixed-doubles team, I figured I'd get a chance to know her much better. You can never tell where long tennis practices and new friendships may lead. . . .

Anyway, I was wrong. Two weeks into our season I knew very little more about Jennifer Krenzwinkle than I did when she first walked into our honors English class in January and amazed Mr. Otto and the rest of us by asking: "Don't you think both Hemingway and Fitzgerald's stylistic innovations were more important contributions to world literature than the actual novels they wrote?" I knew her name. I knew that she was my age, seventeen. I knew that she quickly became the best student in our high school. I knew that her family lived in a nice, new, middle-sized ranch-style house on Briarwood Lane. And that was all.

I probed gently. Jennifer retreated skillfully. I inquired more directly. She managed to duck or turn aside every question with a smile or a question of her own. One afternoon two weeks into the season, I asked directly: "Jen, where did your family live before you moved here?"

We had just finished half an hour of giving each other overheads to smash, and she took her white headband off and shook out her long blond hair. She looked at me, hesitated, and then gave me a tiny smile. "Think we'll win tomorrow?"

"Yes, but that's not what I asked you."

"I know, but that's what I'm answering you."

I would have been angry at her if she hadn't been smiling at me. There weren't too many smiles that pretty in the whole state of New Jersey. "One reason people ask questions is to get to know somebody they're starting to like," I told her.

"That's true," she said. "What's your middle name?"

"Eric."

"Mine's Amanda. What's your sign?"

"Pisces."

"Mine's Virgo. What's your favorite food?"

"Bacon cheeseburgers."

"Mine's fried chicken. Bye, Andrew Eric Logan. Get a good night's sleep—I want to win tomorrow." She turned and started off.

"Bye, Jennifer Amanda Krenzwinkle," I called after her. "Don't worry about my tennis game. Worry about my sanity."

We did win, and we kept winning, but by the middle of the season I was half crazy. Everyone on the team called her the Mystery Woman. Nicknames are fun and mysteries are fine, but when you can't sleep at night because you're lying in bed hour after hour picturing a pair of bright blue eyes floating on the ceiling, a few hard facts would be more than welcome.

"Maybe she's just shy," my big sister, Beth, suggested on a weekend visit home from college. When we were living in the same house, Beth and I never got along, but things got better between us when she moved out, and I even started asking her for advice about girls. "Don't press her. You'll scare her off."

"But she's not shy," I objected. "She seems normal and outgoing, except that she doesn't like to talk about herself."

"Maybe she's hiding something."

"She's hiding everything."

"Give her time."

"It's driving me crazy."

"Then tell her that."

"Really?"

"Sure," my sister said. "If she's really driving you crazy, let her know."

I let her know after the Hasbrouck Heights match. We won in straight sets, and Jennifer raised her game to a new level. She had an amazing first serve for a girl, and against Hasbrouck Heights she served up one blistering ace after another.

After the match, on the bus ride home, several of our

teammates congratulated Jennifer, and old Nutterman told us he thought we were cinches to win the county championships and even had a shot at the state tournament. "There's no chance of that," Jennifer said.

"Why not?" Nutterman asked.

She shrugged, and he didn't push any further—I guess maybe he thought she was just being modest. When the bus let us out at our high school and Jennifer began walking away across the parking lot, I caught up to her. "Hey, Mystery Woman, wait up."

She turned, smiled, and waited.

"You played like a top seed at Wimbledon today."

"Thanks. We make a good team."

"Yeah. Nutterman's right. We're gonna win the county tournament. Maybe the states, too."

She shook her head.

"Why not?"

She kicked a pebble. "There won't be any state tournament."

"What do you mean there won't be a state tournament? Of course there will be. It's down at Princeton this year."

"Nope."

"What do you mean, 'nope'?"

"The state tournament is in May, isn't it?"

"Yeah."

"Well, there won't be one."

"What does it being in May have to do with it?"

"Forget it," she said. "Let's talk about school. Did you start on that report for Mr. Otto yet?"

We were out of the parking lot, on Mason Street. The street was completely empty except for a black poodle on a chain in a driveway a hundred feet up ahead. I stopped walking and Jennifer slowed and then stopped too. "Is something wrong?" she asked.

"Jennifer Krenzwinkle, you're driving me crazy."

"Why?"

I looked her right in the eye and took a deep breath. "Because I'm starting to like you. A lot."

"Don't," she said.

"Why not? You don't like me?"

"I didn't say that. Just don't."

"Give me a reason."

Her palms rubbed together nervously, like she was trying to erase something between her hands. "There wouldn't be any point to it."

"Why? Do you have another boyfriend?"

"No."

"Do you have some problem at home? Are you in some kind of trouble?"

"No," she said, looking more and more nervous. She bit down on her lower lip and tapped her tennis racket against her knee.

"Let's start with something simple. Why won't there be a state tennis tournament?"

"There just won't."

"But there'll be a county one?"

She looked off down the street at the black poodle, which was running in circles, causing its chain to twist around its legs. "Yes."

"And there won't be a state tournament because it takes place in May, whereas the county tournament takes place in April?"

She nodded.

"But if the state tournament took place in April, there would be one?"

"Yes," she said, "there would be. Please don't ask me any more questions."

"You won't even tell me where you're from and why we can't get to know each other better?"

She hesitated, her eyes still on the poodle. "If I answer those two questions, will you let me alone?"

"Yes."

"Promise?"

"Yes."

She swung her eyes from the poodle to me. "I'm from southern California. And I don't like answering questions about myself for reasons of religious freedom."

"What does that mean?"

"You promised no more questions," she reminded me, starting off down the block.

I immediately gave chase. "You're right, no more questions. Could I buy you an ice-cream sundae if I only talk about tennis? We'll discuss backhands. Jennifer, please?"

"No," she said. "I like you a lot too, but it will be better if we just stay mixed-doubles partners."

"Better in what sense?"

"Gotta go. Bye," she said, then lowered her head and took off away from me down Mason Avenue in large, fast strides. I stopped and watched her go. When she passed the black poodle it made a rush for her, but its chain was too short and all twisted up, and all it could do was stand up on its hind legs and bark.

The more I thought about our conversation, the less sense it made. Finally, in desperation, I called my sister and told her all about it. "Aha," Beth said when I was done.

"Aha what?"

"Now it's clear."

"What's clear?"

"She's from southern California. Two girls on my floor here at college are from southern California, and no one can figure them out either. It's not part of America—it's a whole different country, a whole different logic."

"So what do you do? How do you deal with them?"

"We just make allowances for their craziness and go on with our own lives."

"That's the best advice you can give me?"

"No, the best advice I can give you is never take college calculus. I have a test tomorrow and I gotta go study. Bye."

"Bye," I told her. "And thanks for all the valuable insights." I hung up the phone and sat there with my head in my hands, trying to figure out what religious freedom had to do with the state tennis tournament being in May, or not being in May.

After that I made a strong conscious effort to cool it with Jennifer and to spend my time and energy thinking about rational subjects. I wasn't entirely successful, but the less time I spent thinking about her and trying to figure her out, the more relaxed I felt. Jennifer sensed my coolness and seemed to resent it, but she never said anything. As our conversations got shorter and our friendship got thinner, our tennis play improved noticeably.

School wound down to exam periods, and the tennis season ended in the county tournament. Jennifer and I were seeded second, behind a team from Wood-Ridge. We waltzed through our first three matches, won a close one in the semifinals, and found ourselves in the finals against the number one seed.

It was the kind of sunny April day that photographers try to capture on postcards. Bluebirds sang on tree branches and beds of budding tulips and daffodils surrounded the courts where the county finals were held. Jennifer wasn't at all nervous warming up for the big match. I'll say that for her—for all her kookiness she was never nervous or off her game. She was wearing a new outfit, a short pink skirt and a pink and white top, and if it hadn't been the county tournament I would have had a lot of trouble concentrating.

We split the first two sets, so it came down to the final one. Both teams held serve to three games each, and then Jennifer and I broke them to take the lead. The Wood-Ridge duo tried to break back on Jennifer's serve and fought their way to deuce, but she smoked an ace to make it our advantage, and then won the game with a furious two-handed backhand put-away right on the line. The Wood-Ridge team held serve to close to four to five, but I served strongly for set and match, and Jennifer slammed home the winning point with a furious overhead smash.

The hundred or so spectators gave us a nice ovation. Without thinking, I ran to Jennifer and lifted her off the ground in a hug, and she hugged me back. After all those weeks of trying to ignore each other, the hug felt very good. I put her down and we looked at each other, and I guess we were both grinning. "Way to go, Mystery Woman," I said.

"It was fun," she agreed. "I love winning."

A sports reporter from *The Record* snapped our picture, and the assistant head of the County Tennis Association gave us little gold trophy cups.

Our third singles player made it to the county final, so our whole team stayed around to watch him finish. I was still pumped up from winning, and I wanted to savor the feeling, so I watched the final match sitting high up on a bleacher, all by myself. I was kind of surprised, midway through the match, to see Jennifer walking up the bleachers in my direction.

"Hi," she said. "Can I sit down?"

"Plenty of space."

She sat. There was a real strange energy between us—a jumble of resentment and fondness and triumph and confusion. "I never won anything as big as a county tournament before," she said.

"Me neither."

"I just want you to know that I'm glad I won it with you. I do like you."

"I like you too, but you confused me."

"I didn't mean to."

"That's hard to believe. Anyway, we're a good tennis team. Let's leave it at that."

"I guess we won't be seeing each other anymore."

"We still have to practice every day for the state tournament," I reminded her.

"There won't be any state tournament."

"Oh, yeah, I forgot. Well, goodbye."

"I wish you wouldn't be mad at me." I couldn't be sure, but I thought I spotted a little teardrop welling up in one of her pretty blue eyes. "I told you, it's a matter of religious freedom. And if I tried to explain it to you, you'd only laugh."

I looked right at her, and I amazed myself with the seriousness of my voice when I said: "Look, I'll try once and only once. My father was raised Catholic but he's an atheist, and my mother was born Jewish but I don't think she thinks much about religion. I wasn't confirmed or bar mitzvahed or anything else. I'm kind of interested in religion and I've read a little about Buddhism and Islam and Shintoism, but I don't really know what I believe yet. I'm still thinking about it. I guess deep down I believe in some kind of God, or at least I want to believe, but . . ."

"But what?" she said.

"What I'm trying to tell you is that I was born and raised in America and I think everyone has the right to believe whatever they want, and from watching my own parents I think two people from different religious backgrounds can become friends and live together and even get married. So I won't laugh at you, and I won't try to take away your religious freedom. Like I said, I've read about lots of different religions, and I find some beautiful things in all of them."

"I just don't think it's a good idea," Jennifer said slowly, and then broke off. We looked at each other for a long time. "Okay," she finally said. "Okay. Have you heard of Bernard Shaftsbury?"

"No. Who is he?"

"He was a brilliant physics professor at Berkeley. When he was forty he began to have visions."

"What kind of visions?"

She hesitated. "Telepathic messages."

"Messages from where?"

Her face didn't change expression and the tone of her voice remained sincere and constant when she said, "From a UFO orbiting the earth. They were preparing him for his ride."

"He went on a ride in a UFO?"

"Yes," she said. "They came down and got him, and took him all over the galaxy. They went into black holes and came out white holes, they went back in time through intercosmic wormholes and he saw the creation and they went forward in time and he saw the end. And then they let him come back to earth to prepare the faithful."

"And that's you?"

"And my parents, and a few thousand other people."

"A few thousand?"

"We lived in a commune in Shaftsbury Valley, between Los Angeles and San Diego. We were totally self-sufficient. It was beautiful."

"How many years did you live there?"

"I was born there. We had our own school, and organic farms, and a church, and a sacred grove for yoga and meditation, and a tennis court."

I nodded, trying to take this all in. At least Shaftsbury had had the good sense to put in a tennis court. In its own weird way, this was beginning to make a little sense. "If it was so beautiful there, why did you leave?"

"Shaftsbury sent us all out, to each of the forty-nine states, to prepare for the submergence."

"There are fifty states," I told her.

"We only needed to go to the continental ones," she said. "Hawaii wasn't necessary."

"What's the submergence?"

Her shoulders shrugged under the pink and white tennis dress. When she spoke, her voice came out much lower. "The end of the world," she said. "In less than a week. The seas and oceans will rise up and swallow us down, and the surface of the earth will be covered with water, just the way it was at the beginning."

"Why will this happen?"

"Because we've polluted our air and pumped sewage into our water and destroyed our atmosphere. We've killed creatures for their meat and for their hides and for their horns and . . . we just went too far. So what was given to us as a gift is going to be taken away and given to another species."

There were a lot of tears on her face now, and she wiped them off with the back of her hand. "Who?" I asked. "I mean, what species is gonna get the earth next?"

"The dolphins," she whispered. A little April breeze stirred her blond hair around her shoulders. She sniffled a few times and managed to stop the tears. "Shaftsbury says we shouldn't be afraid, so I'm trying my best. Only—" She broke off and looked out across the tennis court and beyond, where the flower gardens were budding and the grassy lawns were like lakes of brilliant emerald. She surprised me by putting her hand in mine. I closed my fingers around it. "Only, it's very beautiful and I hate to see it all go," she said, and her voice quivered and broke.

I kept holding on to her hand with my right hand, and I put my left arm gently around her shoulders. "Listen, Jennifer," I said. "You're not in southern California anymore. You're in New Jersey now. And the world doesn't come to an end in New Jersey."

Her head jerked up and she pulled away a little bit. "Are you making fun of me?"

"No," I said. "I just think that Shaftsbury needs to think this thing over a bit more."

She stood up. "He's the one true prophet."

"Maybe he is," I told her, "but you're so sensible and intelligent, how can you believe this garbonzo?"

She tossed back her head, and her blue eyes shone bright. "I don't think intelligence has anything to do with what you believe or don't believe," she said. "I thought you were sincere when you said you wanted to know about my religion. I never thought you'd laugh at me. But it doesn't matter. Nothing matters anymore. I forgive you." She stomped off down the bleachers, sat by herself on the bus ride home, and took off by herself as soon as the bus let us off at our school.

During the next few days, I thought a lot about what Jennifer had said. At first I thought the whole thing was humorous—her ideas were so wacky it was hard to even know how to take her seriously. But the more I thought about it, the more I began to wonder if maybe I shouldn't have turned her beliefs into a joke. From what little I know about history, there have always been fringe religions, and most people who dare to be different are persecuted. The ancient Egyptians enslaved the Jews and the Romans fed the early Christians to the lions, and if Jennifer had had the courage to share her beliefs with me, maybe I should have been more tolerant. Even if the whole thing was nonsense.

Finally, I called her up. To my surprise, she answered the phone and seemed willing to talk to me. "I'd like to apologize for my behavior the other day," I told her. "I honestly feel bad I teased you about your religion. I'm sorry."

"That's okay," she said. "It doesn't matter now. Nothing matters now. But I'm glad you called, so that we could say goodbye. My parents are almost finished getting everything ready, and we're going to leave."

"What are they getting ready?"

"The world is ending tonight," Jennifer said.

"What time?"

"Ten o'clock."

"And where are you going with your parents?"

"To the highest point in New Jersey. All of the faithful in all of the forty-nine states have to go to the highest points in their states tonight at the appointed time, and perform the Ceremony of the End."

I surprised myself by asking, "Can I come?"

"Tonight? You want to come with us tonight?"

"Yeah," I said. "If it's okay. I promise I won't disturb anything."

"Don't you want to be with your family for the end?"

"I'll say goodbye to them before we go," I told her. "Can I come?"

"One sec, I'll have to check with my mom." She was gone for a few seconds, and then she came back on. "My mom says you're very welcome. We're leaving at eight. Do you know where I live?"

"Sure," I said. I hesitated—I didn't want her to think I was making fun of her beliefs again. "Should I dress casual?"

"Whatever."

"Can I bring anything?"

"No," she said. "Just be on time. See you at eight."

That night at dinner I told my mother that I was going to be out real late, because I was going on an astronomical viewing trip with Jennifer's family. I told her that they had just bought a telescope, and that we were going to try to see the different rings of Saturn.

"Why don't they go earlier?" she wanted to know. "Ten is pretty late to start on a trip."

"They're nice people, but they're a little bit strange," I told her. "They're from southern California."

"Strange how? Like they put ketchup on their hot dogs?"

"Something like that, Mom. I should go. Bye." I gave her a little hug and a kiss on my way out.

"What was that for?"

"For being such a great mom. Just in case."

"Just in case of what?"

"Bye," I said. In the living room I passed my father, who was watching a sitcom on TV. "Bye, Dad."

He didn't look up. "I don't know why I'm watching this. It isn't funny at all."

As I went by I punched him lightly on the shoulder, and the punch made him look up at me. "Bye," I said.

"Goodbye, goodbye," he said. "Have a good evening."

I enjoyed the four-block walk to Jennifer's house. It was a warm, clear April night. The streets were quiet and the air smelled sweet from all the budding flowers and new grass. I passed a whole row of azaleas, each branch decked out with tiny yellow buds. I slowed down and inhaled, and felt the April breeze on my face. It didn't feel like the end of the world—it felt like the beginning of something fresh and sweet and new.

When I reached Briarwood Lane I crossed over to Jennifer's house. A short and pretty blond woman was loading what looked like clothing into the back of a big station wagon. She finished loading it just as I walked up, and turned to greet me. I guess I expected her to look strange in some way or other, and I was a bit startled by her warm smile, direct manner, and firm handshake. "You must be Andrew. I'm Connie, Jennifer's mom. Congratulations on the tennis title."

"Thanks," I told her. "Can I help you load stuff?"

"All finished," she said, and swung the station wagon's door shut. "I think I met your mother. She works at the library, doesn't she?"

"That's her."

"Does your father also work here in town?"

"No, he works in New York. For the city transit system." After all these frustrating months of not getting straight answers from Jennifer, I couldn't contain my curiosity. "May I ask what you and Mr. Krenzwinkle do?"

"I'm an oceanographer," she said. "My specialty is the effects of industrial pollution on freshwater mollusks. My husband is a nuclear engineer. Here he comes now."

Jennifer's father came down the steps carrying three flashlights. He was in his early forties, with boyish features and long brown hair which he kept in a ponytail. I have to admit that the fact that he was a nuclear engineer completely blew me away. Even as I shook his hand, I looked from him to her and wondered how two scientists could bring up their child to believe this junk, let alone believe it themselves.

Jennifer came out of the house wearing jeans and a blue windbreaker, and we all climbed into the station wagon and began the journey. Mostly we drove in silence. Take it from me, there isn't much to talk about when you're riding with three people who believe the world is about to come to an end. You can't say, "So, think the Yankees may take it this year?" because in their opinion there won't be a baseball season. You can't say, "Nice night, think it will rain tomorrow?" because there won't be a tomorrow. So for the most part I just sat in the backseat next to Jennifer in silence, as the big white station wagon roared through the night.

Once, I asked Mr. Krenzwinkle where he first encountered Bernard Shaftsbury. "I took his class at Berkeley, when I was a grad student there. It was the best class I ever took. Every time Bernard opened his mouth, you knew you were in the presence of real genius."

I have to admit that as it got closer to ten o'clock and we began to climb through the foothills of the Kittatinny Mountains toward High Point State Park, I began to feel just a bit nervous. Not scared, but very uncomfortable. I guess part of it was because the Krenzwinkles seemed so bright and sane and decent. I found myself wishing that they had been real weirdos, or stupid, or uneducated. The fact that they were scientists with advanced degrees was a bit creepy.

Not that I was beginning to believe any of this mumbo jumbo. But creepy is creepy.

We reached High Point State Park and drove up the winding road to the mountaintop that is the highest point in the state. Several other cars were already there when we arrived. There were about six other couples and fifteen or twenty small children. As I followed Jennifer away from the station wagon toward a flat grassy area, I checked my watch. It was nine-forty. The world was supposed to come to an end in twenty minutes.

It turned out that Jennifer's father was the ranking priest. Mrs. Krenzwinkle opened the back of the station wagon and began distributing purple robes to all the adults. She offered me one, and I slipped it on. The April night was getting a bit chilly, so it felt good to slip on the thick cotton. Mr. Krenzwinkle put on a special robe of bright scarlet and a pointed hat with a tassel on top. He would have looked comical, except that all the preparations were being carried out simply and seriously. There was no wand-waving or incantation-chanting or anything like that.

By nine-fifty everyone was robed except for the youngest children. Mr. Krenzwinkle told us to form a circle and link hands. Families stood together, with children between their parents. Jennifer's dad stood in the center of the circle, so I got to hold one of Jennifer's hands. It was warm and her grip was firm. At nine fifty-five I gave her a little squeeze and she squeezed back. Then we all just waited.

At nine fifty-seven Mr. Krenzwinkle tilted back his head and made a sound deep in his throat: "Oooooohhhhhh." Everyone standing in the big circle joined him and for several seconds even the children were going "Ooooooohhh."

Then, as if on cue, everyone stopped making the sound at the same moment, and Mr. Krenzwinkle began to speak. He didn't shout, but his voice filled the clearing. "The oceans of the world are beginning to rise. The winds are whirling, the ice caps dissolving. We are grateful for the time we've spent together. Bernard, we thank you for your light. Let us all face the end in peace."

He picked up a musical triangle and held it aloft, then struck it once, so that it vibrated with a pure, silvery sound. We waited. Everyone extinguished their flashlights, making it completely dark, except for the light of the full April moon. As I stood there on the hilltop in pitch darkness, I began to realize for the first time in my life what religion must have meant to mankind in earlier days.

We're so sheltered in our homes, with electric lights and alarm systems and central heating. For the first time I understood why when the ancient Greeks saw the lightning bolt flash out across their farms and fields and heard the thunderclap shake the sky above them, they said it was Zeus, king of the gods, thundering angrily on Mount Olympus, and sacrificed oxen to appease his anger. I imagined what it was like for the Jews when Moses led them out of Egypt across a seemingly endless desert, and then climbed up into the mountains to receive the law from God. And I understood a bit of what it had been like for the disciples in their little boat on the Sea of Galilee when

Jesus rebuked the raging winds and commanded the waves to be calm.

Mr. Krenzwinkle struck the triangle every twenty seconds or so. It was getting very close to ten o'clock. The breeze around the mountain stiffened into a wind that bent the spring grass and whistled through the branches of nearby trees. Far in the distance, I heard a rumbling that could have been thunder. The little hairs stood up all down the back of my neck. My knees got a little weak, and I think I might have fallen down if I hadn't been holding on to Jennifer's warm hand.

And then it was ten o'clock on the nose, and Mr. Krenzwinkle struck the triangle, and, of course, nothing happened. The wind died back down into a breeze, and the distant thunder or whatever it was never rumbled again, and the oceans didn't rise and the world didn't end. We all just stood there, waiting. Every few minutes Mr. Krenzwinkle struck the triangle. Perhaps it was my imagination, but as the minutes crawled by he seemed to strike it less and less frequently and with less and less enthusiasm.

Finally, at about ten-thirty, a little girl—she couldn't have been more than six or seven—looked up at her mother and said, "Mommy, I'm cold."

The little girl's voice was clearly audible all around the circle of bodies. Mr. Krenzwinkle slowly lowered his triangle. I was grateful that I couldn't see his face as he said, "Let's go home, everybody." He took the pointed hat off his head and held it so that the tassel pointed straight down, and began to unbutton his scarlet robe.

I had thought that the ride out was on the quiet and grim side, but the ride back home was much worse. What do you say to three people who have just found out that they've devoted years to a religion that's really just a bunch of hooey? I kept my big mouth shut and listened to the tires eat up the miles of highway.

When we got back to Jennifer's house I said goodbye to her parents and headed home. Jennifer walked with me as far as the corner of her block. She didn't say a thing—but I could tell how confused she was by the way she kept biting her lip. It was like she was relieved and disappointed at the same time, and didn't know what to say or how to act. "Well, bye," she said when we reached the corner.

"Bye," I said. "Maybe we can start practicing for the state tournament soon."

She nodded very slightly. "Maybe."

"Come on," I said, "cheer up a bit. I know you're confused, but it's not the end of the world. . . ." I choked as I realized what I'd said. "What I mean is, try to look on the bright side. . . ."

"Goodbye," she said, and hurried off back to her house.

My mom was still awake when I got home. "How was the astronomy?" she asked. "See any planets?"

"Outer space is a pretty bizarre place," I told her.

"Bizarre in what way?"

I thought for a second of Mr. Krenzwinkle standing on the mountaintop in the funny pointed hat, waiting for Shaftsbury's prediction to come true. I wondered what had passed through his mind when nothing happened—embarrassment, anger, joy? "Unpredictable," I mumbled.

"That's what makes it interesting, I guess," she said. "I'm going up to bed. Turn the lights off when you go up. Night."

"Night," I told her. I made myself a cup of tea and sat

there for a little while, listening to the small sounds that filled up the quiet April midnight. I could hear my father snoring regularly from the second floor. An owl hooted several yards away, its low hunting call a deep, rich sound. Our house was nearly forty years old, and every few seconds a floorboard squeaked or a screen window vibrated. And underlying all these sounds was the endless faint chirping and buzzing of the night insects as they marched back and forth, waging their endless wars through our lawn and garden. I usually take those sounds for granted, but that night I sipped tea and listened to them, and it was nice to hear the raspy snoring and the old house shifting and the endless buzz of the insects. Then I rinsed out my cup, turned off the light, and went up to bed.

Jennifer and I practiced twice in the week before the state tournament, but she just wasn't the same player. She was distracted and uneven, and I could tell just from watching her miss forehands that she was going through a hard time at home. I didn't know exactly what to do for her so I just tried to be friendly and supportive and didn't complain too much when she botched shots.

We got crushed in the second round of the states by a team from Franklin Lakes that we would have beaten handily on a good day. I played pretty well, but Jennifer was off and she knew it. After the match she tried to apologize to me, but I told her not to be silly. "We had a great year. And I can see you're going through a hard time. We'll win the states next year."

"Maybe," she said. "I don't know. . . ."

"Want to talk about it?"

"My parents are thinking of moving back to California."

"When?"

"Real soon, if we go. It's not decided yet."

"If you do, I'll be sorry."

"Me too, a little bit," she admitted. "I told you it wasn't a good idea for us to get to be friends."

"Are we?" I asked.

She shrugged. "I don't know. I don't know much these days. Everything's very confusing. Even my father's confused." She lowered her voice, as if telling me a secret. "Even Shaftsbury's a little confused."

"I'm sure it will work itself out," I told her.

"I'm sure it will," she agreed, but she didn't sound very confident.

I didn't hear from Jennifer for about a week after that, and I took the silence to mean that her family had departed suddenly for their valley in southern California. I tried not to think about the whole thing too much. I got a job at the Burger Barn, and I watched a lot of videos on cable, and a couple of times when I felt like calling her I got my racket and some balls and hit them against a wall for a few hours till the ache went away.

She called me on a Saturday, at about eleven. "Hey, Andy, are you mad at me?" she asked.

"Why would I be?"

"For not calling. Are you?"

"No." I hesitated. "Yes."

"Well, everything's finally settled. We're staying. Are you free this morning?"

"I'm not sure."

"Want to hit some tennis balls? C'mon, please? I have a new can. . . ."

"What kind?"

"Wilson," she said. "Please?"

"I'll meet you at the park in half an hour."

"Great," she said. "Be prepared for a battle."

She was great that day. Her serve was blistering and her backhands were accurate, and she stepped up and ripped forehands back at me with gleeful savagery. It was all I could do to split two sets with her. After the second set, which she won, she jumped over the net to shake my hand. "Anytime you want a lesson, let me know," she said.

"You're in great spirits today. Did you hit the lottery?"

"No," she said, "Shaftsbury found his mistake."

"His mistake?"

"Yes, in his calculations. You won't believe this, but he left out a variable. No wonder the world didn't come to an end two weeks ago."

"So he's gonna come out with a new date?"

"I think so. He's working on it now. It's amazing to think that even Shaftsbury could make a simple mistake like that."

"It could happen to anyone," I told her. "But I guess that gives us some time."

"Sure," she said. "My dad's been talking to Shaftsbury, and he says it looks like we have at least five years." She smiled, and it was a joy to watch. It was like the sparkle in her blue eyes ignited her entire face. "Maybe even ten."

"I'll settle for an hour," I told her, "if you'll split an ice-cream soda with me. Since you've been the holdout, I get to choose the flavors."

"Okay," she said, putting her racket away. "But no strawberry. I hate strawberry ice cream."

"So do I. What do you know, we have something in common besides tennis."

"You never really believed Shaftsbury, did you?" she

asked. "Tell me the truth. You think my whole family's crazy?"

As we walked to the ice-cream parlor, I gave her a careful, but true, answer. "Actually, I don't really have any philosophical differences with Shaftsbury," I told her. "He built the valley and the schools that produced you, and you turned out all right. And we *are* polluting the water and the air and the atmosphere, and I'm perfectly willing to believe that eventually the gift that was given to us may be taken back."

"And given to the dolphins?" she pressed.

"I have trouble with the dolphins," I admitted. "But aside from that, Shaftsbury and I pretty much agree. The only place we differ is in the matter of timing." I took her hand in mine, and I guess my answer was okay, because she didn't pull away.

That was a great hour. We sat in that ice-cream parlor side by side, laughing and talking and making pigs of ourselves, eating every variety of ice cream except for strawberry. And as Jennifer finished off a banana split, I realized that Shaftsbury and I disagreed on one other minor point.

Maybe he did have telepathic visions, and maybe he did go on a UFO ride through the galaxy, and I guess it's possible that his calculations about the future and the end of the world may someday come true. Who knows? By all accounts he's brilliant. For me, speaking as a seventeen-year-old who hates physics and likes tennis, I believe that most of the things worth knowing in the universe are contained within the bounds of the pretty blue eyes of a girl you like very much. And as Jennifer scooped up the last of the banana split, licked the spoon, and grinned at me, the future that I glimpsed in her eyes looked very encouraging, to say the least.

David Klass

David Klass is known for novels whose main characters are involved in sports. He is the author of *Breakaway Run, A Different Season, The Atami Dragons,* and *Wrestling with Honor,* which the American Library Association has included among its 100 Best of the Best Books for Young Adults published between 1967 and 1992. In *California Blue,* Mr. Klass combines the world of high-school track with ecological concerns and parental conflicts in a story about seventeen-year-old John Rogers, who discovers a new species of butterfly on land owned by the lumber mill at which his dying father works. Mr. Klass's most recent novel for young adults is *Danger Zone,* in which a worldwide junior basketball tournament becomes very dangerous for the American team.

As a teenager David Klass played baseball and soccer at Leonia Public High School in New Jersey and went on to do the same at Yale University, from which he graduated. In Los Angeles, where he now lives and writes, he swims and "occasionally limps up and down the basketball court."

Mr. Klass says the relationship between Andrew and Jennifer in "The Gospel According to Krenzwinkle" was inspired by his moving to Los Angeles and meeting some smart people who had unusual views of reality.

Handling Disappointments

Nobody was as good as Vicik. He was the strongest, the fastest, the best. And unlike Lenny, Vicik could stay out and play as long as he liked.

Falling off
the Empire State Building

Harry Mazer

➤ **Vicik** never came to my house and I never went to his house, but he was my friend, and it was like God was my friend. He was strong as a truck. He could run faster and hit a ball farther than anybody. He'd dare anything. Nothing could ever touch him.

What I remember best about him is stickball, the way he held the bat, waving it in a little circle over his head, just daring you to get the ball past him. He could hit a ball three sewers, from one end of Britain Street to the other.

Britain Street was the best place to play stickball because there was hardly any traffic. All you needed was a taped-up broomstick and a rubber ball. Every game had a season. There was a squirt gun season, a yo-yo season, and a season when we played street hockey on roller skates that we clamped to our shoes and tightened with special keys we kept on cords around our necks. We played stickball all year round.

Vicik and Dov were the leaders. Vicik tossed the bat to

Dov, who tossed it back. They went fist over fist up the stick. Last hold got the first pick.

Dov was tall and skinny. He talked fast and stuttered, spattering spit in all directions. He always picked his pal, Jack, first. Vicik picked Leo. I would have picked him, too.

The strongest were chosen first, the fastest, the best hitters. The scare in my belly was big. "Choose me," I prayed. I didn't care if I was the last, as long as I played. It was shameful not to be picked. Vicik finally saw me and gave me the nod. "Okay, Lenny, you play out."

I ran out almost to the end of the street. I counted two manhole covers. "Hit the ball," I yelled. I slapped my hands together. I was small, but everyone said I had a man's voice. "All the way," I yelled, "hit it all the way to me!"

Vicik smiled at everything I did. If I missed the ball, he winked at me. And when I caught it, he said, "Thataway, Lenny."

My father never smiled at anything I did. All he said was, "I don't want you to play in the street." Where he came from, you either went to school or you went to work. He called my games "foolishness." Everything I did was "foolishness." He wanted me to stay in the house, do my homework, study, and listen to the opera like him. He always wanted me to do something I didn't want to do.

He didn't get it. We had to play in the street or we didn't play. Growing up in New York City, there were just the streets, the cement sidewalks, the stoops, the brick walls. No Little League, no grown-ups supervising games. Hardly any playgrounds.

We got chased by everyone: storekeepers afraid for their windows, and people who couldn't stand us playing stoopball against their steps. "Chickey!" Chickey was the call when a cop was coming. We ran, the cop after us. He got the bat, broke it in a sewer grate, and dropped the pieces down the hole. It was bad. A heavy-duty stick with a good taped handle was hard to find.

It was all part of the game. The only place that belonged to us was the middle of the street. Us and the cars. "Heads up. Car coming!" Play stopped. We jeered at the drivers, dared them to brush against us. "Go on, move, get outta here!" we yelled.

You had to have nerve. And never show fear. Once, on my bike, I grabbed the back of a moving truck. I was on one side and Vicik was on the other side. The truck went so fast my heart was down between my legs. I had to let go. But Vicik never let go.

We hopped rides on the trolley cars that ran up and down White Plains Road. If the motorman didn't see us, we could ride all the way to Burke Avenue or even Gun Hill Road. Every time the trolley stopped, we jumped off. When it started, we jumped on again. Hook a hand through the window, but keep ducked down. If the motorman spotted you, he'd whack your hand off. A kid in my class got bounced off the hood of a car that way and broke both his arms.

We flew kites on the roof and chased each other over the top. Being on the roof was like being on top of the world. We looked out over the rooftops. At night you could see the stars.

"Chicken! Let's see you walk the edge." Vicik walked the edge like it was nothing. On a dare, he hung over the edge, seven stories in the air, and let go. The fire escape was right under him, but it scared me just to think about it. Once I'd seen a dead man on the sidewalk, covered with a canvas. He'd been working on the building and slipped off a scaffold. His paint-stained boots stuck out from under the canvas.

My father didn't like me to go out. "Where are you going? Put something on." Like I was going out naked. I wasn't cold; he was. He never went out without getting all dressed up—suit, tie, hat, his shoes shined. He was like a soldier in uniform.

The first thing my father did in the morning was comb his hair. He combed it straight back, smooth and flat behind his ears. Then he exercised. He opened the window. My mother told him not to stand by the window in his underwear, in front of all the neighbors. "What neighbors?" he said. "Who's looking?"

He stretched, he took deep breaths, everything deliberate and slow. He bent his knees, straightened up, then touched his toes. Then he combed his hair again.

He rubbed his hand over the bristle on his cheeks, then took out the shaving cream and the razor. That was the part I liked best. When he was done, he'd hand me the razor, but without the blade. I foamed up and ran the razor up and down and all around my face like a sled in the snow.

One time I decided I was going to teach my father how to play. We were on the street together, and I was bouncing my ball. "Catch," I said. "What?" he said. I showed him the ball. I put the ball in his hand. "Now you give it to me, Pop." He handed me the ball, then wiped his hands on his white handkerchief.

I bounced the ball on the sidewalk, then threw it to him, nice and easy. He caught it. "That's the way, Pop, good."

My dream was that my father would learn about games

and play catch with me. He could pitch to me and I could practice my batting, which was not too great. I threw the ball again, and it got away from him. He was wearing a coat and a hat, and he couldn't bend. The ball slipped like water through his fingers and rolled out in the street. "Grab it!" I yelled. But he didn't move. He stood there like a dope.

I dove for the ball. It was my pink Spaldeen, the best ball in the world. I saw the car coming, I had plenty of time, but my father went nuts. "Stop!" His voice was like an explosion. "Are you crazy?"

"Pop, my ball . . ." The car rolled over it and split it in half. "My Spaldeen . . ." I picked up the pieces. The insides were pink like bubble gum and it smelled like new rubber.

"How many times do I have to tell you: Stay out of the street," my father said. "All you do is play. Play is not important. School is important."

I didn't say anything. Underneath everything, I knew I didn't have to listen to him, because he wasn't a real American. When I thought that, it made me feel sorry for him. I was born here and he wasn't. I knew I was going to leave him behind.

There was never a moment when I felt he understood. He was from another world. He had nothing to teach me. I learned from my friends, from Vicik. There was nothing I needed from my father, except maybe to teach me how to shave or make a tie.

• • •

On Saturday I was out of the house early. Out of the dark rooms, the corridors, the tension. "Stop! Stand still a minute." They were both on me. Mother and Father.

306

One of them says, "Where are you going?" The other one says, "You didn't eat anything yet."

I hardly heard them. I was out, up the stairs and over the roof. It had rained overnight and there were puddles in all the dips. The air was clear and clean and taut as a wire. I couldn't breathe enough of it. One last breath and I dove down another dark, spooky staircase. I pounded on a door. "Let's go, Mutt." He was my real friend.

He wanted me to come inside. I looked past him down the dark corridor of his apartment. His mother was in the kitchen, and he had to finish eating before she'd let him out.

I waited in front of the building. Mutt and I were handball partners. I was left-handed and that was an advantage, because our strong arms were on the outside. I liked to watch the older guys play. They played the same game we did, only they played with gloves and a small hard black ball. Those were things I really wanted, a pair of leather gloves and a regulation handball.

I had a ball in my pocket. I bounced it, threw it up, caught it. Besides the ball, I carried marbles in my pockets, trading cards, a pocketknife, coins. We played marbles in the dirt. I used my biggest, smoothest marble as a shooter. The little ones were emmies, and there were steelies and clearies you held up to the light. We matched pennies, playing odds and evens, or pitched them against a wall. Or you could put a coin on the crack in the sidewalk, then try to hit it with a ball to the next crack.

Sometimes, if no boys were around I'd play potsie with the girls. You chalked the game on the sidewalk, eight numbered squares. You dropped a bottle cap or a stone into square one, hopped on one foot through all the squares, picked up the marker, and hopped out.

Mutt and I played handball all morning. When I got home my hands were swollen, my fingers fat like sausages. Nobody was home, but my mother had left me a sandwich, a glass of milk, and a big piece of yellow sponge cake. I ate and then fell down on the bed, sank down into pillows and quilts. I heard cars honking through the open window, sirens, kids calling. The window curtains blew in and out.

When I woke up, I didn't know where I was. I staggered out to the other room. My mother was cutting a pattern for a dress on the table. My father was telling her she was going to ruin everything. I ate noodle pudding and washed it down with a glass of milk.

"I'm going out." I had the door open.

"Where are you going? Shut the door and come back inside."

"My friends are waiting."

"You've been out enough. Sit. Read something."

My father read the paper. I went to the refrigerator and got the white bread and butter.

"Are you eating again?" he said. "If you're eating, sit down. Only animals eat standing up."

I sat down. My father turned a page, wet a finger, and turned another page. I could hear the kids outside through the open windows. It was getting dark. I leaned on my elbow. In the distance, along the horizon, along the edge of the sky and the rooftops, I saw a train creeping along the elevated track.

The paper rustled, then slipped from my father's hand. I waited till his eyes closed. I had my sneakers off. I held them up for my mother to see as I tiptoed out of the room.

In the bedroom, I looked out the window. The sky was

still bright above, but below in the courtyard it was dark. I hung out the window and saw Vicik's blond head shining. I bird-whistled. "Vicik, up here."

I dangled my sneakers out the window, let one go, and then the other. They fell five floors, straight down. Vicik caught them. He motioned for me to come down. I went out the fire escape window, down the narrow metal stairs. On the last landing, I was still too high. Vicik reached up. "Leggo." He had his arms out. "Leggo, Lenny."

I let go, fell into his arms, and we both went down. I laced on my sneakers, and we ran off to find the others.

There were a million moths around the streetlights. The best game at night was Johnny on the Pony. We divided into two big teams. I was on Vicik's team. Dov's team made itself into a horse first.

The fattest boy, the pillow boy, stood with his back to the wall. The other boys on his team bent over and locked together, head to tail, making the horse. The last boy tucked his head between the legs of the boy in front of him. "Anyone who farts gets killed."

Our team was across the street. I was the first one to run, because I was the smallest. "Go, Lenny!" Vicki yelled. I sprinted, picked up speed. I got my knees high, let my arms swing. "Go, Lenny!" I vaulted over the bent back of the last boy and threw myself as far forward on the horse as I could. I came down hard on somebody's bony back. The next boy landed on top of me, and the next, and the next, one on top of the other, digging in, hanging on.

I looked back. There came Vicik. His arms were pumping. His feet were shooting out like a duck's. His eyes were popping out of his head. He went up higher then anyone and came down on top of us like a ton of bricks.

It was like an earthquake. The horse trembled. It started to shake and crack and fall apart.

"Johnny on the Pony," the other team chanted. They had to say it three times. "Johnny on the Pony. . . . Johnny . . ." But they couldn't. The horse swayed one way and then the other. And then it fell. We won.

After the game broke up, a bunch of us hung around the candy store. Vicik sat on a fire hydrant and poked at his teeth with a straw. He was telling us a joke and laughing in the middle of it. "What did the moron say when he jumped off the Empire State Building?" Vicik was laughing so hard he could hardly get out the punch line. "He's falling, and someone says, How's it going? And the moron says, So far so good."

Gradually, everyone went home, but I was still there with Vicik. I knew I should go home, but it was Vicik, and I couldn't. He bought a candy bar and we shared it. We walked around Allerton Avenue, all the way up to Boston Post Road. It was late and there was almost nobody on the street. Vicik's house was off Mace Avenue. I'd never been on that street. The sidewalk was all broken up, and there were no apartment houses, just a lot of trees and old wooden houses.

The lights were on inside his house, but he didn't go in. "Is your father waiting up for you?" I knew my father was going to kill me. Vicik just shrugged.

We walked along the edge of the curb, talking a little. I kept waiting for him to say he was going in, so I could leave. He kept talking, telling jokes. He sat down on his steps, leaning forward with his head in his hands. He stopped talking.

"What's the matter?" I said. He shook his head.

Finally, I couldn't stay another second. "I'm going," I

said. I knew I was letting him down, but I couldn't help it. When I looked back, I saw him go into his house. I didn't know why, but I went back and stood on the sidewalk and looked in the window. I saw a man. He looked like Vicik, only bigger. I saw him push Vicik against the wall. Vicik fell back. He didn't raise his hand. He didn't defend himself. He stood with his back to the wall, his eyes on his father. When his father swung at him he ducked, and ducked again, but his father kept hitting him.

I ran all the way home. There was no traffic, nobody on the streets. When I got to my building, I took off my shoes and went up the stairs like a burglar. I turned my key in the lock and slipped inside. Then stood there, just inside the door, listening. I didn't hear anything but my own breathing.

Where were they? What if they were gone? It was the same thought I scared myself with sometimes when I woke up in the middle of the night. What if they said, Enough! They were sick of waiting for me, sick of my games, sick of trying to make me be good.

Then I heard something from the living room, where they sleep. Something moving, something big and dark, and creeping toward me. "Who's there?" It was white and big, and in the doorway. A ghost wearing white underwear.

"What are you doing?" my father said.

"Nothing."

"What are you standing by the door for?"

"I'm not." I laughed. It was dumb to laugh. I should have been sorry. Made an excuse. *There was an accident. . . . We had to go to the hospital . . . and the police station. . . .*

"You're laughing? You come home at this time and you're laughing?"

From the other room, my mother called, "Don't get excited."

My father held the alarm clock. "You see what time it is?"

"I don't know."

"It's twelve on the clock. What were you doing till twelve o'clock?"

"Playing Johnny on the Pony."

"With horses, you play with horses at twelve o'clock?"

"We're the horses, Pop. It's only a game."

He sat down. "You're a horse now? What kind of game is that?"

"It's teams, Pop. It's like tug-of-war. It's fun."

For a long time he sat there, rocking forward and back with the clock in his lap. "A game." He repeated it several times, rocking back and forth.

"Gonif," he said, finally. "American gonif." American thief. "In this country, you can get away with anything." Then he told me to go to bed, and I did.

Harry Mazer

Handball was Harry Mazer's favorite sport when he was a kid—one-wall handball against the side of buildings, until the city built six courts in his New York neighborhood. After school and on Saturday mornings he lived at those handball courts, he says. He played four-wall handball for years, until he dislocated his thumb and switched to racquetball. After tearing his ankle a few years ago, he reports, he only "plays catch and throws rocks and hard green apples at signposts" near his home in central New York State. "I love throwing things," he admits.

He also enjoys writing novels for teenagers, something he has been doing for nearly twenty-five years, starting with *Guy Lenny*, a story about a boy who lives with his divorced father. *Snowbound*, a winter survival story that was made into an NBC television movie, remains one of his most popular books. Among his other novels are *The War on Villa Street*, *The Dollar Man*, *When the Phone Rang*, *The Island Keeper*, *The Last Mission*, and *Someone's Mother Is Missing*. Romance plays a role in several of Mazer's novels, including *I Love You, Stupid!*, *The Girl of His Dreams*, and *City Light*. With his wife, Norma Fox Mazer, he has published *The Solid Gold Kid*, which the American Library Association named one of the 100 Best of the Best Books for Young Adults published between 1967 and 1992; *Heartbeat*; and *Bright Days, Stupid Nights*. His most recent novel, *Who Is Eddie Leonard?*, is about a boy who believes Eddie is not his real name and that the Leonards are not his real family.

"Falling off the Empire State Building," Mazer says, was inspired by the recent death of a neighborhood boy he knew in childhood. "He was a good athlete, and like all the really gifted, physically, he seemed to live in a state of grace, like a prince, relaxed and easy. Nothing got him excited and he never got mad. He was so good, an ideal person . . . somebody to admire."

There's money to be made in sports. If you can't be a professional player pulling down several million dollars a year, you can still purchase a little piece of those superstars. Sports memorabilia is where the action is.

The Hobbyist

Chris Lynch

You were not born into physical greatness and all the love and worship and happiness that are guaranteed with it. But fortunately you were born American. So you can *buy* into it.

You have Paul Molitor's special rookie card from 1978. Who knew he'd be such a monster when he got to be thirty-seven years old? Alan Trammell's on the same card. Again, who knew? Those two could just as easily have wound up like the other two rookie shortstops on the card, U. L. Washington and Mickey Klutts. Mickey Klutts? Was he a decoy? A you-can-do-it-too inspiration for the millions of Mickey Kluttses in the world?

So nobody knew, which is good for you. You got it at a yard sale, along with a thousand other cards that some scary old lady was dumping. Her scary old man had died. As far as she was concerned, he'd taken all the cards' value with him. She didn't know. Bet there was a lot more she didn't know.

You have complete sets of National Hockey League

cards from everybody for the last three seasons. Fleer, Topps, O-Pee-Chee, Pinnacle, Leaf, and Upper Deck. *Two* sets of each, in fact, one you open and look at, one that stays sealed in the closet to retain its value because you're not stupid. You're a lot of things, but you're not stupid. Hockey, understand, is the wave. That's where it's at for the future, collectiblewise.

Anything that has Eric Lindros's picture on it, or his signature, or his footprint, you own it. Big ol' Eric Lindros. You own him.

Ditto Frank Thomas. Big ol' Frank Thomas. You own him.

You just don't own you. Because you're not going to be on any card. Because you have to be on a team first, and you're not going to be on any team, are you? Six inches. You were so close. "You're a good kid, boy, and you busted your ass harder than anybody who's ever tried out for me, no lie. If you were just six inches taller, you'd have made that final cut for the jayvee."

You're six feet six inches tall. Thanks, Coach.

When you're six feet six inches tall, everybody asks you, "You playin' any ball, kid?" If you cannot answer yes to that question, looking the way you do, you let everybody down. It's like asking an old man, "So how've you been?" and he answers, "No good. Prostate's blown to hell. Incontinent. Impotent. Death's door." You bring everybody down.

You can't do that. Bring everybody down. Because even though they don't know it, when you bring them down, you bring you down. Only lower. You always go lower down than everybody else. Where no one else goes, where no one else knows. So you learn. You go around the whole thing.

"So, you playin' any hoops?" your uncle asks when he comes by to take his brother, your father, to the Celtics-Knicks game. You don't answer yes, you don't answer no. You smile sagely, nod, and hold up a wait-right-here finger to your uncle with the beer and the electric green satin Celtics jacket. You go to your room and come back with a ball. The ball is a regular $20 basketball with a $295 Bill Russell autograph on it.

"Holy smokes," your uncle marvels. "*That* bastard? You actually went to that card show for this, huh?" He pretends, like a lot of people in Boston, to hate, or at least not care about, Bill Russell, who is famous for hating, or not caring much for, Boston. "I heard they had to pay him two million damn dollars just to come back here for two lousy card shows," he says with obvious disgust. But he doesn't let go of the ball. He stares and stares into it, turning it around in his hands, as if he's reading his future or his past in there. He shakes his head and mutters something about watching, as a kid, Russell eating Chamberlain alive. Then he offers you $100 for the ball.

You take your ball back with a silent knowing smile. You feel the power and satisfaction, exactly the same rush as blocking a shot, swatting it ten rows up into the stands, you are sure. You get a little crazy with cockiness and attempt a dribble on the kitchen tiles as you head out. You bounce it off your instep, then chase it down the hall feeling stupid, tall and stupid.

Your father does not get the autographed picture of Patrick Ewing you ask him to get at the game, even though his brother, your uncle, explains the whole Russell-Ewing historical continuum. Your father just doesn't get it. Oh, he *gets* Russell, and he *gets* Ewing. What he doesn't get is the whole "autograph thing," the "collectibles thing," the thing where a big healthy kid can reach *over* the protective fence around the players' parking lot at Fenway Park to get a hat signed by Mo Vaughn, but that same kid could not learn to grab a rebound. Couldn't even rebound. "Even Manute Bol catches a rebound once in a while, for God's sake," your father points out.

You have two jobs to pay for your hobby. That's what they call it in *Beckett* magazines, the Hobby. You are a hobbyist, or a collector. Football isn't a sport, it's a Hobby. There are two slants to every article—what a player's achievement means to the game, and what it means to the Hobby. You, you are a most dedicated hobbyist, paying for it all by shoveling snow/cutting grass and by working in, of course, a card shop. You long ago lost contact with the other stuff, the game.

Vic owns the shop, the Grand Slam. "Listen, kid," he says after sizing you up in about thirty seconds. He always calls you something diminutive—kid, boy, junior—as he looks straight up at you. "Listen, kid, the shop, it don't mean nothin', understand? It's a front. I mean, it ain't illegal or nothin', but it ain't a real store, neither. The real business goes on back there." He points to his little cubbyhole computer setup in back. "That's where I work on the sports net. I'm hooked up to every desperate memorabilia-minded loser in all North America, Europe, and Japan. But you gotta run a store to belong to the on-line. So this"—he points to the glass counter he's leaning on, like a bakery case, only filled with cards—"is where you will work. All you gotta do is look big, look kinda like an athlete, 'cause my customers like that, they like to feel like they're dealing with a honest-to-God washed-up old pro or somebody who almost coulda been somebody. You can do that?"

You assure him that you can.

"Talk a good game, boy," Vic said that first day and many days since. "Talk a good game and the whole world'll buy in."

"Buy in." You know "buy in." You're in, way in. Your dad hasn't been in your bedroom, not once, in three years, so he doesn't know about your achievements. Your mother has, so she does. She's the only one who does.

She does the cleaning, and all that polishing. The caretaking and the secret-keeping.

"Check it out, kid," Vic calls from the back of the store. "*The Hockey News*. Classifieds. Ken Dryden, okay? *The* Ken Dryden. Probably the best money goalie of all time. He's in here begging for a mint-condition Bobby Orr 1966 rookie card. Says he *has* to have it. Practically he's cryin' right here in *The Hockey News*. Look, you can see his little tears. . . ."

Vic is at the safe now. The squat safe he keeps under his desk. He keeps all the really big items, his personal stock, in the safe. Whenever he has a chance, Vic cracks open the safe to show what he has that somebody else wants.

Ken Dryden. 1970–71 O-Pee-Chee rookie card, $300.

"There," Vic says, placing the tissue-wrapped, wax-paper-enfolded card on the counter. He slides it out of the wrapping. It is pristine, like it's fresh out of a pack. "Poor Kenny Dryden has to have this. He's offering ten thousand dollars for this. Kid, you know what I say to Ken Dryden? I say get a life, Ken Dryden, or get yourself another ten grand. 'Cause I ain't even picking up the damn phone on this card for less than twenty thousand dollars."

You've seen this all before. You've seen the card, seen the posturing, heard the patter. It is the closest Vic ever gets to emotional. Bobby Orr is the only thing that does it.

"I was gonna *be* Bobby Orr, y'know, kid. You have no idea what it was like, growin' up around here in them days. It was *crazy*. The guy meant so much to me . . . so much to everybody. I just swore, you just swore, that he could do absolutely anything. Final game of the playoffs, Bruins down four-nothin' with a minute to go. I just knew, you just knew, that Orr was gonna pot those five goals in that last minute and make *my* life so perfect. . . ."

And you've seen the daze before too. Vic gently wraps up his precious card and mumbles, "Musta spent five solid years pretending I was him. . . ."

"So what happened?" you ask, trying to get him back.

"What happened. What happened was I grew up. Orr didn't score the five goals, and I grew up."

"Card means a lot to you, huh?" you ask.

He doesn't look back at you as he returns to the safe. He holds the card daintily between thumb and middle finger, raising it over his head. "Ya, it means a hell of a lot. It means a nice new car for Vic. Some loser's gonna come up on the computer one day and pay the bill."

You hear that a lot too. Vic talking back to the computer. *Loser. Chump. Fool. Rube.* "There are exactly two types of people in this game," he says. "Businessmen and fools. The businessmen sell memories to the fools who don't have nothin' else."

He is explaining this, adding one more coat of shellac to your shell, when she comes in.

"Manon Rheaume" is all she says. You don't exactly hear her because Vic is ranting and you are staring.

"Manon Rheaume," she repeats. "Do you have her card?"

"Uh . . . how 'bout some Gretzky? We have a rare . . ."

You go into your spiel, pushing the stock of Wayne

Gretzky items like Vic said to. "That guy hasn't done anything for years. What's he win lately, the Lady Byng Trophy? Ohhh, please. Only us hobbyists keepin' his career alive. He's like a bug with his head pulled off, he keeps wigglin', but it ain't exactly life."

"I don't want any Gretzky," she says. "I want Manon Rheaume, and only Manon Rheaume. If you don't have her, just say so and I'll go someplace else."

"No, no, wait," you say, finally registering. You don't want her to leave. You don't get that many customers in the store during the week. You don't get many girls. You don't get many beautiful girls who are six foot two.

"Sure we have Manon," you say, pulling out a drawer. "Manon is hot." You mean it in more ways than one. Manon Rheaume is the first woman to play in the NHL, a goalie. She's much prettier than the average hockey player and one card even has her lying belly-down in a come-on pose that has never before appeared on a sports card to your knowledge. You've prayed no one would come in and buy it.

But she does. She makes a grunt of disgust when she comes across the cheesecake picture, but she buys out all six different Rheaume cards. And the poster where she looks like a real goalie, and the back issue of *Beckett Hockey Monthly* with her on the cover.

"You a hobbyist?" you ask.

She laughs. "No, I'm a feminist."

"Me too," you say, though you have no business saying it.

"Do tell?" You make her laugh again. You find that it's easy to make her laugh, and you want to keep doing it.

"Do you play hoop?" you ask, and she stops laughing.

It seemed a natural enough question, and one of the few things you felt capable of discussing. But you should have known better.

"Yes, I play it," she sighed heavily, "but I don't discuss it."

Your mind makes little crackling noises as she starts backing away from the counter, and you desperately search for a new topic. "You have grass?" you blurt.

"Pardon me?"

"I do that. My other job. Cutting grass. Or shoveling snow, but I figure you don't have any snow to shovel in July so I figured I would ask if you had grass. To cut. He lets me—Vic—ask people if they need yard work. Nothing personal."

Her smile comes back, and your palpitating slows. "You know, if I talked to you on the phone, I'd have known how tall you were," she says.

You don't have to ask, because you know exactly what she means. You slide your own card, a business card your mother had made up for your birthday, across the counter. MVP YARD WORK, it reads, with your name and number and a silhouette of a little man pushing a mower.

She takes it. "We have grass," she says. "But I cut it." She puts your card into the stack with the Rheaume cards. "But I'll keep this, for the collection. Maybe it'll wind up valuable someday when you're a big somebody." She waves and leaves.

"Don't waste your time," Vic yells after listening to the whole thing. "She's a brute. Looks like that Russian basketball freak."

He is wrong. She is lovely.

• • •

"For me? Are you sure?" you ask. Your mother is grinning with excitement when she hands you the phone.

"Well, like I said, I don't need your services, but I told my next-door neighbor about you, and he'd like you to come by and, if you're cheap enough, do his yard."

You thank her, take down the address, then lie awake all night thinking about what to wear. You are so nervous that you get out of bed at five A.M. and start ripping open all your packs of Upper Deck Collector's Choice cards. The 1994 series contains a bunch of prize cards in which you can win shirts and hats and pictures, but that is nothing. You want the grand prize—getting your picture on Junior Griffey's 1995 Collector's Choice card, where you will be right there inside the package for all the world to rip open and see. You have been pacing yourself at a pack a day, just to have a little something for the summer days, but this morning you break out. After twenty-five packs and no winner, you quit.

• • •

Though it is hot out, high eighties, you wear sweats to cut the grass. Bulky sweats. You wear them because they are beautiful and well cut with the logo and breezy tropical colors of the Florida Marlins. They give you the illusion of size, as opposed to the reality of just height. The illusion of fluid motion, that sleek fish cutting through the surf, as opposed to the reality of robotic jangling elbows and clomping flat feet.

You wear it because you figure she'll be watching, and she is. Part of the time sitting on the steps, part of the time walking alongside as you push the man-powered old mower over the quarter-acre lot. She makes small talk, mostly about you and your jobs and your independence which she envies. She may notice, but she makes no mention of the sweat running down your face all over. She sweats, but neatly, a bubbly glistening contained on her lip and brow.

You try not to, but you do occasionally steal a glance sideways to look at her, talking and moving at the same time, gesturing even, comfortable with it all, with those long long legs of hers loping along serenely like a giraffe's. Through the fog of the heat vapors rising and the perspiration falling from the tips of your eyelashes you look, and you want to get to her. To reach out your spidery arms which aren't good for a great many things but which could certainly reach from here and bring her in closer. You know it's unreasonable, you know it's very soon yet, and you know you don't actually do that sort of thing, you know all that. You want to do it just the same. You don't, of course.

You finish your work, frothy as a farm beast, drench yourself with the hose, and collect your pay.

She invites you. Across the lawn, with its fresh clippings sticking to the black leather sneakers you wear for the same reason fat people wear black shirts. The smell of the cut grass is a bit of a revival, filling your head, giving you the feeling, as it always does, that something has been done, that something is improved in your wake. She offers you a Jolt cola or a Gatorade, your choice, and you say that both together sounds like a good idea.

As you sit on the upturned wheelbarrow in her driveway sipping your drinks, she absently scoops up a basketball and dribbles it. Then she flicks her wrist and the ball clangs off the rim mounted above the garage door. She chases it down and lays it in. She takes it back out fifteen feet, wheels, and drops the shot.

You watch her for a while and enjoy it like you've never enjoyed basketball before. Because it's not quite basketball. You watch it the way you figure people watch ice dancing. She is grace, all her moves just one long continuous extension of all her other moves. She shoots with one hand, the other hand, both hands. She looks like the Statue of Liberty for a second, then like Gregory Hines splitting in midair. Even when she misses she looks good, rebounding with an explosive two-step and putting the ball back up while she's still in the air.

"Twenty-one?" she asks mischievously, squeezing the ball with her elbows pointed straight out in either direction.

You turn and look down the driveway behind you, to see who she's talking to. When you find no one you turn back to see her grinning, pointing at you, with the ball on her hip now.

First you shudder. But you've got the Jolt in you, and the Gatorade. And you're at least four inches taller than her.

"Take that sweatshirt off at least, will you? You're going to die right here in my driveway."

You laugh, but there's no way you are going to take off your shirt in front of her. "It's not so bad," you say, and push up your sleeves to the elbows.

She offers to let you have first possession. You decline. You are the man, after all. And you don't *want* first possession. She shrugs, takes the ball, doesn't move her feet at all as she floats a shot over your head. It doesn't go in, but by the time you've turned to see, she's already blown by, picked up the ball, and rolled it in.

She takes it out again, dribbles to her right. You keep your hands up. That's all you know, keep your hands up like a human letter Y and keep yourself between her and the hoop. Desperately you try to do that, but you can't manage to sidestep, sidestep, and you wind up running awkwardly cross-body, foot over foot. You manage the small victory of not falling, but watch as she passes directly under the basket to come up for a reverse layup on the other side.

She cannot believe you are as bad as this so she laughs, thinking you are toying. You laugh along, dropping your hands. As soon as you do, she races by. You chase. She stops short. You fly past. She pulls up and banks an easy jumper.

She's into double figures and your Florida Marlins sweats with the leaping fish are soaked by the time she seems to gather that you have nothing. *Nothing*. You don't laugh anymore, don't smile. You try like hell. Only halfway through a game neither one of you wants to finish. But she's kind enough not to offer, and you're stupid enough not to quit. You sweep at the ball and actually tick it, knocking it out of her hands. She doesn't chase, and you get it. You are an impossible twenty feet from the basket, but you heave the ball from where you are. Air ball, of course, and she looks irritated that you did it.

She stands practically in your shoes as she squares up to take the midrange jumper. You are looming over her, the shot begging to be blocked. If there is one thing you should be able to do, this is that thing. She goes up, you go up. You can see the ball, you can see your outstretched hand, you can see her outstretched hand as the ball leaves it.

It has always been this way. It has never mattered whether the shooter was a foot shorter, or could not jump, or didn't even try to jump. It's as if there is just something, something about trajectory, something about time, that everyone else knows but that you do not. You have never arrived at that point in the air at the same time that the ball has. Never.

What you need here is a cold-blooded killer, someone willing to stick the dagger in, twist it, beat you soundly and quickly. What you have, unfortunately, is a girl with a heart. She tries to joke again, but the pity is clear on her face and in her game. As she creeps toward twenty-one, she tries mightily to get you some points. She dribbles the ball off her foot, expertly booting it right into your hands. You fire up another brick. She hauls in the rebound out of instinct, but stands flat-footed and lets you take it away from her. It is a gimme, but you panic and roll it off the rim.

"Why didn't you just stick it, for God's sake?" she yells, angry like a coach. She's mad at having to work harder for your points than for her own. "You're that close to the hoop with the ball in your hands, you jam it in. It's not even regulation height."

Out of her exasperation come more baskets. A bank shot, a hook shot, a short baseline jumper—all rain right over your head. It feels better than the charity, though.

She needs only one basket to finish it, to skunk you finally, a shutout. "Don't forget, gotta win by two," she says, a tired smile relighting her game face. She dribbles once behind her back, between her legs, to her right, to her left. By most standards, she is not a great ballhandler, very shaky and off-balance with the show-time moves that seem unnatural to her. But you can't touch her.

Suddenly for no good reason she pulls up from long range. She doesn't penetrate at all, which she has already proven is easy enough to do. Instead she lets it fly, from three- or four- or five-point land. A line drive, a bullet. You turn to watch the shot ricochet off the front of the rim and bounce all the way straight out to you. She hasn't moved for the hoop, so there you are with the ball and nothing but air between you and the basket.

You put the ball on the floor. It works once. You bounce if successfully a second time, then manage a third, fourth, fifth consecutive off-balance dribble as you lumber toward the hoop.

If you were alone, you would have taken some small pride in having come within five feet of the basket before having the ball trail off harmlessly in one direction while you and your empty hands go flailing off in another.

You don't try to talk to her as you angle off the side of the driveway, across her front yard, toward home. You stare straight ahead and compulsively keep pushing your sleeves back up. They slide back down over your forearms; you push them back up.

"It's not important, you know," she says from right behind you. You don't want to hear it. She comes up alongside, locked into step with you, the two of you marching along like a pair of string-bean soldiers. She marches and swings her hands, a little comedy, as she tries to catch your eyes with hers. You see her clearly in your peripheral view, but you will not turn.

"Really," she says, "I really don't think it's a big deal. I beat guys all the time. We're not all athletes, you know."

None of it means anything, until she touches your arm. You have just pushed the sleeve back up, again, and her fingertips feel cool and wet there. You stop walking.

"I *can* do stuff," you say, a little desperately. "People just think because of the way I look that I'm supposed to play ball. But I can do stuff. I can do lots of other stuff. I'm not a loser, you know. I'm not a geek."

"Nobody said you were," she says.

"You want to see? I have a lot of stuff, back at my house. I'd love to show you. I have a ball signed by Bill Russell, did you know that? I shook his hand. He hates this whole city, and he shook my hand. I paid the money and he signed the ball and shook my hand and laughed that spooky cackle laugh even though I didn't say anything at all to the guy. You want to see it?"

She nods, impressed. "I'd like to see that, sure."

It seems like no one is home when you bring her in through the front door. "Mom," you call out tentatively. You get the no-answer you hope for.

"You have a very nice place," she says. "It's so clean and airy. Really nice."

"My mom," you say, leading her up the stairs. "My mom is wild for cleaning and straightening. This is nothing, though. Wait'll you see my room."

It was something you hadn't thought much about, something you just took for granted after so long. You smile at her as you stand for a second before your door, which is almost entirely taken up by a life-sized poster of Evander Holyfield, who is perfect and sculpted and smiling and a half foot shorter than you. The poster is signed. You own Evander Holyfield.

But as soon as you swing the door open and look at her astonished face, you remember. You feel yourself go flush as she beams.

"This is unbe*liev*able," she says, scanning the brilliance of the room. "It's like opening a door on the Academy Awards show."

"Oh, never mind that," you say, but it is too late. She

rushes to the tall chest of drawers, covered with trophies. She careens over to the dresser, blinding with the trophies themselves and their reflections off the mirror behind them. The nightstands on either side of the bed, covered. Small brass loinclothed men standing atop pedestals, arms raised triumphant, at attention all along the baseboard of four walls.

"Hey, let me show you that ball," you say, even your voice sweaty now. You make for the closet.

"Track." She points at one modest third-place plaque hanging on the wall. "Tennis?" She points at a trophy, the player bent over backward in midserve. "Football, boxing, hockey. Sailing? Who *are* you?" Her voice, momentarily filled with awe, changes as soon as she gets up close and begins reading. You are buried in the closet, but you can tell. You take your time.

"Wait a minute. Oh, I know who you are. You're Sven Lundquist. Oh no, you're Eamonn O'Rourke. Wait, wait, you're Jamaal Abdoul."

When she starts laughing hysterically, you come out of the closet.

"This is soooo cute," she says, delighted. "You're a funny guy."

"No it isn't," you answer coolly. "And no I'm not."

"Come on now, you're kidding me, right?"

"No, I'm not."

"Well, then, what? It's a hobby, right? It's a cool idea, I think. You'll probably wind up with an unbelievable collection, the way you're going. A real conversation starter, to say the least."

"No, they're mine."

"They're yours. You *won* them? All?"

You nod.

"Stop pulling my leg. Okay, so you won, ah"—she browses—"the American Legion baseball championship in 1990? You also won . . . the New England regional Golden Gloves middleweight title in . . . oooh, you were a busy boy in 1990, huh?"

"They're mine," you say.

"Sure they're yours, because you bought them, or swiped them, but not because you *earned* them."

"Please. I earned them. I did, I earned them. Can we not talk about them anymore? Look, here's the Russell ball."

"Just, okay, for my peace of mind, before we move on, just can I hear you tell me you know these are somebody else's awards?"

You know the stakes, you know the true facts. You know you don't want her to leave, and you know the appropriate answer. You open your mouth, and some words come out.

"They are mine. Really. They belong to me."

She backs toward the door, talking calmly, sadly. Pity again. "Being a geek is okay, you know. Being a psychopath is not. You can *be* a lovable geek. . . ."

"They really are mine," you say, almost following her. She's on her way down the stairs. You get to the threshold of your bedroom but you don't cross it, unable to go out even though you'd like to bring her back.

You hear your mother say hello as they pass each other at the front door. The response is a polite but rushed hi as she speeds out.

When your mother reaches your room you are rapidly tearing open all your remaining 1994 Upper Deck Collector's Choice packs. You are certain that the prizewinner is in there, the ticket that puts you on Griffey's card for the millions of hobbyists and girls to see next year. As each pack comes up a loser, you drop it to the floor. Your mother looks at your face and she knows the story. You can see your fractured heart in hers.

"Son, I told you. I told you you shouldn't let anyone in here." She stands in the doorway holding a crinkled brown shopping bag. She pulls out a small but different-looking prize, the figurine on top made of white marble instead of metal. "This was at the thrift shop today. I thought you'd like it, thought you could make room for it. You don't already have anything from soccer, do you?"

When you don't respond, she comes on in. Even with her standing up, you have to sit on the bed for her to cradle your head in her arms.

Chris Lynch

The holder of a master's degree from the writing program at Emerson College in Boston, Chris Lynch is the author of several highly acclaimed novels about teenagers, beginning with *Shadow Boxer,* an American Library Association Best Book for Young Adults. With humor and sensitivity, *Shadow Boxer* explores the rocky relationship between two brothers whose father died from injuries received during his boxing career. The older brother, George, is determined that twelve-year-old Monty will not follow in their father's footsteps.

Family relationships also figure prominently in *Iceman* and *Gypsy Davey.* In *Iceman,* Eric's father lives vicariously through his son's violent hockey games, and Eric's only close friend is a man who works at the local funeral home. Eric's violence on the ice brings his team victories, but to him they become increasingly meaningless. In *Gypsy Davey,* the title character grows up in a tattered household whose members are too busy to love one another because they are desperately trying to escape the misery of their own lives. So Davey sets out to find love elsewhere.

Mr. Lynch's most recent novel, *Slot Machine,* grew out of the same issue that inspired "The Hobbyist": the attitude that American males are somehow inferior if they are not neck-deep in sports. The novel is about three friends who go to a camp run by their new high school. The camp's leaders try to slot the campers into manageable, comfortable, stifling categories, but not everyone is willing to be shaped into the expected roles. Like all Mr. Lynch's novels, this one focuses on identity and self-worth.

When he himself was a teenager, Chris Lynch participated in all kinds of sports, with special interests in baseball, street hockey, soccer, and football, until he grew distant from the "organized" part of organized sports. Understandably, his current athletic passion is running. Alone.